Telling Incest

Telling Incest

Narratives of
Dangerous
Remembering
from Stein
to Sapphire

Janice Doane and
Devon Hodges

ANN ARBOR
THE UNIVERSITY OF
MICHIGAN PRESS

Copyright © by the University of Michigan 2001
All rights reserved
Published in the United States of America by
The University of Michigan Press
Manufactured in the United States of America
♾ Printed on acid-free paper

2004   2003   2002   2001   4   3   2   1

A CIP catalog record for this book is available from the British Library.

Library of Congress Cataloging-in-Publication Data

Doane, Janice L.
    Telling incest : narratives of dangerous remembering from Stein to
Sapphire / Janice Doane and Devon Hodges.
        p.   cm.
    Includes bibliographical references and index.
    ISBN 0-472-09794-6 (Cloth : alk. paper)
    ISBN 0-472-06794-X (pbk. : alk. paper)
    1. Incest.   2. Incest in literature. I. Hodges, Devon L., 1950–
II. Title.
HV6570.6   .D63   2001
306.877—dc21   2001002649

A small gift in exchange for large ones—

To Bill and Camille
—Jan

To David and Laurel
—Devon

Acknowledgments

This book was authored by Janice Doane and Devon Hodges, Inc. Incorporated in our work are the contributions of a large group of friends and colleagues. From the beginning, Tania Modleski encouraged us onward. Zofia Burr, Dina Copelman, Sandy Grayson, Carol Lashof, and Alok Yadav read the book in whole or in part, asking probing questions and making productive suggestions. Thorell Tsomondo provided stimulating conversation that helped keep the book going, then read a draft at the start of a busy term. Michelle Massé, after reading the manuscript, sent us meticulous, insightful comments. To these friends, generous and scrupulous scholars all, we owe a lasting debt.

Devon Hodges would also like to thank the National Endowment for Humanities for a fellowship that gave her time for research and writing. She also is grateful for a study leave from George Mason University. And to the other friends who have shared the travails and triumphs associated with the writing of this book—especially, Carmela Ciuraru, Lorna Irvine, Rosemary Jann, Deborah Kaplan, Barbara Melosh, Eileen Sypher, and Ellen Todd—she offers heartfelt tribute.

Janice Doane adds her thanks to Saint Mary's College for a sabbatical in spring 1999 and for the generous support provided by the Faculty Development Fund. Thanks also to the librarians at the College, especially Sharon Walters, for their help with research. The "Gang of Four" listened, advised, and celebrated; their friendship was a source of sustenance in every way.

LeAnn Fields, our editor, has been constant and constantly helpful. We greatly appreciate her confidence in our work. Two anonymous readers also provided wonderfully useful feedback. Their comments made revision less daunting. Acknowledgment is also made to the following: Hacking, Ian; *Rewriting the Soul: Multiple Personality and the Science of Memory.* Copyright © 1995 by PUP. Reprinted by permission of Princeton University Press. Passages from Gertrude Stein's *The Making of Americans* are reprinted by permission of the Estate of Gertrude Stein.

Introduction

Just thirty years ago, a good local library might have been able to provide its patrons with two or three books on the topic of incest. Today, incest is the subject of innumerable films, novels, memoirs, scholarly articles, and self-help books. The word *incest* might still provoke anxiety, but it is no longer as unspeakable as it was when feminists in the late 1970s proclaimed: incest is not the taboo, speaking about it is. It may even seem that incest is now talked about too much. Such a concern is based on the assumption that women's testimonies about incest have become formulaic, marketable products. Yet the belief, reassuring to some, that women's stories of incest are all alike, and most likely inauthentic, may work to muffle stories that women have only recently dared to tell. To encourage readers to think again about why telling incest might be both difficult and productive, this book charts some of the significant historical shifts in the discursive models available for telling and hearing about incest, shifts that have taken place in the last hundred years. We hope that this history will inspire readers to keep listening when women "tell" incest.

By the mid-1990s, women's incest stories were the subject of much public attention and controversy. This debate centered on narratives of the recovered memory movement (in which daughters recall long-forgotten experiences of incest) and opposing narratives of the false-memory syndrome movement (in which therapists are attacked for encouraging daughters to develop false memories). At issue was the truthfulness of a dominant form of women's "telling," what we call the "recovery story." In this particular type of narrative, a middle-class woman suffers amnesia about an incest experience until a therapist helps her to retrieve lost memories of it and eventually heal her life. Perhaps in response to notorious court cases, the favored response to such accounts, as witnessed in the national media, has been to debate their truth or falsehood: thumbs up or thumbs down?[1]

Doubts about the legitimacy of incest narratives and the motives of those who tell them are nothing new. We will show how incest narratives are formed under conditions of uncertainty not only about "what happened" but about who will listen. In our view, questions about the truth and falsehood of incest stories have tended to limit understanding of the pressures shaping these narratives. We also need to ask: why does an incest narrative inspire particular forms of resistance or acknowledgment? How have forms for telling incest changed? Under what conditions does a model for telling become dominant?

Telling Incest emphasizes clusters of incest narratives defined in relation to specific historical contexts, cultural politics, and kinds of reception. The form of incest that we explore in this study occurs when fathers (or close surrogates) have sexual intercourse with their daughters. This framing of incest will be neither precise nor broad enough to satisfy all of our readers, but it allows us to focus on characteristic forms of father-daughter incest. Though this book studies narratives, all of them marked by the gap between the experience of incest and its narrative representation, it argues that the experience of incest must be acknowledged as an actuality that puts significant pressure on models for telling. In first-person memoirs about incest, the narrative negotiation with an experience of incest is obvious. But the actuality of incest—what we call "the thing" (borrowing from Toni Morrison, who uses the term to gesture toward bitter historical realities associated with slavery)—also puts pressure on fictions about incest.

One way in which the power of "the thing" is demonstrated is in the persistence of the belief that incest is something that happens to *other* people. Which other people? Them.[2] The projection of the actuality of incest onto cultural others, often the poor and black, is a sign of "the thing's" danger to imaginary, moralized communities. Fantasized moral havens provide a sense of order and safety for their inhabitants, that is, for most us. Another sign of "the thing's" destabilizing power is the commonplace belief that incest happens more often in the fantasy life of individuals than it does in real life. Of course incest may be fantasized, no doubt often is, but what is interesting is the extent to which an emphasis on the place of fantasy functions as a disavowal of "the thing."[3] In our cultural moment, for example, the idea of incest as fantasy is often invoked to discredit the truth of narrations of incest and to call into question memories said to be conjured up in therapy. As we will show, many incest narratives are marked not so much by memory lapses, although these may be evident, as by the difficulties of finding a workable framework for telling. These difficulties include gaining a sympathetic audience, avoiding retaliation, and finding a way around the familiar and debasing personae associated with tellers: the liar, the seducer, the hysteric, the victim.

Our book will argue that there is a wide range of ways to tell incest. We focus on fictional and nonfiction narratives, although there are other genres in which telling occurs.[4] For heuristic purposes, we have given names to several distinctive types of narratives—the "feminist incest story," the "recovery story," the "false-memory story," the "incest survivor memoir." However, when we discuss the specific differences between groups of stories, we hope not to enclose them within one reductive narrative paradigm, understood as particularly faddish or conventional. Clearly incest narratives produced under different historical conditions are distinguishable from one another, but even roughly contemporaneous stories that share generic similarities are not simple clones of one another.

Our own process of coming to understand incest narratives may serve to illustrate why it may be difficult to acknowledge the complexity of stories located within a single genre. When we first decided to study the incest survivor memoir, for example, we were confident about what we would find even before we started reading. We were primed by the debate about recovered and false memories to expect that memoirs about incest would be stories about recovered memories. For this reason, we also assumed that our response to them should be to decide on their truth or falsehood. After all, because incest is defined as a horrifying crime and evil act, the credibility of an accuser and the factual basis of the accusation are matters of serious concern. But focusing on truth and falsehood kept us measuring the credibility of narrators and the credulity of audiences rather than asking why our response was so constrained.

Because our response to women's incest narratives was shaped by the public outcry about the dangers of false memories, we feared that incest survivor memoirs might well be exploiting women's various experiences of distress, making them formulaic and undercutting the seriousness of earlier feminist political analyses of incest as about power. We were surprised to discover that there was a significant gap between these often thoughtful and carefully crafted memoirs and their representation by many critics as self-pitying and naive victim stories. In addition, we discovered far fewer full-length memoirs than we expected to find, which led us to question the accuracy of the widespread perception that narratives of sexual abuse have reached an "epidemic frequency" (Crews, 129).[5] Sobered by our experience of reading and analyzing incest survivor memoirs, we were reminded that even feminists, perhaps especially feminists, may abet such fears when trying to separate themselves from women who are assumed to be hysterical and invested in victim culture. We have learned to take to heart Tania Modleski's slogan about women in patriarchy: "One is a hysteric; two are a movement" (*Old Wives' Tales*, 22). Read more than two incest survivor memoirs, we discovered, and their class analysis and their challenging experimentation with narrative conventions of telling suddenly become visible.

Analyzing our initial skepticism about memoirs of incest, we were reminded how much the socially powerful rhetoric of the media reflects and plays upon our fears about being duped, fears exacerbated in an age in which unreliable and unverifiable information proliferates. Our effort to understand women's tellings of incest was thus complicated by our repeated efforts to supply the fairness usually lacking in media accounts of sensational events. However, we came to understand that our hope for magisterial judiciousness reflected an unconscious desire to meet requirements for credibility that the debate about true and false memories has vividly dramatized. As women and feminists, we are speakers who are, in the cultural imaginary, doubly linked to hysteria and unreason: No wonder that we were trying so hard to be reasonable and that other feminists in this debate often bend over backward to articulate an absolutely sensible position.

An important aid to discovering our voice was Janice Haaken's fine but obsessively responsible book, *Pillar of Salt*. Haaken's work on the sexual abuse recovery movement has been important to our own understanding of the political and social tensions fueling the memory wars. Although she is a therapist working in the trenches, and her perspective and concerns are thus somewhat different from our own, Haaken shares our desire to "move beyond the poles of 'true and false' recollections of child abuse" (2). Her method is to find a "third position" (8); but finally, it is hard to discern what that position is. Haaken attempts to be completely responsible, to address every point of view. Unfortunately, this practice makes her book confusingly inclusive, with the result that its interpretative stance is difficult to discern. Haaken's book showed us that the way out of the true-false dichotomy is not to be found in a narrative that aspires to an incontrovertible reasonableness.

As we have discovered, reason itself is a partisan in the recent controversies about the status of recovered memory. To show how the voice of reason is deployed in these debates, **Chapter 1, "Ordinary Doings,"** begins with a discussion of *Rewriting the Soul* by Ian Hacking, a prominent philosopher who has been influential in debates about how to understand claims of child abuse. Hacking tries to establish a historical genealogy for phrases such as *child abuse* and *sexual harassment* so that reasonable people might come to some agreement about what these terms properly refer to. Like many social constructionists, Hacking hopes to emphasize, in a productive way, the postmodernist understanding that reality is constructed by language. Yet to counter the new—and threatening—discursive practice he names "memoro-politics," Hacking himself scurries back to foundational entities—"character" and "the soul"—as places of refuge. His argument relies upon the solid truth of these terms, a truth that memoro-politics, allied with a coercive therapeutic science of the self, apparently undoes by encouraging women to rename and thereby invent the past.

Similarly, Allan Young, in *The Harmony of Illusions*, argues that post-traumatic stress disorder, sometimes assumed to be a timeless and universal problem, became "real" through the use of narratives, such as the various *Diagnostic and Statistical Manuals of Mental Disorders* and developing medical practices. Like Hacking, Young offers a disturbing history of "a new language of self-deception" that justifies "the emergence of a new class of authorities" (4). Young's investment in the determining power of language and social practices thus shapes his reading of traumatic memory narratives: they require "self-deception." How, then, can he consider the impact of actual events, events that victims may not be able to name?

For us, incest is not simply an intrapsychic event, and it is not simply a narrative invention. Although we share with social constructionists an awareness of the constitutive role of language, and our book considers the social contexts for telling, we challenge the so-called reasonable story about *child abuse* by showing some of what such a story silences. Using case records of incest, the letters of Maimie Pinzer, the narrative of Sojourner Truth, and the writings of Gertrude Stein, we explore accounts, written in the late nineteenth and early twentieth centuries, in which women manage to narrate incestuous experiences even before those experiences are given the name *child abuse* or *incest*. These new interpreters of experience create a space for telling that is almost ghostly, so tenuous is its authority and its claim to be something other than an assault on public morality.

In the late nineteenth century, the dominant narrative about incest locates the actuality of incest in homes of the poor and the racially other, understood to be sites of immorality. So, for example, for a black man or woman to speak about incest is to reinforce the notion that the black family is a "tangle of pathology," to use the words of the Moynihan report (*Negro Family*, 30). In **Chapter 2, "Signifying Incest,"** we discuss how two celebrated African-American writers, Ralph Ellison and Toni Morrison, tell incest. In Ellison's *Invisible Man*, an African-American father, Trueblood, tells a story about incest that both reveals the white father (as embodied in Mr. Norton) to be a perpetrator and allows Trueblood, as a perpetrator himself, to enhance his own paternal authority. This paternalistic narrative is challenged, we argue, by Toni Morrison in *The Bluest Eye*, a novel that attempts to narrate the story of incest from what was, in the late 1960s, the almost unimaginable position of the black daughter.

The cultural work done by these narratives is enormous, and this is why we devote a chapter to African-American incest novels in this book.[6] They rewrite the received incest story so as to shift the responsibility for incest from marginalized and poor people to those whose social status and authority allow them to commit acts of incestuous violence and to silence speech about them. The African-American incest narrative thus gives shape to a realm of experience occluded by the dominant story, namely that slavery was a paternalistic institution in which white men economically and sexually exploited people that they defined as their dependents. While this rewriting of the official story may itself become a moralized enclosure, one that makes it difficult for African-

American women to tell about incest in their own families, it defiantly makes visible the larger social field in which incest takes place and explains why incest is projected onto culturally marginal people as something only *they* do.

In the late 1970s and early 1980s, white feminists drew upon the writings of African-American women, not only *The Bluest Eye* but also Gayle Jones's *Corregidora* and Maya Angelou's *I Know Why the Caged Bird Sings,* in order to formulate what we call the "feminist incest story." **Chapter 3, "It's about Patriarchal Power,"** focuses on two influential nonfiction books, Louise Armstrong's *Kiss Daddy Good Night* and Judith Herman's *Father-Daughter Incest,* that tell a story about incest as an effect of patriarchy. The feminist incest story challenges official claims about incest that are predominant and pervasive in the professional discourses of anthropology and psychology: the claim that the incest taboo founds culture by requiring the exogamous exchange of women, making incest seem rare and outside culture; the claim that daughters who tell about incest are projecting their own transgressive desires for their fathers; the claim that cold wives and collusive mothers are to blame. Authors of the feminist incest story made these familiar claims seem strange by turning the tables. They collected women's stories to show that incest was not rare but ordinary; they challenged Freud's focus on the daughter's desire by focusing on the father's desire and power, an emphasis that lifted blame from mothers as well as daughters.

Patriarchal myths seemed to be replaced, at last, by women's truth. But producers of the feminist incest story did not see that by effecting a reversal, their story was shaped by the culturally powerful narratives that they had rejected. The feminist incest story, disseminated at a moment of high feminist expectation, assumed that speaking out is telling all—and that telling all would make possible revolutionary change. In this way, the feminist incest story was a paradigmatic instance of that smart but somewhat dated feminist sound bite: "The personal is political." Showing how gendered forms of social inequality distorted family life, feminists who wrote about incest were impelled by a belief that women's testimony about incest, the feminist incest story, would be productive of massive political change.

While these hopes were not satisfied, the feminist incest story did create cultural space for paying new attention to what happened to victims of incest. In **Chapter 4, "The Canonical Incest Story,"** we look at a few of the best-known books about incest written in the 1980s: Alice Walker's *The Color Purple,* Ellen Bass and Laura Davis's *The Courage to Heal,* and Jane Smiley's *A Thousand Acres.* These incest narratives offer versions of the "recovery story." The word *recovery* has a double meaning. It refers to the act of recapturing memories of incest that have been disassociated and forgotten, and it also suggests the process of healing from a traumatic event.[7] These narratives appropriate elements of the canonical American story about a beset individual's (here an abused woman's) heroic resistance to a constrictive social order that leads to the creation of a newly redeemed community. The revolution promised by the feminist incest story never happened in the real world, but it happens rhetorically in the incest recovery story. This narrative model thus incorporates the energies of the feminist incest story in its promise to free the beset incest victim from an oppressive past.

The wide success, the marketability, of these recovery narratives has evoked both acclaim and condemnation. While some readers were grateful for narratives that celebrated new possibilities for survivors of incest—the word *survivor* itself suggesting a separation from a past scene of injury—detractors maintained that incest was now all too easy to tell, and perhaps the *only* story of women's distress that could be heard. In **Chapter 5, "The Science of Memory,"** we look at narratives that attempt to demonstrate that the proliferation of women's stories about recovering memories of incest is a symptom of the invidious power of therapists. We call these stories "false-memory stories." To readers unfamiliar with this jargon, "false memory" is shorthand for "false-memory syndrome," a syndrome that purports to describe the process by which patients come to believe in the truth of false memories, that is, in incest memories that are fabricated rather than recovered within a therapeutic session. In false-memory stories, the recovery of memories of incest never leads to healing. Instead, the false-memory story describes how therapists lead patients to believe that they are incest victims and then how parents come to be considered monsters by their deluded daughters.

By the early 1990s, the lineaments of the false-memory story were beginning to solidify. In this genre of narrative, a writer attempts to provide scientific evidence about how easily memories are distorted in order to invalidate women's claims to have recovered true memories of incest, especially in therapy. False-memory stories often provide thoughtful descriptions of the malleability of memory. Yet an insistence on the distorting properties of memory also becomes a source of anxiety for producers of this kind of narrative. Writers who attack "recovery stories" believe that they can locate the truth, which is that these stories are false. But because these writers have dramatized the power of narrative frameworks in constructing the past, they also reveal their own work to be highly mediated. Furthermore, false-memory narratives, which highlight the role of the market in promoting therapies and claims of abuse, also participate in the consumption and exchange of popular narratives about victims, a discourse they decry.

Nonetheless, the false-memory story, which structures a dichotomy between true and false memory, has demonstrated its dominance by effectively defining incest tellings as something to be debated. As Mike Males notes, although "sexual and other violent abuse of children" is a documented and severe problem, the supposedly false memories of those who tell incest now seems to be a bigger crime (10). One way to think about the size of the problem is by looking at its coverage. In 1994, according to Mike Staunton, "more than 80 percent of the coverage of sexual abuse" in prominent weekly magazines "focused on false accusations involving supposed false memory" (44).[8] Given this public framing of the topic of sexual abuse, it is not surprising that readers might have doubts about the truthfulness of women's incest narratives.

Yet heightened skepticism may defeat understanding of new contributions to the expression of women's subjectivity and oppression as still incompletely tellable. As we have already discussed, our skepticism initially made it difficult for us to understand the contributions made by incest survivor memoirs, the subject of **Chapter 6, "The Incest Survivor Memoir."** These memoirs occupy a discursive space opened up thanks to the political and intellectual gains made by both "feminist" and "recovery" stories. However, they also challenge the view that healing is easy by emphasizing the damaging, long-lasting effects of trauma. These new stories thus make visible the difficulty of remembering and telling that many other tellers had downplayed. With the acknowledgment of lasting trauma in these new tellings also comes an increased understanding and analysis of the limitations of language and, therefore, of the inevitability of uncertainty, paradox, and reconstruction in giving public expression to private wounds. Incest survivor memoirs also offer a layered representation of both the event and the way fantasy can give shape to both the victim's and the perpetrator's understandings of an event. These stories thus contest the belief, further promulgated by the now familiar practice of couching the understanding of incest in terms of truth and falsehood, that fantasy is a falsehood and an event is the raw truth.

But if the literature of trauma disputes the possibility of a *fantasized* event causing trauma, is the reality of trauma thereby exalted and the fantasy life of trauma victims consequently ignored?[9] Our reading of work on trauma suggests that trauma theorists strive both to consider the social and experiential sources of trauma and also how trauma is internalized and narrated. This negotiation often leads not to a forgetting of the place of fantasy but to an emphasis upon it, upon mechanisms of repression, dissociation, denial, and repetition. Interestingly, these are mechanisms that allow the incest victim and her therapist to direct their attention away from rather than toward the finding of facts.

It might also be said that psychoanalysis as an institution sometimes deflects attention from large-scale social problems like incest abuse. As Michelle Massé has pointed out, a focus on individual psycho-pathologies can blind us to the "larger cultural production of discipline and punishment" shaping "the individual psychodrama" (5). "Our repression-based analyses," Massé writes, "thus construct a reassuring critical fiction," one that draws attention to psychic mechanisms and thus relegates to the margins the external, social sources of trauma (11). Critics like Mark Pendergrast believe that analysts of trauma unduly emphasize the factual basis of women's narratives about traumatic events, but Massé's words are a reminder that the psychoanalytic understanding of trauma may lead to forgetting as well as to remembering past traumatic experiences.

Although they highlight the artful reconstruction involved in narrating a terrifying past event, producers of the incest survivor memoir still insist upon the truth of their memories of incest, that "the thing" really happened, thus continuing to provoke incredulity and outrage. In **Chapter 7, "On the Borders of the Real,"** we discuss Dorothy Allison's *Bastard out of Carolina* and Sapphire's *Push*, novels that also mix fiction and truth within the more hybrid genre of autobiographical fiction, a genre that is "not biography and yet not lies," as Allison describes it (*Trash*, 12). These novels seem to confirm expectations that incest is likely to be found in homes of the poor. They also might seem to favor traditions of the "recovery story" that exalt central characters as individuals who rise above their circumstances, or, in the case of contemporary incest narratives, who move from trauma to recovery and become "survivors." We explore Allison's and Sapphire's use of the resources of the recovery story to endow a culturally marginalized incest victim with full humanity and subjectivity, thereby allowing her to voice a believable account of the *difficulty* of rising above oppressive circumstances. At the same time, these novels encourage readers to believe in the exceptional individual: protagonists of these novels "push" impressively far. The uneasy but productive way in which the recovery plot is used against itself in these two novels offers another instance of a complex form of telling.

By the end of our book, readers will not have found a litmus test for deriving the truth or falsehood of incest stories. Instead, we hope to offer strategies for thinking about the multiple ways in which women have told incest stories and gained a hearing. In order to locate the historical shifts in the dynamic of telling and listening, it has been helpful to think about fault lines where the unsayable disrupts a dominant paradigm for telling. Cathy Caruth explains that deconstruction (which we could understand here as a method of struggling to express what cannot be spoken) comes to understand any text as a site of the possibility of a new reference, one that cannot be accounted for in "preconceived conceptual terms" (Caruth and Esch, 3). This way of understanding a text challenges the more constricted view adopted by Hacking and Young, which implies that only what is named can be real. Our own strategy for listening is to notice where emerging realities—new references—are marked in narratives about incest. These references disrupt familiar patterns of narrating and understanding incest.

One way to understand what Caruth means by "preconceived conceptual terms" is to see these filtering terms as a master narrative, one that shapes expectations about narratives and their relation to a specific referential field, for us, incest. Texts that resist normative understandings, for example, the belief that incest is a taboo and rarely happens, may initially seem to be mistaken and then come to seem normative, for resistant stories themselves often give rise to a dominant narrative that will itself be disrupted by yet new tellings. This process is a complex and open-ended one, and our book only provides a limited set of examples. Nonetheless, we hope that it offers suggestions for rethinking and revising familiar ideas about what incest narratives sound like and what they mobilize. In the effort to describe, remember, and re-create the unspeakable, these narratives point to historical doings and fantasized residues of women's experience, both authoritative and uncertain, about which we always need to think again.

Chapter 1
Ordinary Doings

Recent debates about the truthfulness of belated memories of incest have highlighted the role of narrative in memorial representations of the past. As a result of this emphasis on narrative and the constructedness of memory, many feminists—and many of their detractors—have come to the conclusion that women's stories about incest may tell us more about the distorting lens of memory and powerful ideological forces than about authentic experiences of incest. All narratives reflect social and political interests, but confessional narratives, more than other kinds of stories, evoke contradictory responses. While they seem at first to be urgent and authentic outpourings, upon reexamination they appear to be shaped by the needs of powerful inquisitors and hungry audiences. In the last decade, women's memorial accounts of incest have increasingly been understood by many academics and journalists to be disturbing products of therapeutic intervention rather than independent accounts of real events.

Some feminists have seen this reading of incest stories as an antifeminist attack on women's authority as reporters of the past, but others insist that skepticism about incest stories cannot be antifeminist—because they, too, are worried. Recovered-memory stories, in particular, have been described by feminists such as Carol Tavris and Elaine Showalter as debilitating tales featuring women as victims, not agents. These feminists, along with members of the False Memory Syndrome Foundation, have argued that it might be in everyone's best interest if women's incest stories were reprivatized: kept not only within the sphere of the therapist's office but understood as bound by the even more private space of personal fantasy. The desire for a reconfinement of stories about incest is linked to fears about what telling incest has supposedly wrought: broken families, children suing parents, a growing number of disturbing novels and memoirs.

In this chapter we are going to suggest why it is nonetheless worth taking the risk of trying to uncover the complex ways in which incest narratives are told and embedded in the world. Despite the inevitable problems with narratives that attempt to uncover the truth of the past, the denial of any reliable historical itinerary has its own dangers. As we will show through an analysis of Ian Hacking's *Rewriting the Soul,* which offers a sustained argument about the costs of talking too much about childhood sexual abuse and trauma, the effort to limit talk about the past is a gesture that often serves to consolidate the power to remember legitimately in the hands of a few.

The debate about recovered memories has produced, in a competitive way, intricate narratives asserting and contesting the links between sexual trauma and memory. The analogies used on both sides of the debate are dramatic, historical, and very rhetorical. So, for example, a segment of the recovered-memory argument, found in popular books such as Bass and Davis's *The Courage to Heal* and Herman's *Trauma and Recovery,* is constructed by pieces of the debate about the truth of the Holocaust. Because Holocaust deniers peddle a falsely benign past, recovered-memory advocates have found it useful to deploy the power of the Holocaust metaphor to suggest that deniers of recovered memories of child abuse are counterparts to Holocaust revisionists. And given the amount of media attention bestowed upon a vague concoction, "False-Memory Syndrome," a term invented by the False Memory Syndrome Foundation to suggest the craziness of those who claim recovered memories of incest, this analogy was perhaps inevitable. For recovered-memory advocates, the Holocaust provides a moralized lesson from history that lends support to the argument that false-memory proponents "abuse survivors" with contrived arguments, while it also emphasizes the truth of recovered memories of abuse (Lipstadt, 3).[1]

Members of the false-memory movement employ another metaphor, the "witch hunt," to attack the recovered-memory movement. This metaphor transforms women with recovered memories into sexual hysterics. These crazed women apparently enjoy victimizing innocent people, "the falsely accused," who are charged with crimes and convicted despite a lack of evidence: "we are now experiencing the United States' third great wave of hysteria. I believe that more have suffered in its course than all those who suffered in Salem and the McCarthy era combined" (Gardner, 425).[2] Here, again, a moralized history lesson, involving powerful American communal stories about group-think and persecution, lends support to the argument that innocent people are suffering at the hands of recovered-memory victimizers. Simplified references to past events, especially the Salem witchcraft and McCarthy trials, emphasize the embattled reasonableness of proponents of false memory in the face of a resurgent and feminized form of American irrationality.

Such charged rhetoric makes it difficult, yet all the more desirable, to talk about the issue of sexual abuse and memory in a quiet, reasonable way, though reason is also a partisan in the debates about memory. Ian Hacking has written a philosophical work, often cited by analysts of women's incest stories, about multiple personality disorder and its links to concepts of child abuse, *Rewriting the Soul: Multiple Personality and the Science of Memory.* In this book, Hacking attempts to separate the contemporary language of multiples, child abuse, and recovered memories from the words and meanings attached to childhood trauma in the last half of the nineteenth century and the first half of the twentieth. Yet though his self-described "archaeological" scholarship promises relief from careless historicizing, his "distanced view of child abuse" (67) is actually part of the fray. In this chapter, Hacking's discussion of child sexual abuse will be juxtaposed with American women's stories of abuse written during the period that interests Hacking. These narratives do not emphasize psychic repression, and this means that we have chosen to examine transgressive stories, drawn from case records, letters, autobiography, and literature, that do not follow the familiar analytic plot line about women's stories of sexual abuse as having a simple origin in the nets of psychoanalytic discourse. The stories that interest us thus provide a challenge to Hacking's usefully representative assumption that tellings of child abuse have a very specific origin in late-nineteenth-century narratives about "shock," in accounts of physical wounds that were transformed by Janet and Freud into narratives about psychic trauma. Hacking presents contemporary discourse about child abuse and trauma as a fabrication of the past, unlike the discourse found in archives, which supposedly reveals the actual past. We will challenge this way of framing the divide between past and present and offer a more dynamic account of how experiences are estranged from language and how they are recovered. We are thus creating another perspective on what constitutes responsible remembering. Since memory wars may be irritating, it is useful to bear in mind that a unified view of the past is only possible if alternative views are unspoken—or unacknowledged.

Of course, skeptics, observing the recent proliferation of incest stories, might well turn to Ian Hacking's *Rewriting the Soul* for confirmation of their fears that contemporary narratives of child sexual abuse would be better left unspoken. Hacking argues that these new stories have a dangerous agency: "One should not dismiss the possibility that some of the increase in child abuse is due to the publicity itself, in that it makes available new descriptions under which to act, and then, by semantic contagion, leads on to yet worse actions" (238). Apparently, the present language used to describe child abuse does more than bury the past under an edifice of signs, "new descriptions." These descriptions are capable of corrupting the present. Hacking makes those who attempt to address the problem of child abuse partly responsible for causing it through a process of "semantic contagion" (238).[3]

Certainly representations—the language we use, the images we see—do shape our desires and actions, though not in a simple cause-and-effect way. The relation between individual acts and the set of cultural representations and material conditions informing those acts is enormously complex. Hacking, because he is interested in isolating structures of causation, often makes things too simple. To isolate the contemporary use of the phrase *child abuse* as a cause of child abuse reductively limits discussion of causes. For one thing, Hacking's focus deflects attention from perpetrators: why do perpetrators forget the desires and interests of daughters? under what conditions does sex become a form of disciplinary violence? what cultural definitions of the erotic inform their desires? Furthermore, a focus on the dangers of the phrase *child abuse* masks the significant ways in which, historically, a prohibition on speaking about abuse has served not to stop incest from occurring but to occlude responses to it. Silence frees the field for perpetrators. As Wendy Evans and David Maines point out, "the collaboration of clinical and social scientific theories" in the late nineteenth century supported a rhetoric about the incest taboo and dysfunctional girls that made incest and male perpetrators nearly invisible (306). Louise Barnett explains how these prohibitions shaped the reception of incest tellings: "The easiest attitude for a public that never spoke about such things was to assume that an accusation of incest could not be true. Even if it were, many would maintain, bringing it to light was the greater scandal, a corruption of public discourse" (22). By decrying the "semantic contagion" caused by speaking about child abuse, Hacking's rhetoric implicitly works to support a prohibition on telling in the name of public morality, without suggesting any alternatives.

Hacking not only attempts to chill present discussions of child abuse by arguing that our new descriptions contaminate the present, he also suggests these descriptions contaminate the past: "retroactive attribution of modern moral concepts" may make the past seem more corrupt than it really was. Hacking offers the following "trite" example.

Imagine some plain, but not entirely gross, case of sexual harassment that took place in 1950, behavior that contravened no law nor custom of 1950, and which hardly even infringed the canons of taste then current, in the social milieu where the event took place. If you tell me about the episode in 1950 terms, you certainly will not use the expression "sexual harassment." What was the man doing? You answer by identifying the action, telling me what the man was doing to his secretary, perhaps, and the way in which he said it. But now you can also answer the question "what was the man doing?" with "He was sexually harassing his secretary." This is the same action as the one you first presented in a more neutral way, but it is that action under a new description. On the other hand, when we ask whether the man intended to harass his secretary, most of us are less sure what to say. Today, in many milieus, we hold in contempt the man who says he did not realize he was harassing. And if he will not stop behaving that way, he is finished. But when we reflect on the 1950s man, there is a certain diminishment to the accusation if the very idea of harassment was not available to him. (*Rewriting the Soul*, 243)

Hacking's implicit question is: how can we now condemn the 1950s man if he could not have understood his actions as sexual harassment?

The ghostly neutrality of the man's actions, however, is being produced by Hacking's writing, though it seems at first only an artifact of a "doing's" necessary namelessness. Hacking asks his readers to imagine a "plain" case of sexual harassment, but he does not provide a clear description of what the "man was doing to his secretary." Of course, he cannot be "clear" because the point of this exercise is to refuse to name what is happening and so remain, presumably, chaste, innocent of contemporary namings. At the same time, Hacking's refusal, one made in the present, may also be read as an aggressive suppression of information. The passage only admits that the action was something "said." A "plain case of harassment," as definitions of sexual harassment insist, would occur within a specific context in which one person has power over another and exercises it, often repeatedly, through unwelcome, sexually provocative words and actions.[4] In a "plain case" of harassment, it would be difficult for a woman—in Hacking's example, "his secretary"—to resist such "doings" without jeopardizing her job. Hacking's troubling focus on the man's doings and complete lack of interest in the secretary's response (the classic male boss and female secretary roles thus repeated in the narrowness of Hacking's concern) allow him to blandly assert that in the 1950s "you" (which "you" is this?) would have had a neutral description for actions that "we" (which "we" is this?) would now identify as harassment.[5]

To accept Hacking's belief that a clear divide exists between "them" in the past and "us" in the present requires a good deal of confidence in the homogeneity of both cultural moments. Was the 1950s a decade in which there existed a consensus about "canons of taste"? Hacking insists that if a man did not think he was harassing, then "there is a certain diminishment" to present accusations about his doings (243). Because he takes as a given the absolute dominance of the boss's point of view (though he thinks he offers a universal perspective), Hacking can claim that in the 1950s, the man's doings were more or less "neutral," which is a way of saying that they were, at the time, not simply unnameable but also incontestable. His implicit belief that there would likely be no resistance to the man's doings requires that Hacking forget the point of view of the woman who was the recipient of these acts.[6] The secretary, of course, might have felt scared and angry about "what the man was doing." She might not have agreed that the man's actions were "hardly" an infringement of taste; she might even have said something. The lacunae in Hacking's example reflects his own blind spot. Despite his claims to be conducting a Foucauldian archaeology, he does not engage in Foucault's effort to map not only what a dominant discourse creates but what it excludes and subjugates. In other words, Hacking pays insufficient attention to the dynamic of power and resistance.

From a feminist perspective, the 1950s have long been linked to women's experience of a "problem that has no name," as Betty Friedan so memorably put it. That Friedan's book focuses only on the plight of educated, affluent, white women is proof that even this painfully articulated effort to name women's problems also rendered invisible the language and experiences of women with less visibility and social power. Indeed, it has only been very recently that writings of African-American women in the 1950s have been recognized as articulating resistance to the status quo. Examining contemporaneous reviews of Gwendolyn Brooks's only novel, *Maud Martha* (1953), Mary Helen Washington notices their inability to perceive the novel's "compelling themes," "the struggle to sustain one's identity against a racist and sexist society, the silences that result from repressed anger, the need to assert a creative life" (31). Hacking's imposed consensus, like the one operating in reviews of *Maud Martha,* simply ignores the feelings and words of those women in the 1950s who resisted and ultimately transformed normalized practices (ones that "contravened no law" and seemed not to infringe "canons of taste"). A feminist critic, Maureen Cain, pushes that subjugated knowledge into view: "Did not the relations which constitute sexual harassment exist before they were named and did not the women in those relations have an experience? Is not that . . . experience the reason that women wanted to take the personally risky and politically fundamental step of giving the experience a name?" (89).[7]

Hacking's "trite" example seeks to demonstrate the epistemological and moral problems associated with describing past actions in new terms such as *sexual harassment.* Indeed Hacking believes that commentators falsify the past by describing old, unnamed actions using such new terms. His point is that *sexual harassment* is a recent term and must mark a new category of experience. But do new terms always work this way? That someone did not know that she suffered from a disease called "diabetes" did not mean that diabetes did not exist. Naming, then, may not always falsify the past, and trying to avoid naming, as Hacking does in the interests of fidelity to history, has its own dangers. By fabricating an example that is "not entirely gross," he necessarily uses description to construct and contain the meaning of what happened in the past: in this case, men doing nameless things to women. Despite his anxiety about false attribution, Hacking himself uses signs to build an image of the 1950s that he believes represents the truth of the past itself. His descriptions are contrived and interested, but the real problem is his inability to acknowledge that anything lies outside them. In a sense, he has too much confidence in his own authority.

In a predictable extension of his argument, Hacking suggests that recovered memories of sexual abuse involve the falsification of the past. He writes: "Old actions under new descriptions may be reexperienced in memory. And if these are genuinely new descriptions, descriptions not available or perhaps nonexistent at the time of the episodes remembered, then something is experienced now, in memory, that in a certain sense did not exist before" (*Rewriting the Soul*, 249). Hacking is here developing a postmodern argument that explains that recovered memories are false insofar as our present discursive milieu (our "narrative truth") separates us from the past: new descriptions create new pasts. For Hacking, remembering involves finding the historically correct words for invoking the past (the "historical truth"). These are two forms of linguistic absolutism. In addition to arguing that narrative and historical truths are not so easily separated, we hope to show that nondiscursive conditions— historically contingent forms of embodiment of, and resistance to, power relations—have an instrumental relation to language. As previously unspoken doings emerge into representation, they challenge the comprehensiveness of dominant forms of language and knowledge.

Having drawn a historical line at the 1960s, the time before which charges of past abuse cannot "in a certain sense" be accurate, Hacking moves to what he sees as the real problem: women in therapy, especially "multiple personality therapy," are using their "apparent memories" to fashion false selves. In this way, therapy leads women to "false consciousness."

> Not in the blatant sense that the apparent memories of early abuse are necessarily wrong or distorted—they may be true enough. No, there is the sense that the end product is a thoroughly crafted person, but not a person who serves the ends for which we are persons. Not a person with self-knowledge, but a person who is the worse for having a glib patter that simulates an understanding of herself. Some of the feminist writers . . . appear to share this moral judgment. They add that too much multiple therapy implicitly confirms the old male model of the passive woman who could not hang in, who retroactively creates a story about herself in which she was the weak vessel. (*Rewriting the Soul*, 266)

Women, it seems, are more harmed by therapeutic practices than by their "true enough" painful memories. Implicit here is another prohibition on women's stories (or "glib patter") about victimization, this time in the name of the laudable stoicism of the woman who "hangs in." Notice how passive is the form of agency—"hanging in"—that Hacking extols.[8] Yet for Hacking, "hanging in" is a powerful moral operation that protects a woman's very soul, the core of her being, from the emptying-out process of therapeutic self-fabrication.

While feminists such as Carol Tavris, Wendy Kaminer, and Janice Haaken have expressed concerns about the political effects of women's identifying themselves as victims who need to be saved, all such concerns are not feminist. Indeed many false-memory proponents unilaterally blame feminism for *encouraging* women to think of themselves as victims, an argument that is meant to make all survivor stories seem deplorable, victim posturing.[9] Hacking's language, which often follows the contours of the false-memory argument about the power of therapists to elicit false memories, dramatically features women losing their souls as they become pseudovictims. Indeed, the extent to which he represents women as pseudo-victims is stunning given that he is willing to acknowledge that their memories may be true. By emphasizing women's loss, Hacking also refuses claims made by female patients that recalling/narrating their experiences of abuse is empowering and a source of new discursive authority. For Hacking, these claims too become fabrications, glib patter, false consciousness. Yet it is useful to remember that other interpreters place the scene of a woman's "soul murder" *before* therapeutic intervention, in acts of violence, rather than after it. Leonard Shengold, for example, describes "soul murder" as an effect of an abused child having either felt too much to bear or having been exposed to too little (2). When "soul murder" is positioned this way, then the locus of dangerous fabrication lies in those who disavow the terrors of the familial past, not the therapeutic present.[10] In Hacking's work, the individual as well as the social past is a place of greater integrity than the present, but it is important to recognize that this assumption is a crucial site of contestation in the memory wars.

Although Hacking sometimes aligns himself with feminists who are skeptical about the effects of therapy, his argument differs from theirs in its implicit effort to protect a discursive regime that operated in the past to privilege the boss's point of view by rendering it neutral. Remarking upon the problem of viewing one's discursive positions as neutral, Dean MacCannell and Juliet Flower MacCannell point out, "That some are privileged to think of their power as neutral, to think of themselves and those with whom they enter into power relations as free is based on the suppression of violence" (206). Actions in the past rendered blandly neutral by Hacking were contested by women struggling against forms of oppression without a name. Because he dismisses this struggle, Hacking's admonition against naming the past using new descriptions begins to seem a powerful move to enforce his reading of the past against the claims of new interpreters. As Hacking's book demonstrates, the inevitable process of rereading the past is disconcerting, especially to those who would like to settle on one authentic, seemingly apolitical and neutral meaning for past events—the one *they* provide, of course.

In another effort to draw a clear distinction between past and present, Hacking offers a brief history of child abuse that attempts to explain what can be accurately said about such past "doings." "The phrase 'child abuse'—that exact phrase—is seldom found before 1960; its predecessor was 'cruelty to children'" (56). Unlike *child abuse*, which is now supposed to be a classless evil, "cruelty to children" was connected to poverty and "not felt as the outstanding evil" (58). Furthermore "the man who beat or raped his daughter may have been called a beast, but there was no expert knowledge to help, cure, or manage that type of individual. He was a wretch to be punished" (59). This summary, which he expands elsewhere, accurately emphasizes the former centrality of the phrase "cruelty to children." This phrase was often used by the late-nineteenth-century protection agencies that were indeed directing help to the poor, though Hacking ignores the importance of the growing professionalization of social-work "experts." Entirely missing from his summary, however, is any effort to think about the victim of the "beast," to whom Hacking is as indifferent as he is to his imagined "secretary." He also refuses engagement with the multiple and shifting determinants of acceptable speech during this period. Not only does he not explain why so little discursive pressure was put on the "man who beat or raped his daughter"—deference to paternal authority? beliefs that sex with children cured venereal disease?—but he does not pay sufficient attention to the texts of new interpreters, located outside of scientific networks, who were challenging the fixed picture of the social universe offered by privileged male subjects.[11] It is to examples of these narratives, rather than the much-analyzed accounts of Freud and Janet, that we now wish to direct attention.

One set of narratives revealing the language women used to destabilize, though not defeat, the prohibition on speaking about incest has been developed and analyzed by Linda Gordon in several articles, as well as in her book *Heroes of Their Own Lives*. These narratives are drawn from the archives of three private social-work agencies in Boston during the years 1880 to 1960; about 10 percent of the case records in her sample were cases of incest, and most (98 percent) involved the sexual assault of a girl by an older male relative, usually the father (Gordon, *Heroes*, 207; Gordon, "Incest and Resistance," 253). Acknowledgment of these cases was "in part based on [the] notion that it was exclusively a vice of the poor." Yet although there were class boundaries placed on discourse about incest, the eventual cross-class legitimacy of this discourse was inevitable once the prohibition against speaking about ordinary incest was partially lifted. Perhaps that is why an organization that worked with the poor, the Massachusetts Society for the Prevention of Cruelty to Children "considered incest cases 'too revolting to publish.'" Moral opprobrium clearly was attached to incest long before 1960 and could be used to ban information about its frequency and ordinariness (Gordon, *Heroes*, 215). One of Gordon's goals is "to situate incest socially and historically, in the ordinary conditions of girls' lives" ("Incest and Resistance," 254). The ordinary pattern of incest in the case records between 1880 and 1930 will be familiar to readers of Herman's *Father-Daughter Incest*, a book that we will analyze more fully in a later chapter. The pattern involves families in which a socially isolated oldest daughter with an absent or weakened mother has to function as a wife (housekeeper, baby-sitter, sexual partner) for a moralizing, tyrannical father. The earliest testimony about an incest victim that Gordon includes in her book comes from records in the 1920s that corroborate the incest experience of an oldest daughter. Social workers recorded many exchanges, like this one, that compel belief for several reasons. First, they are mediated through agency workers who often disdained the culture of their clients (*Heroes*, 14) and so cannot be accused of offering excessively sympathetic accounts. Second, these caseworker reports have the directness associated with the "note": "About 2 or 3 wks after mo's death one night fa came to the kitchen and locked the door, and made [Silvia] get on his lap, and had relations with her." Though the father initially denied the charges and tried to get the other children to testify on his behalf, he was eventually convicted and sentenced to ten to twelve years (206–7). In her study of similar cases, Gordon found that girls, despite "canons of feminine acquiescence" (253), actively reported attacks, and child-protection workers helped convict perpetrators, though then, as now, there were concerns about false allegations (216). Between 1910 and 1960, attitudes toward victims shifted; preventative work became less active, and the crime of incest lost visibility as the problem of incest became "redefined as a problem of sex delinquency" (219). This new definition—*sex delinquency*—shifted blame from male family members to daughters, while still marking the resistance of abused girls, who often became "sex delinquent" to get the money to leave home.

There are other examples of partial narratives that can help illuminate how women both challenged and respected the prohibitions—linguistic, social, and economic—on telling stories about sexual abuse. Between 1910 and 1922, Maimie Pinzer, a working-class woman, wrote letters to Sophie Howe, a wealthy and charitable Bostonian. These now well-known letters were published by the Feminist Press in 1977 in an effort to restore to visibility the lives of "ordinary and powerless people" whose perspectives were not, at that time, often included in historical accounts (Rosen, xiii). Maimie's letters include a revelation of abuse by an uncle that functions to challenge the moralizing voice of a male relative. Maimie, remembering the actions of her uncle, who argued at a hearing that she was incorrigible, writes: "This uncle is the same one who did me the first wrong, when I was a tiny girl, and any number of times since then" (193). Maimie's first-person account surely gains credibility, though it could be seen as a way to explain her "fall," because early abuse has been linked to later prostitution, for her an occasional occupation.[12] Further, the simplicity of this quasi-private revelation powerfully dramatizes the gap between her power to narrate her experience in a letter and her uncle's power to narrate it in a court of law.

Providing another example of this kind of belated, almost invisible testi-

mony about nonincestuous sexual abuse, the historian Nell Painter sugges-
tively reads the silences of Sojourner Truth's *Narrative* (1859) and finds a story
about Sojourner's abuse by her mistress. With the help of an amanuensis
whose presence is revealed in the *Narrative*'s distanced point of view, Truth
describes "a long series of trials in the life of our heroine, which we must pass
over in silence; some from motives of delicacy, and others because the relation
of them might inflict undeserved pain on some now living" (20). These trials
may have included sexual abuse. Painter writes: "the sexual abuse came from
her mistress Sally Dumont, and Truth could tell about it only obliquely, in scat-
tered pages in her *Narrative*. Truth spoke straightforwardly about most of her
suffering in slavery, "'this putrescent plague-spot,' but only vaguely about this"
(Painter, 16). Truth's story was about things that she called "so unacceptable,
so unreasonable, and what is usually called so unnatural" that readers who
were not "initiated" might doubt her veracity (16). Painter points out that abo-
litionist literature actively circulated slave narratives about the rape of slaves by
male slave owners, and Truth was unlikely to be reticent had this been the story
she wanted to tell. There remained, however, abuses that were "unseen" by
abolitionists and thus less credible (16). Truth knew her audience. Her story
strategically omits what cannot be believably told, without allowing the
"believable" to entirely determine what she says. Her "vague" tale points to a
place of a "doing" that cannot be told because it cannot be credibly heard.

These narratives in which women tell about their experiences of nearly
unspeakable doings are, by definition, spoken by social actors who assert themselves against the grain of a culture that suppresses such reports, even if, as
Hacking correctly notes, exemptions were sometimes given to the poor
because they were understood to be immoral and thus required to "confess."[13]
Yet though these women's narratives were fragmentary and did not often serve
as the basis for public condemnation of an abuser, they mark an intervention
of the kind that will eventually gain enough cultural authority to make
women's incest stories a powerful form of contemporary women's memory, a
form with the power to inspire a backlash. In early narratives of abuse, of
course, that power is only nascent. Maimie's story was written long after her
uncle had successfully spoken at the hearing that would define her sexuality as
delinquent. Yet she did contest his story in a letter to a woman with considerable social status, exposing her uncle's hypocrisy. In alternative archives that
are explored by feminist "archaeologists," new stories about child sexual abuse
emerge at the turn of the century in the context of a changing cultural grid. As
John D'Emilio and Estelle Freedman have pointed out in their book *Intimate
Matters,* sexual practices and their meanings became more heterogeneous as
they were dislocated from a primary association with reproduction in late-
nineteenth-century and early-twentieth-century America. Women, supported
by feminist reformers, protective agencies, and news media interest in sex

crimes, began to mobilize their own narratives about sexuality and gender. This mix of emerging subjectivities, expert discourses, and scandal was both volatile and productive (D'Emilio and Freedman, 166).[14] Contemporary women's narratives of abuse thus have historical antecedents in the final decades of another century, one that shared with our own anxious time a fascination with and suspicion of women's narratives, especially those about sexual threats.

Gertrude Stein is the exemplary figure of innovative women's writing at the turn of the century, so it is not surprising that she self-consciously explored the limits of what was narratable about a father's "doings" to his daughter. Buried at the center of Gertrude's Stein's mammoth book *The Making of Americans* (1925) is an innovative vignette about a man's "doings" and a daughter's response.[15] Though located in a novel that employs deliberately digressive and repetitive textual practices, this vignette is narrated in a surprisingly simple way. It has characters, dialogue, and a clear teleology.

It happens very often that a man has it in him, that a man does something, that he does it very often, that he does many things, when he is a young one and an older one an old one. It happens very often that a man does something, that a man has something in him and he does a thing again and again in his living. There was a man who was always writing to his daughter that she should not do things that were wrong that would disgrace him, she should not do such things and in every letter that he wrote to her he told her she should not do such things, that he was her father and was giving good moral advice to her and always he wrote to her in every letter that she should not do things that she should not do anything that would disgrace him. He wrote this in every letter he wrote to her, he wrote very nicely to her, he wrote often enough to her, and in every letter he wrote to her that she should not do anything that was a disgraceful thing for her to be doing and then once she wrote back to him that he had not any right to write moral things in letters to her, that he had taught her that he had shown her that he had commenced in her the doing the things things that would disgrace her and he had said then when he had begun with her he had said he did it so that when she was older she could take care of herself with those who wished to make her do things that were wicked things and he would teach her and she would be stronger than such girls who had not any way of knowing better, and she wrote this letter and her father got the letter and he was a paralytic always after, it was a shock to him getting such a letter, he kept saying over and over again that his daughter was trying to kill him and now she had done it and at the time he got the letter he was sitting by the fire and he threw the letter in the fire and his wife asked him what was the matter and he said it is Edith she is killing me, what, is she disgracing us said the mother, no said the father, she is killing me and that was all he said then of the matter and he never wrote another letter. (488–89)

Although this story does not use the new description "father-daughter incest," old taboos against speaking about incest are nevertheless resisted in this tale of a father who commences doing things that would "disgrace" his daughter. Indeed, in a small space, Stein provides the contours of a case study of sexual abuse in "ordinary middle class existence" (34), where such abuse was not supposed to exist. Elizabeth Wilson has written perceptively that in the nineteenth century, one of the ways in which the ideology of the white middle class justified the dominance of this class was by implying that "incest occurs more often in other classes or racial groups because these groups are morally inferior and are unable to restrain their animal impulses" ("Not in This House," 41). This ideology, she suggests, continues to inform the false-memory syndrome movement and its denials that incest has occurred in the nice white families that make up the bulk of its membership.

Stein's narrator tells the reader that a man engages in repetitive behavior: "he does a thing again and again in his living." This generalized repetitive "doing" at first seems to be exemplified by an action that can be named: writing. The father repeats, and so does Stein, uncovering "the thing" through repetition. "There was a man who was always writing to his daughter that she should not do things that were wrong that would disgrace him." This man seems to be giving "good moral advice to her," to the daughter, whose morality we question since we are initially viewing her through the eyes of the father. Stein insists on the repetitive qualities of his letter writing: "always he wrote to her in every letter." He wrote this in "every letter," he wrote "often enough," so that his morality and writing both come to seem weirdly obsessive.

The daughter, however, just has to write once, puncturing her father's confidence in his own virtue, perhaps secured only through repetition. She reminds him of other, unacknowledged scenes of instruction, "that he had taught her that he had shown her that he had commenced in her the doing the things things that would disgrace her and he had said then when he had begun with her he had said he did it so that when she was older she could take care of herself with those who wished to make her do things that were wicked things." The daughter's stunning reminder of the things he has done to her causes his paralysis, a symptomatic revision of the trauma that transforms him into a victim and thus provides a defense against recollecting his role as the initiator of "wicked things," though he never denies her account. Repeatedly performing his new victimhood in an emotional style usually associated with discredited, hysterical femininity, the father says "over and over again that his daughter was trying to kill him and now she had done it." The father's language here is eerily familiar because the false-memory movement has popularized emotional narratives of fathers who claim to be victimized by their daughters.

In Stein's vignette, the father's announcement of his daughter's attempted parricide is a moment of apparent power reversal in which the daughter, now given murderous agency, is provided with a name, Edith. The mother, a bystander who announces her allegiance with the father in her use of the pronoun *us,* asks, "is she disgracing us." The father's answer, "no," narrows the scope of interpretive possibilities to what has happened between himself and his daughter, and he repeats, "she is killing me." The emotional impact of the scene is created by the surprising strength of the daughter's intervention, which challenges her father's moral explanation for "commencing in her" things that would disgrace her. The father's rationalization of his actions seems to hinge upon a distinction between what is acceptable for him to do in private and what she can do in public. Although this narrative is very wispy and oblique, it contains many features of later incest narratives. First, the mother's position is uncertain. She seems unaware of what has taken place between the father and daughter yet predisposed to align herself with her husband: "is she disgracing us." Second, the father rationalizes himself as a moral "teacher," and he believes that he is a victim of his daughter's hurtful accusations. Third, the father focuses on the daughter's sexual propriety in the public sphere—or her lack of it. The focus on her sexual behavior deflects attention from his own behavior. All of these features help illuminate why it is difficult for the daughter to tell her story.

This vignette occurs in the "Alfred Hersland and Julia Dehning" section of the novel where a "new way to me of feeling living" begins to emerge (621), following the clearly autobiographical "Martha Hersland" section of *The Making of Americans.* Indeed, Stein scholars have long assumed that the narrator who proclaims, "I write for myself and strangers" at the beginning of this section is simply Stein herself. Yet this "I" is a more complex construction that becomes a subject of increasingly explicit concern in the "Alfred Hersland and Julia Dehning" section. What is the place of the real event in such a project? How has Stein both relied upon and transformed her own history in the act of self-consciously composing it? By asking these questions, we are suggesting that in *The Making of Americans* the boundaries of fiction and personal history are blurred. In this way, we are responding to the complexity of Stein's project and also deferring to pressures to provide corroborating evidence for the truth of an incest story.

The personal experiences that Stein might have been drawing upon as she wrote this "incest" vignette have been documented by biographers, most notably by Linda Wagner-Martin in *Favored Strangers: Gertrude Stein and Her Family,* which places a new emphasis on Stein's childhood and family life. This new form of feminist interpretation is itself highly controversial because of the way it turns a female author's—Virginia Woolf's, Edith Wharton's, Anne Sexton's and now Stein's—purported experiences of incest into the "keys" to her literary work. But surely it is arguable that such autobiographical readings are meaningful even if they are not foundational truths. The story Wagner-Martin tells about behavior in the Stein household suggests that Stein may not have been a happy Buddha, the other popular picture of her life, because of her experiences within what looks like one of the "incest families" described by Judith Herman and Linda Gordon. In these families the mother is absent through death and the sexually abusive father is erratic and domineering. While Wagner-Martin does not mention the vignette we have included here, she does provide evidence from Stein's notebooks pointing to incidents where male relatives made sexual advances to her sister Bertha, and perhaps to Gertrude herself, when both girls were in their teens. Drawing upon the notebooks, Wagner-Martin comments that following the death of Stein's mother, "not only was Daniel [Stein's father] courting women but much more disturbing—he had approached Bertha sexually, 'coming in to her one night to come and keep him warm'" (25). These words drawn from the notebooks seem to be reworked in a passage of *The Making of Americans* where the narrator comments on old men's desire for warmth:

> Many old men do things to keep themselves warm then, when they are old ones and they are needing to be warm then. Some of them are cold then and they need to be warm then and need to be warmed up then, and some are shrunk away from the outside of them then when they are old men and need some one to fill them and they do concrete actions then and their generalised sensation is keeping warm then, their generalised intention is of keeping warm then. (490)

Old men understand their concrete actions as defined by their generalized intentions to keep warm. But how would these doings be understood from the point of view of the "some one" who must warm them?

Apparently Bertha Stein was not the only female in her family to be approached by a male relative, though Gertrude Stein's language about her own experience is elliptical. Wagner-Martin points out that

> writing [in the notebooks] about an attempted sexual encounter was dangerous for Gertrude, particularly since she had been reared to avoid such topics. She added to the risk by combining her account [of Bertha's experience] with her memory of "my experience with Uncle Sol." . . . In another note, Gertrude fused the branches of her father's and uncle's families to implicate both men in this pattern of abuse: "Father's loving children young girls. Uncle Sol, Amy [one of Sol's daughters], uncle to them?" (25)

The halting language of the notebooks suggests a tale of sexual abuse—father "coming into her one night to come and keep him warm" or "father's loving children young girls"—that struggles to be told. In these passages, the tentativeness of Stein's remarks reflects her doubt (note the question mark) about experiences that were not openly discussed by "children young girls" and, in this communal way, provided with legitimation. Though much disparaged as places where false memories are fabricated, survivor support groups today offer ratification of experiences that might otherwise not get a hearing. Stein's story, then, reminds us of what may be at stake when these groups are attacked as functioning only to create fabricated memories.

The inaccessibility of Stein's writing has been justly celebrated by postmodern critics, many of whom have privileged her later works that powerfully challenge conventions of realist writing. Yet attending only to the aesthetic achievements of Stein's writing may downplay her long struggle to give voice to silenced, personal pain—and the extent to which this struggle shaped her experiments in writing narrative. Indeed, much of *Making of Americans* is devoted to her narrator's digressive discussions of how hard it is to write when no one is listening, to her despair about her project: "I am important inside me and not any one really is listening" (595), or "I am in desolation and my eyes are large with needed weeping and I have a flush from feverish feeling" (729). Indeed, Stein was one of the few woman writers of her time who devoted a great deal of space within her texts to the explicit consideration of how to speak what should not be spoken or cannot be said.

The "incest" vignette provides one powerful example of a Steinian narrative that works against and within prohibitions against women telling stories about incestuous abuse, but it is only one of many in *The Making of Americans* that attempt to tell about nameless "doings." In the autobiographical "Martha Hersland" section, one hundred pages before the "incest" story, the narrator writes that

> many do something to a little girl who does not like it, she shows just then no sign of reacting to it, the little girl who does not like it. She is not angry, she seems not to remember then to be angry, her reaction is not there then to it. Then she does something violent to show it and often then the one that did something to that little girl is surprised at it, that one then has forgotten all about it. (379)[16]

In recent testimony about recovered memory, women claim to have recovered memories of events to which they long had no conscious access. But the little girl in Stein's story does not forget what happens. Instead, she forgets to react to what is done: "she seems not to remember then to be angry." This kind of "not remembering" might be described as an artifact of a child's familiar vulnerability ("many do something to a little girl") that inhibits an independent judgment of a doing. A gap also exists between the "doer" and conscious recognition of a doing. As in the vignette, the one "that did something to that little girl" is the one who forgets and is surprised by the forceful expression of the girl's delayed anger.

This little story is interesting because it offers another way of thinking about why perpetrators forget *their* acts. In part because the little girl's expression of anger is delayed, the original event has no troubling significance as far as the "doer" is concerned. At the moment when something is "done to a little girl," no explicit, dissenting point of view challenges the doer's interpretation of events. The little girl, on the other hand, knows something happened that she "does not like." The issue for her is how to express her anger. Her response is delayed, violent, and still not fully narratable. In different ways, then, the doer and little girl are disconnected from the significance of a "doing." The doer forgets an event that seemed ordinary; the child's anger is out of sync with her experience. It takes the work of the narrator to connect the act and the girl's anger. As the girl's response becomes coherent, the past takes on a new meaning, especially for the doer, for whom the doing was never before explicitly resisted. In recent psychoanalytic literature, that gap between the event and its understanding within a comprehensible story is described as "trauma," and it accounts for the victim's rather than the perpetrator's delayed comprehension of an event.

As these examples show, Stein's effort to narrate women's experiences provoked and explored fruitful difficulties. In one amusing but pointed demonstration of how women's stories are occluded in a patriarchal culture, the narrator pokes fun at the Puritan heritage that constricts women's sexuality as well as their ability to know what is happening to their bodies:

> One once who was a very intelligent active bright well-read fairly well experienced woman thought that what happens every month to all women, she thought it only happened to Plymouth Brethren, women having that religion. She was a child of Plymouth Brethren and had only known very intimately Plymouth Brethren women. She had known other women but it had not happened to her to have known about this thing. She was a child of Plymouth Brethren and she thought that what happens to all women every month only happened to Plymouth Brethren women, women having that religion, she was twenty eight years old when she learned that it happened to every kind of women. This is not an astonishing thing that she should have believed this thing. (495–96)

Stein clearly understands the limits of class, community, and beliefs on what a woman can either say or know. Yet despite her broad perspective, the narrator still does not use the word *menstruation* to describe "what happens every month to all women." While she acknowledges this "happening," she does not name it. As a result of prohibitions on speaking, women's recollection finds a language of not quite knowing and not quite telling.

With this tension between the narratable and the unnarratable in mind, let us return to the "incest" vignette. This scene emphasizes the point of view of the father, with Edith's perspective entering through the contents of a letter that is summarized by the narrator. The narrative form of Stein's story thus dramatizes the centrality of paternal power. Yet though Stein does not give Edith a point of view and a story, *per se,* she does give her letter agency that is violent in its repercussions: the father is a "paralytic" ever after. While his body is explicitly immobilized, what seems to "kill" him is the way Edith's intervention undoes his "virtuous" feeling, his way of understanding his own actions and securing a moralized identity.

Stein describes the father not as a hypocrite, or self-righteous, but as an ordinary man, among those who are "good enough men, good enough fathers, good enough husbands, good enough citizens" (491). And given this framework of ordinariness, these men have a generalized conviction that their concrete actions reflect their goodness and virtue. Further, their sense of their own integrity lends them authority to believe in their concrete acts that are "instructing to others so that other ones will know something" (491). Rather than using the language of true and false so pervasive in the contemporary memory wars, Stein emphasizes a dynamic process in which this morality is subject to reinterpretation. The father of the story is shown to have done something and rationalized it as an activity conveying useful knowledge to his daughter, even as what he has done contradicts the tenets of the moral code he believes he is enforcing—and to which he wants her to conform. His rationalizations are a dangerous form of forgetting, and he suffers the consequences when his daughter provokes his "killing" reinterpretation of his past behavior. He loses his socially constructed identity, his categorization of himself as a virtuous, good-enough father. He also loses his potency both as an authority and as an author ("he never wrote another letter"). The vignette explores the gap created between the father's frame of reference and his nameless doing, a gap forced into view by Edith's powerfully resistant perspective.

Stein makes clear that the father's moralized framework is not individual and personal but culturally sanctioned, "ordinary." Stein, then, is documenting evolving historical formulations of character and morality and the ongoing resistance provided by both concrete actions and emerging points of view. The dynamics of such a process have implications for understanding the past. In a discussion of the rise of new sexual stories, Ken Plummer describes a process that begins with the envisioning of a "feeling, a thinking, a doing." These inarticulate preconditions for stories are blocked or fragmented; "nothing unusual is happening at one moment and then some trouble appears at another" (126). He adds that the first narrations of a "doing" may be "little crimped tales" (127). Stein's vignette and the other fragmentary abuse stories that we have included are examples of narratives that mark a moment when networks of social activity have shifted just a bit, rearranging conventional patterns enough to allow space for a story that accommodates experiences that are not supposed to be tellable without the provision of "new descriptions." These new stories are fabrications, but they are fabrications linked to feelings, thinkings, and concrete doings that are slowly becoming narratable, defining a counterdiscourse that has not yet linked up with psychoanalytic expertise—and in some ways defies it by forgetting to forget and, eventually, remembering to tell.

When women start telling much more coherent incest stories to a much larger audience than Stein ever did, they do so because they have more cultural power (derived from complex sources) to attack paternal authority and morality, even to claim disciplinary power. Yet they continue to elicit sharply corrective analyses. In other words, stories representing the daughter's perspective, although much easier to hear now than they have ever been before, still inspire resistance, as they did in Maimie's uncle and Edith's father. They are seen as sources of unfairness, of violation, of institutional oppression both by feminist writers who worry about the confessional and depoliticizing effects of survivor stories and by antifeminist writers who prefer more fixed and friendly accounts of the past, ones that do not challenge figures of traditional authority. The consolidation of these corrective texts is worrisome given the continued social power of normative views about women's hysteria, tendency to lie, and vulnerability to manipulation (or willingness to participate in "witch hunts"). No wonder that feminists such as Rosaria Champagne and Judith Herman have decided that the best response is to assent to the truth and significance of survivorship. We want to suggest a more nuanced response, one that concentrates on the complex narrative transactions that inform a woman's telling.

Foucault remarks on the usefulness of a discursive dynamism that opposes formerly entrenched truths without simply substituting another entrenched truth: "And if we want to protect these only lately liberated fragments, are we not in danger of ourselves constructing, with our own hands, unitary discourse?" (Foucault, *Power/Knowledge*, 86). In this chapter, we have charted a dynamic process in which occluded memorial fragments begin to claim the narrative authority to challenge the neutrality and morality of those with privilege and power. In the following chapters, we continue to show that the meaning of incest—and the memories associated with it—is not simply located in mass hysteria or mass denial. Who has the power to tell a believable story of incest and in what context? This book's project is to examine the production and reception of women's incest stories, resituating these narratives so that it is easier to recognize different forms of telling, hearing, and remembering.

Chapter 2
Signifying Incest
African-American Revisions

As we have already seen, the dominant nineteenth-century incest story worked to construct the virtues of the white middle class, embodied in the strong patriarch, in opposition to those whose narratives about incest only confirmed their immorality: young girls, the poor, and racialized others who are understood to be sexually deviant. The culturally dominant story, then, made it easy for the prosperous and white to understand incest as a problem of the poor and black. This way of understanding incest is related to another similarly powerful and deeply wounding narrative that has also found sexual "aberration" in black families, which are themselves described as aberrant. Maxine Baca Zinn describes this narrative about the dysfunctional black family as based on a "cultural-deficiency" model, which, among other things, "assigns the cause of the growing underclass to the structure of the family" (72). So, to use the most infamous example, the 1965 Moynihan report focuses on the poor black family as at the "center of the tangle of pathology" with a "weak family structure [a female-headed family]" now the principal source of "most of the aberrant, inadequate, or antisocial behavior" (*Negro Family*, 30).[1] When family structure becomes the cause of the economic and social marginality of poor black families, the more distant cause of slavery (and its aftermath) almost completely disappears. As a result of this occluding of the past, the African-American family can be constructed as a place where the victims of slavery and racism are portrayed as their own victimizers.

The idea that poor black families are "doing it to themselves," so to speak, is incorporated into the metaphor of the incestuous black family, an inbred breeding ground of deviant black men, too strong yet easily preyed-upon women, and illegitimate children. In telling the incest story, an African-American novelist always risks making the structure of the family rather than other racialized structures in transition—such as patterns of employment, educational opportunities, provision of housing—an isolated origin for the impoverishment and violence in poor black communities, communities that are often imagined in opposition to a fantasized white norm.[2] In fact, illegitimacy rates among white youths were, in 1965, rising very rapidly, a fact masked by the Moynihan report's emphasis on black family "deviance" (D'Emilio and Freedman, 300).

African-Americans, aware of the way the "cultural deficiency" model blames the black family for what Hortense Spillers calls slavery's "*prescribed internecine degradation*," have sometimes felt that incest in the black family cannot be discussed without confirming myths of black deviance. It may be better not to tell. This form of silence, silence as social discretion, is one that tacitly supports racialized, patriarchal prerogatives. (Ann duCille has recently called this silencing the "discourse of deference," female deference to the cause of a "masculinist ideology of uplift" [65].) The "cultural deficiency" model insists that the forms of patriarchal dominance historically enjoyed by white men (and described by feminists as a *cause* of abuse) would, when claimed by black fathers, *cure* aberrant, because female-headed, African-American families. In other words, "not telling" ultimately functions to legitimize forms of gendered inequality within the family that have been linked not only with incestuous abuse but with slavery, a white, paternalistic system in which dependents were "cared for" and also sexually and economically exploited.[3] Indeed it was precisely the discourse of paternalism, of caring, that allowed slave owners to understand their harsh abuse of slaves to be a form of benevolent, parental diligence.

Of course, given especially high rates of black male unemployment and incarceration, it may seem particularly difficult for black women to criticize patterns of patriarchal dominance in the black community, no matter what their social and historical contexts. As Melba Wilson, a black incest survivor puts it, by talking about incest, "some may feel that I have breached an even greater taboo, crossed a bigger boundary . . . than incest" (1). For African-American novelists, "telling" similarly involves a complex racial and gendered politics that threatens to exact a real and familiar price: the further marginalization of African-American life and the exacerbation of tensions caused by the different ways in which black men and women have experienced economic and social disenfranchisement. This chapter will attempt to show how the African-American incest novel negotiates the risk of saying the wrong thing, or saying "the thing" the wrong way.

Despite anxiety about the representation of blackness and concerns about how an incest story will be understood by black as well as white audiences, African-American writers, perhaps because of a long tradition of resisting discursive unfreedom by signifying on dominant and excruciatingly painful cultural myths, have artfully told and revised the incest story. Indeed, they were among the first writers courageous enough to substantially explore this topic. Their revisions have eventually made the incest narrative available to many other writers, such as white feminists, who use accounts of incest to articulate a history of subjugation. African-American incest narratives thus affirm "Ellison's law": "First something happens to us; and then, just wait, it happens to every other group in America" (Fabre and O'Meally, 4).[4] Through African-American novels, the story of incest begins to signify, in racial and gender-specific ways, a once culturally unspeakable and horrific collective past that might, as Barbara Christian puts it, "terrify" readers by exposing the vicious predations of a patriarchal, white culture (331). In other words, these texts shift the site of what is "unspeakable" from the marginal to the dominant culture.

The contradictions and pain that are central to the African-American incest novel are narrated from different perspectives as they become thinkable and sayable. This chapter will describe the changing contours of the silences integral to this narrative by examining the "mistakes" (telling the wrong story of incest or telling the story of incest the wrong way) made in two well-known novels: Ralph Ellison's *Invisible Man,* Toni Morrison's *The Bluest Eye.*[5] These novels, which have been visibly woven into the text of public culture, usefully highlight the dangers and possibilities of narratives that offer to reveal secrets about incest in the African-American family. The African-American incest story, precisely because of the way it explicitly operates as a narrative that undoes boundaries and violates taboos, is a useful discursive strategy for opening up and reconceptualizing the dynamics of public power and private speechlessness. In African-American novels, this process of undoing crucially involves a blurring of the culturally sanctioned place given to a speaking subject, usually a paternal figure, with the place of a devalued and objectified person: for example, Trueblood (Ellison's black male shareholder) and Pecola (Morrison's violated daughter). Through the reconfiguration of the incest story, what emerges is the formerly hidden perspective of a violated, objectified person into whom something unwanted has been put. This unwanted substance—a residue from a violent past and the seed of the future—becomes the basis of a new social subjectivity. The formerly dehumanized person, most dramatically the incest victim but to some extent the emasculated perpetrator as well, becomes increasingly vocal as shifting social and political relations transform the constraints on what can be said and who can be heard. Indeed, the incest novel functions as a polemical and pedagogical device, one specifically concerned to understand how past histories are effaced and how these silenced narratives are recovered. This process is represented as having the power to transform the future, often figured in the possibility of new life, children resulting from incest.

An early instance of this kind of destabilizing telling of incest occurs in Ralph Ellison's *Invisible Man,* an immediately acclaimed best-seller that was published in 1952 as the civil rights movement was about to begin.[6] The novel explores and violates the rules governing who can claim the position of an authoritative speaking subject in a segregated America. For example, early in the book, the narrator describes a traumatic memory of a "battle royal," in which the town's leading white men sadistically entertain themselves by watching blindfolded black schoolboys, including the narrator, fight each other. Yet even while blinded and bombarded with punches, the narrator cannot stop worrying about whether or not he will be allowed to give the valedictory oration that a school administrator has asked him to present to the same town dignitaries who are now terrorizing him. What is really important is the chance to speak and be heard, even if the topic, "social responsibility," is one sanctioned by hostile and culturally dominant whites who want to hear "that humility was the secret, indeed, the very essence of progress" (20). When, bleeding and fearful, the narrator finally gets to speak, his audience alternately taunts and ignores him.

As the narrator explains his understanding of "social responsibility," it becomes clear that "responsibility" falls mainly upon blacks to understand that they live in the midst of plenitude and have but to "cast their bucket" into this well of possibilities to better themselves. This safe message succeeds in placating, though just barely, his white audience, and the narrator must swallow his own blood to go on speaking. Taunted to repeat the phrase "social responsibility" one too many times, the narrator slips and substitutes the phrase "social equality." This verbal slip makes the white audience dangerously uncomfortable and even more hostile. As Eric Sundquist points out, the phrase "social equality" meant desegregation, which would seem to lead to "racial mixing— the right of blacks and whites to date, intermarry, and to have children" (66).[7] The narrator's "mistake" violates a taboo by suggesting an invitation to miscegenation, the prohibited sexual relations that secured the Jim Crow logic of racial segregation.

Sexuality is an important register of the history of American race relations. The taboo on miscegenation, situated in proximity to incest (another form of prohibited sexual relations), functions to obscure the fact that it was primarily white men, who, by raping objectified "dependents," were responsible for racial mixing. This inability to acknowledge that the sexual rule-makers are the primary rule-breakers emerges in the language of a nineteenth-century Southern sociologist, Henry Hughes:

> Impurity of races is against the law of nature. Mulattoes are monsters. The law of nature is the law of God. The same law which forbids consanguinous amalgamation forbids ethnical amalgamation. Both are incestuous. Amalgamation is incest. (qtd. in Rogers, 166)

This passage is extremely incoherent, but the gist of it, as David Rogers points out, is that the mulatto becomes the consequence of mixing qualities that are at once too different, an "ethnical amalgamation," and at the same time too much alike and "consanguinous." Here even the notion of mixture becomes mixed. The idea of "making monsters" has been appropriated in the recent memory wars to describe how therapists have led daughters to turn their fathers into monsters. Hughes's language demonstrates that the metaphor for creating incestuous mixtures—"making monsters"—has historically had a cultural function: to mark places where dominant groups discover that the other is within. Rather than black families "doing it to themselves," this incest metaphor points to something else: the mixings caused by slavery in which the culturally dominant white patriarch is deeply implicated as a source of violent sexual abuse.

In Ellison's novel, a verbal "amalgamation" takes place through the simultaneous blurring and separation of dominant and tabooed stories, both involving the masked culpability of white men for the plight of troublesome "charges" who are encouraged to take "responsibility." Once again, the image of blood is crucial to this process of conjoining, marking a linkage occasioned by a verbal lapse on the narrator's part. In the first story, Ellison's narrator struggles to get a hearing at the cost of swallowing his own blood and ignoring his bleeding body, metaphors symbolizing the legacy of slavery's savage wounding that is repressed in the discourse of "social responsibility." This invisible story of a social wounding is available to the reader but the hostile white audience hears a social violation only in what the narrator might say about "social equality," desegregation, and the threatened purity of racial bloodlines. Without the narrator's "mistake," the two stories would stay separate rather than bleeding into one another, linking "social responsibility" and "social equality," creating a form of a discursive impropriety that anticipates social change. In a later episode, another speaker, sharecropper Jim Trueblood (whose name plays on the yearning for an essentialized racial bloodline and for discursive purity) makes an even more dramatic "mistake." This time the discursive "mistake," telling an incest story, seems irresponsible to the narrator because of its appeal to a white audience at the expense of a black one: "How can he tell this to white men . . . when he knows they'll just say that all Negroes do such things?" (57).

Trueblood seems to confirm the dominant story about incest. By including the Trueblood story, Ellison, then, runs even more risks than does the young narrator when he gives his valedictory speech. While the narrator makes a significant verbal slip, it is protected by the phrases of a coded language. And although that language carries dangerous sexual and social connotations, it establishes the narrator's resistance to his white audience and his alliance with a black one. Trueblood's story, on the other hand, is sought after by white men, an audience presumably soothed by Trueblood's assumption of responsibility for acting upon their own forbidden desires. Giving the white men what they seem to want, his story also runs the risk of alienating a certain black audience, who, like the blacks at the college, demand stories of racial uplift featuring positive images of African-Americans. Yet despite all of these problems, Trueblood's incest story, like the young narrator's valedictory, shows that discursive "mistakes" can be a useful abdication of social "responsibility," already shown to be a loaded word. Indeed, Trueblood's incest story is a way of claiming "social equality."

Freud interpreted linguistic mistakes or slips as moments when a censored past slips into the present. What he considered a personal and psychic process has a social dimension. Under conditions of political repression such as those operating in the segregated south, the moralized rules of the "proper" social order incite forms of subversion that may look like acts of iniquity and deviance but that may have another function as social critique. Incest, for example, is usually understood as a universal violation of a foundational taboo, but given the way this rule is racialized, a violation cannily narrated by a black man has a more local, historical significance. Certainly Mr. Norton sees Trueblood's incest as an experience of "chaos," a violation of fundamental social laws by a sexually deviant "other." This sense of incest as out-of-the-ordinary usefully protects Norton from acknowledging his own incestuous desires for the daughter whose "purity" and "beauty" are at the center of his own story.[8] Indeed, his investment in a black college—a "living memorial to my daughter"—is, as Peter Hays suggests, an act of propitiation for those desires. But it is also yet another form of guilty paternalism in which the white father acknowledges and covers over a history of exploitative relationships with racial "dependents."

Because he assumes incest is a sacrilege, Norton shouts to Trueblood with a mixture of "envy and indignation," "You did and are unharmed!" (51). Sacrilege is supposed to be punished, but Trueblood does not even feel guilty, perhaps because his desires are not, like Norton's, defined as sexual. He is, then, not precisely reproducing the incest story about sexual desire that Norton wants to hear. He is also actively composing a tale that defies some of the expectations of its audience. Indeed, according to Trueblood, his act of incest is committed while he is sleeping with his wife and daughter to stay warm (this phrase recalls Stein's discussion of men's desire for warmth in *The Making of Americans*)—and while he is dreaming of something else. Both his feelings of powerlessness and his desire to become powerful are evoked by his dream of entering a white man's, Mr. Broadnax's, house. In this dream, as Hortense Spillars vividly describes it, "Ellison's narrator has so loaded the dream sequence—the major portion of the tale—with an invaginated symbolic plan that we seem justified in reading the breach of the incest taboo, as it is elaborated in this scene, as a symptom of an inverted castration complex" (134). Entering the house, Trueblood violates a now feminized white space where he experiences—and repudiates—the white man's attempts to emasculate him. As a result, Trueblood's incestuous act can be interpreted as a heroic moment of resistance to and escape from what Houston Baker calls the "castrating effects of white philanthropy" (179). Understood this way, by committing incest and telling his dream tale, Trueblood momentarily rights an imbalance of power, much as the narrator does in his valedictory when he mistakenly says "social equality."

Of course, while Trueblood attempts to right one imbalance of power, an enabling condition of Trueblood's telling is that both he and Norton find in the incest story, and the daughter's subjugation, a fantasy of freedom from restraint. This is not a generic fantasy that transcends gender. Invisible, and essential to this shared male story, is the ordinariness of patriarchal prerogatives that both men assume. Of course, though Trueblood shares these prerogatives with Norton, the millionaire enjoys the privileges of patriarchal power to a far greater extent. But in Freudian fashion—and Ellison plays with psychoanalytic theories of social evolution—Norton's achievements carry him further from his ability to act upon his instinctual desires.[9] These disavowed desires, systematically embodied in the black man, provide the ground for Trueblood's powerful—and lucrative—narrative authority. But the story should not, for this reason, be read simply as a parody or a white scapegoat ritual. Trueblood does tell Norton some of the story he wants to hear, but he also discursively breaks through restraining racial and sexual codes that would forbid his dream-tale of miscegenation and incest. When Trueblood's story is finished, Norton is clearly weakened rather than strengthened by what he has heard. Furthermore, the money Trueblood gets from the tale enhances his paternal authority by enabling him to be a better provider; his wife gets a pair of eyeglasses and a dress. Only from the position of an audience of violated women, one largely excluded as Trueblood tells his tale, is Trueblood's assertion, "I'm a man and a man don't leave his family," a scary rather than responsible claim to power (64).

Trueblood's is a perpetrator's story that demonstrates how rural impoverishment, a legacy of slavery, has undermined a father's ability to be a powerful provider without extinguishing his aspirations to fulfill that role. In other words, Trueblood's telling at once repudiates Norton's patriarchal power and also works to claim it. So strongly does Trueblood speak from the moralized position of the perpetrator that he makes the act of incest and its effects on his daughter and wife seem much less important than his dreams of finding "fat meat," dreams that are fulfilled by telling a story that white men think they want to hear. Even when, in the margins of the story, Trueblood's wife Kate is allowed to voice and act on her outrage, she is a character created by Trueblood and one who ultimately joins her daughter Matty Lou in silence.

In Trueblood's story, women are not just spoken for, they are metaphors for larger, dangerous forces that the women themselves do not understood. (When his wife attacks him, Trueblood thinks to himself, "You ain't guilty, but she thinks you is" [60].) For example, Trueblood's struggle with the power plant, a dream figuration of his rape of his daughter as a castrating assault on *him*, recalls the narrator's fight with Monopolated Light, the novel's symbol of white visibility and power. No wonder, then, that Trueblood will not give up the fruits of this battle. He refuses to let Aunt Chloe interrupt his daughter's pregnancy, reasserting in this way his paternal ownership of his womenfolks and progeny. Indeed, as Houston Baker puts it in an analysis whose male-bias has been noted elsewhere, "the Trueblood encounter reveals the [black] phallus as producing Afro-American generations rather than wasting its seed upon the water" (183).[10] In this reading, Trueblood's family becomes the "entire clan . . . of Afro-America," while incest is made a figure for "a type of royal paternity" (183) that is linked to Ellison himself as an "untrammeled creator" (197). Incest, here, is a way of signifying the black man's claim to an originary and potent symbolic authority.[11] But as Ann duCille sharply observes, though the "phallus may not be a material object, its action, its 'phallic energy' is not immaterial—certainly not to Matty Lou Trueblood or to Pecola Breedlove [the incest victim in *The Bluest Eye*], and other objects of its power" (68). At the same time, remembering the power of the black father may also lead to forgetting that he might inhabit the vulnerability of a daughter in relationship to the white man's authority.[12]

Trueblood tells an incest story that gives him a certain phallic power, but this empowerment requires that his daughter be objectified and that he must experience a form of self-violation by performing as the mythically barbaric black man. In moving women to the center of incest narratives, African-American women writers challenge the African-American male's precarious and tainted narrative and paternal achievement by bearing witness to his compromised symbolic authority. As a result, black women's rescriptings would, in the 1980s, produce a backlash within the black community. Deborah McDowell has noted that it is "for narrating, for representing male abuses 'within the family' that contemporary black women are most roundly criticized" (78). As she also argues, this criticism of black women's narratives minimizes the complexity of their reception within a political structure in which black and white men fight over "the bodies/texts of black women" in a manner that "reproduces an older meta-narrative written in the history of the slave master's hand" (96).

Although Toni Morrison has not escaped criticism for writing novels whose gender politics are said to undercut black male authority, *The Bluest Eye*, published in 1970, is often praised for its thoughtful understanding of the incestuous father's point of view and motivation.[13] For example, Madelon Sprengnether writes:

> Among Morrison's many achievements as a writer, one of her bravest, to my mind, is her characterization of Cholly Breedlove, who rapes and impregnates his eleven-year-old daughter Pecola. While a lesser writer might have concentrated solely on Pecola's plight, which is achingly grim, Morrison chooses to enter into Cholly's mentality in such a way that we cannot help perceiving this father-daughter tragedy as mutual. (533)

Far from attacking black men for horrifically abusive behavior, the narrator of *The Bluest Eye* notifies us within the first few pages that "mutual accusations about who was to blame" are the stuff of childish quarrels and that the question the novel will raise has more to do with "how" such horrifying abuse happens.

Given the present celebrity of African-American women writers, it is easy to forget how recently this visibility was attained and how fragile it may be. Toni Morrison's experience with *The Bluest Eye* provides one example of the complex task of claiming symbolic capital, of moving from the margins to the center of that province known as "serious literature." In order to establish her credibility with a white literary and critical audience, Morrison contended with the aesthetic criterion to present reality as the repository of complicated yet timeless truths, for to do otherwise would appear limited and sociological, those labels often placed upon African-American literature. At the same time, Morrison explicitly hoped to challenge the timelessness of American notions of beauty in order to explain how Pecola has been subjected to symbolic murder in the American culture of the early 1940s. Circulating in the reviews of *The Bluest Eye*, which was Morrison's first novel, are these competing demands for aesthetic universality and historical realism. In one review her book is said to contain too much "poetic imagery," though Morrison is said to be worth encouraging because she conveys "beauty and hope" (Frankel, 47); another review claims that the novel "embodies a reality" and is recommended for "social caseworkers" (Marvin, 3806); and in the most favorable review, one by John Leonard, *The Bluest Eye* is shown to have achieved timelessness as "poetry, history, sociology, folklore, nightmare and music" (35).

Morrison's juggling act is complicated by her desire both to represent and to speak to her black audience without losing the white audience of reviewers and readers that are crucial to a novel's success. For her black audience, Morrison uses the language and, as she has put it, "codes embedded in black culture" (215), while also remaining attentive to codes of white readers. In praising the *Bluest Eye*, one white reviewer applauded Morrison for writing "a novel instead of a harangue," explicitly noting that other "black writing," presumably not sensitive enough to white readers, has a "forensic" tone (Solokov, 95). This kind of praise, of course, reveals the operation of ideological filters, shaped by white fears of black power movements of the 1960s, and most likely directed at

African-American male authors, such as Eldridge Cleaver and Richard Wright, who might be seen to have made "black writing" an irritating polemic. Morrison not only must anticipate the expectations of such reviewers but also speak to a black audience that is not a homogeneous entity. *The Bluest Eye* figures the black community as split within itself: class and skin color, for example, create forms of segregation that exacerbate those imposed from outside. And gender considerations complicate the matter further: to represent and speak to women, Morrison was "pressing for female expressiveness" (215), a perspective supported by the emerging women's movement. But this emerging possibility contains its own danger, alienating her black male audience by defying its notion of the "right" perspective on the black father's role, a perspective illuminated in Ellison's novel.

Making matters more difficult, while also symbolizing constrictions on speaking, Morrison chose to write about incest, a topic still very much tabooed in the 1960s, the period in which she wrote the novel. Maya Angelou's autobiography *I Know Why the Caged Bird Sings*, which includes an account of her rape as a child, was published the same year as *The Bluest Eye* (1970) but Louise Armstrong's *Kiss Daddy Goodnight*, an early mass-market book featuring the stories of incest victims, was not published until 1978. And though Toni Morrison may have been engaged in a deliberate regendering of Ellison's Trueblood story, written much earlier, such a revision was especially difficult because it required sympathy with a black, female victim. How was that sympathy to be voiced?[14] The narrative problems facing Morrison may have drawn her to empathize with the incest victim's experience of silence and pain. Trying to tell the victim's story before it was popular, Morrison had many cultural and internal restrictions to overcome. As Morrison puts it in her new afterword to the novel, "In some sense it [overcoming the conspiracy of secrecy around incest] was precisely what the act of writing the book was: the public exposure of a private confidence" (212). She goes on to say that the political climate in which the writing took place made the publication of her book feel almost like a betrayal of her community: it "involved the exposure . . . the disclosure of secrets, secrets 'we' shared and those withheld from us by ourselves and by the world outside the community" (212).

So, rather than seeing Morrison's sympathetic representation of the incestuous father only as a sign of her bravery and greater artistic achievement (because it represents more than a *woman's* point of view), we might see it as a sign of the greater difficulty, if not the near impossibility of representing the experience of incest and the incest victim's story at the time when *The Bluest Eye* was written. For Sprengnether and others writing in the 1990s, a "lesser writer" might have "concentrated on Pecola's plight" as if this were easier than representing the father's point of view. Yet to call such a task easier is to skate over a history of obstacles to speaking that we have discussed in the previous chapter and that affected Morrison as she composed *The Bluest Eye*. In her afterword, she writes that the novel "does not in its present form handle effectively the silence at its center: the void that is Pecola's 'unbeing'" (215). Morrison attempted "the novelty" of telling "this story of female violation . . . from the vantage point of the victims or could-be victims of rape—the persons no one inquired of (certainly not in 1965): the girls themselves" (214). But she herself believes that the task was so difficult that she failed at this "attempt to shape a silence while breaking it" (216). Whether or not we think that she "failed" in any way, focusing upon Morrison's difficulties and perceived "mistakes" is illuminating.

As one initial difficulty with adopting the "vantage point of the victims . . . of rape," Morrison notes that Pecola "does not have the vocabulary to understand the violence" (214). Like Matty Lou, Trueblood's silent daughter, Pecola cannot tell the story of incest and her own violation. To mediate this unspeakable point of view, Morrison invents a number of narrative voices: Claudia McTeer, a young girl who is subjected to many of the same outrages of racism, sexism, and poverty as Pecola but who is from a more financially stable and loving family; an omniscient third-person narrator who has an intimate knowledge about the history and thoughts of both Cholly and Pauline, Pecola's parents. Pauline and Pecola get a voice toward the end of the novel. Pauline's recollections about her own past interrupt the omniscient narrator's account and Pecola's hallucinatory dialogue concludes the story. Morrison constructs other narrative frames as a way to give shape to the silence of the victim's "unbeing": the Dick and Jane reader provides a prefatory frame and chapter titles—and suggests the oppressive expectations represented by the institutionalized ideal of white family life; the seasons—autumn, winter, spring, summer—provide titles for each of the book's four parts and link the story's theme, in ways that are problematic, to nature. All of these narrative voices and frames provide the reader with a broad cubist-like canvas that encourages understanding of the problem of incest from a variety of perspectives. Yet, at the same time, the multiple perspectives also tend to keep the reader at a distance from "the *Thing*" itself.

The voice of the omniscient narrator is at odds with a narrative strategy that elsewhere uses separate narrative voices to undercut the expectation that a unified truth is available. Of course, this voice, if it is to tell "how" Pecola is annihilated, must claim authority, sometimes explicitly conjuring up other, embedded individual voices to support the omniscient narrator's larger social critique. For example, when the omniscient narrator has taken over in the chapter describing Pecola's mother Pauline, Pauline's disembodied voice, marked by italics, suddenly emerges as if beamed down from a distant place, beckoned, perhaps, by a longing for the kind of testimony that would compel commitment to the narrator's embattled, because culturally marginal, vision of the truth. Another strategy for supporting the truth of her critique is provided by the school primer that locates a historically specific and recognizable way in which the dominant white American culture was internalized by black children. In *The Bluest Eye,* this process of socialization is experienced as an assault that leaves behind a legacy of self-loathing. Pecola is the novel's dominant figure of this ideological rape that gives birth to her desire for blue eyes. These "offspring," the phantasmic traces of the white father's molestations, mark her as a scapegoat for her community's feelings of self-hatred and rage.

Pauline's black and female voice and the Dick and Jane primer, because they suggest the importance of specific contexts in the construction of meaning, are in tension with the seasonal frame, which lends a timelessness to the events that both unifies and distances them. In classic fashion, macrocosmic nature is meant to be a metaphor for a microcosmic social order: the marigold seeds that do not bloom in Lorain, Ohio are figures for the beliefs planted in African-Americans that inhibit the production of healthy self-images. Through incest, what is left behind in Pecola is her father's seed that fails to thrive. Through white patriarchal ideology, what is left in her is a desire for bluest eyes that devalues as it eradicates her racial identity. Yet naturalized metaphors always function to universalize political structures as well as to politicize natural ones. As a result, metaphors of seasonal change, growth, flowering, and deflowering provide a perspective that can leave the reader contemplating events at a great distance as inevitable moments in a wheel of change: "This soil is bad for certain kinds of flowers. Certain seeds it will not nurture, certain fruit it will not bear, and when the land kills of its own volition, we acquiesce and say the victim had no right to live. We are wrong, of course, but it doesn't matter" (206).

These sentences, among the last words of the narrator, now a Claudia McTeer with powers of omniscience, do not just distance us from the intimate tragedy of Pecola's rape and madness. More significantly, they seem to keep distant a deep fury at the seemingly implacable social and economic forces that have destroyed Pecola. Measured tones and natural metaphors are also a gesture to appease an audience that might not accept a story that directly communicated rage, which would make the novel sound like a harangue. Morrison herself has talked about her desire not to participate in the processes of dehumanization that "trashed Pecola," hence her efforts to forgive and understand how victims become victimizers. But there is more than forgiveness and understanding motivating this novel. Morrison distances the enemy—"All the time we knew that Maureen Peal was not the Enemy and not worthy of such intense hatred. The *Thing* to fear was the *Thing* that made her beautiful and not us" (74). But intense hatred is felt even if, for safety's sake, it must be displaced and muted in elegiac, aestheticized language that was described by reviewers at the time of the novel's publication as "angry sadness" (Leonard) and "acid prose pungent with metaphor" (Marvin).

Toni Morrison has written that her effort to solve the problem of Pecola's voicelessness by breaking the narrative into parts was only partially successful, though we are suggesting that this "problem" helps us to understand Morrison's complex sense of the possible audience for her first novel. And she has discussed the problems of a language that is meant to both hold and sabotage "the despising glance" (211), the task partially accomplished by Trueblood's story. She also notes that "it is interesting to me now that where I thought I would have the most difficulty subverting the language to a feminine mode, I had the least: connecting Cholly's 'rape' by the whitemen to his own of his daughter" (215). Her "feminine mode" depends on a loosening of the boundaries between masculine and feminine: "This most masculine act of aggression becomes feminized in my language, 'passive'" (215). The white men who force Cholly to have sex in the glare of their flashlights effectively castrate him, stripping him of his manhood by rendering him helpless and small, and with a "vacancy in his head . . . like the space left by a newly pulled tooth" (150). Left a life of passive, "free" movement, he acts on instinct, finally raping his daughter out of a sequence of emotions, "revulsion, guilt, pity, then love" (161) in which Pecola is confused with his memories of his wife Pauline. Cholly's "rape" of Darlene, and later Pecola, is then indirectly linked to his "rape" by white men, symbolically connecting the black father's acts to a history of racial subjugation by whites.

Morrison writes that she had the least trouble feminizing Cholly, and perhaps this ease of representation is explained by the existence of Trueblood as a model. Trueblood, too, is feminized, but Morrison makes Cholly's feminization more explicit, blurring past and present and blending feminine passivity and masculine aggression so that her narration of the perpetrator's story is easier than Ellison's to understand—and to listen to. Morrison's use of the omniscient narrator also expands the frame within which the perpetrator's action is placed. The success of this vision depends on accepting Cholly's actions as a socially created form of what might seem to be an instinctive action. The novel's narration of the white men's voyeuristic pleasure at compelling Cholly's sexual performance makes it clear that Cholly is not rewarded for providing this entertainment, but rather disabled and disempowered. In this way, Morrison makes the black perpetrator's story less assimilable to white pleasure and even more linked to the abused victim than is Trueblood's. "The saddest reality in the novel," writes one critic, "is the naked father like Cholly" (Dickerson, 123). This critical judgment involves an identification with the perpetrator that demonstrates again how hard it is both to tell and to hear the daughter's story.

If the omniscient narrator is thus capable of making Cholly's point of view coherent, without completely embracing it, Morrison faces a greater difficulty when she tries at the end of the novel to give Pecola the words to represent her own perspective. By the time that Pecola speaks she has received her blue eyes and is totally mad. Drawing upon Du Bois's model of double consciousness and doubling the psychic weight of that split identity by adding the experience of incest to the molestations wrought by racism, Toni Morrison brilliantly attempts to narrate Pecola's fragmentation of self through what Michael Awkward calls "a schizophrenic double voicedness" (176). This split self anticipates the model of dissociation later used to describe the psychic trauma of incest victims, while it also forcefully rewrites Du Boisian double consciousness to show its potentially psychotic possibilities. Whiteness, "blue eyes," enters Pecola as a hallucinatory false consciousness. *The Bluest Eye* is implicitly a novel sympathetic with the black nationalist movement, yet it also registers a shift toward locating social injustice in individual psychological states.

Charged and inventive as this chapter is, Morrison herself describes it as a "problem": "the fact of [Pecola's] hallucination becomes a kind of outside-the-book conversation" (215). The problem is not just that the story is over before she begins to speak but that Pecola, because deep in madness, is absent from the scene of this narrative experiment in which one voice badgers another for information about her mistreatment, including the possibility of a second, less violent, sexual encounter with her father. Of course, Pecola's madness and disintegration allow readers to understand how thoroughly she has been "assassinated," annihilated by her experience. There is no grounding self and hence no "voice" is possible. This is the darkest view imaginable and it is also a vivid demonstration of the extent to which the incest victim's perspective remained discursively attenuated—almost unsayable—even as late as 1970.

In a recent review written for *Harper's* magazine, Katie Roiphe directly links the current trendiness of the incest novel to the "excessive" writing of African-American women:

> The graphic sexual abuse in Toni Morrison's *The Bluest Eye* (1970) and Maya Angelou's *I Know Why the Caged Bird Sings* (1971) offered the prototypes for the modern incest scene. After that came Alice Walker's *The Color Purple* (1982). . . . By the early Nineties incest had swept across the literary map of America . . . (68)

This language implicitly endorses the view that women's incest novels are unusually "graphic" and that this quality of the genre is a legacy of African-American women's writing, beginning with Morrison's *The Bluest Eye*. Here Roiphe employs a familiar model of associating black writers with deviant sexuality, which is useful to her larger effort to discredit women's incest novels as opportunistically pornographic. She also makes a clear association of incest narratives with "otherness" and with a degrading process of undoing aesthetic values. From Roiphe's point of view, "Ellison's law" works to make the incest story a sensationalist literary fad that is very marketable but also censored as superficial and pornographic.

As we turn to an examination of other incest stories, it is useful to challenge Roiphe's comfortable condemnation of incest "tellings." Women writers have now achieved acclaim for incest novels, spoken from the victim's point of view, that give shape and visibility to forms of "unbeing" that are gendered, racial, economic, and social. Toni Morrison writes at the end of her afterword: "With very few exceptions, the initial publication of *The Bluest Eye* was like Pecola's life: dismissed, trivialized, misread" (216). Of course, in the decades since then, her novel has gained respectful attention. But we should not forget how hard it was for Morrison to tell Pecola's story or how hard it may still be to recognize the complexity of Morrison's effort to break a culturally enforced silence. Roiphe worries that there are too many women who tell, but we might find in this phenomenon some reason to hope. Largely thanks to the work of African-American writers, the persons "no one inquired of (certainly not in 1965): the girls themselves" have finally found a voice and an audience.

Chapter 3

It's about Patriarchal Power
White Feminists Speak Out

A few years after *The Bluest Eye* (1970) was published, white feminists begin to publish political and psychological accounts of incest emphasizing the despotism of patriarchal power as the cause of incest. Father-daughter incest becomes "a paradigm of female sexual victimization" within a radically unequal patriarchal society (Herman and Hirschman, 4). Through a broad emphasis on gender and power, the "feminist incest story" undercuts the claim that incest is only a problem of the poor and ethnically other. More dramatically, this emergent narrative shifts the responsibility for incest from the "seductive daughter" and the "collusive mother"—key actors in clinical explanations of incest in the 1960s—to the "seductive father" and the social and psychological supports for his incestuous behavior. As a result, the strong patriarchal family, often idealized as the origin of white, middle-class values, is represented as pathological and dangerous. This reversal of the dominant story contains within it legacies of the discourse it rejects, yet in this way too, the feminist incest story is marked by its struggle to tell incest in a new way.

Individual transgression is at the heart of understandings of incest as a sexual act, but who is the transgressor? A familiar answer, once a staple of psychoanalytic literature on incest, is the seductive daughter. This seductive girl also transgresses in telling an incest story; if she were innocent, she would not tell disgusting tales. The girl or woman who tells is thus doubly marked as a propagator of scandal. Inspired by the courage of African-American women writers such as Toni Morrison, Maya Angelou, and Gayl Jones, white feminists in the 1970s began to publish women's accounts about their experiences of incest in order to challenge these normative beliefs about incest victims and incest narratives. "Many of the first, most daring, and most honest contributions to the public discussion of incest were made by black women," writes Judith Herman, "and much of our work has been inspired by theirs" (Herman and Hirschman, 67). Feminist writers hoped to follow the example of black women writers by shifting the blame for incest, this time from daughters to fathers, making a scandal of male privilege instead of women who tell. What we are calling the feminist incest story evolved in the 1970s and early 1980s, when feminists placed great confidence in the power of women's narratives to speak truth to paternal power and so undo it.

In this chapter, we will focus on two nonfiction books about incest: Louise Armstrong's *Kiss Daddy Goodnight* (1978), one of the first mass-market collections of first-person stories of incest to offer a political analysis, and Judith Herman's *Father-Daughter Incest,* an early and still influential feminist study of the psychological effects of father-daughter incest (1981). Both books assume that father-daughter incest is more prevalent than analysts and anthropologists had ever acknowledged, and both emphasize the importance of women's incest stories as a vehicle of social critique. They include no postmodern reflections on the "story" they are telling and, indeed, the power of these books is linked to their unassailable conviction that feminism has made it possible for women to tell formerly tabooed "real" stories and to uncover their significance for a larger analysis of patriarchy.[1] There is an odd sense these days that imperfectly reflective feminist narratives should be censored, as if there were perfect, "correct" stories to put in their place. A more flexible approach, one emphasizing cultural contexts, might understand that the representational strategies of the feminist incest story place it within a specific social context.

In the 1970s women's stories of incest took the shape of a critique of patriarchy because of the existence of a popular women's movement. The new authority of feminism can be read in its considerable success in changing the response to the incest story from a salacious grin to a raised fist. A crucial, authenticating claim of the women's movement has long been that women can come to understand their political subjugation by recalling instances when they were silenced and harmed by the men who ruled over them at home. Feminists have theorized that behind the sexual abuse of girls by fathers, uncles, and brothers is a system of unequal gender relations, patriarchy, that provides the ideological rationalization for male exploitation of the bodies and labor of women. Crucial to this political story is that well-known feminist slogan: the personal is political. The feminist incest story teaches its intended audience— women—that fathers are powerful and they, not mothers, are to blame for the harm done to daughters in the private sphere as well as the public one. Implicit in this reading of patriarchal power and violence is the message that women need to work together for political change.

With the benefit of hindsight, this analysis may seem mistaken in some obvious ways. It universalizes the incestuous father, who comes to represent all men, and the victimized daughter, who comes to represent all women. The powerful feminist critique of father-daughter incest thus squeezes as well as expands the allowable range of male and female identity and subjectivity. Yet the feminist understanding of incest is nonetheless persuasive. Using incest as a paradigmatic example of the sexual exploitation sanctioned under paternal rule, feminists explain not only why patriarchy must be challenged but why such change is difficult. In a paternalistic system, the ruler father is also the provider. Because the father's ownership of property extends to his relationship with people living in his domain, he may certainly exploit them, but he may also be a source of benevolent caring. The father, then, may make sexual use of his daughter, but he also is her protector and provider. This patriarchal social system, then, creates the psychological conditions that encourage the reproduction of unequal relations between men and women. As Phyllis Chesler puts it: "Women are encouraged to commit incest as a way of life. . . . As opposed to marrying our fathers, we marry men like our fathers . . . men who are older than us, have more money than us, more power than us, are taller than us . . . our fathers" (qtd. in Herman and Hirschman, 57–58). By arguing that male supremacy creates conditions that encourage father-daughter incest "as a way of life," the feminist incest story works to break the bonds of gratitude and identification that, in a paternalistic system, lead subordinate subjects to accept a system of unequal power relations. In other words, the feminist incest story argues that the desires of the seemingly loving father are ultimately in conflict with the interests of the daughter. The idea that the father metonymically embodies the institution of patriarchy thus leads to a severe judgment about father-daughter relationships, which is misleading as well as enlightening. Not all fathers have the same power; not all daughters are equally powerless; not all gendered power inequalities within the family result in incest.

As an explanatory tool and form of protest, the feminist incest story does not always work, but in the late 1970s, it seemed more full of potential than of problems. Indeed, the telling of prohibited stories about incest once promised to galvanize a feminist social movement that could make the world a dramatically better place. Such first-person accounts of sexual abuse, highlighting the exploitative behavior of fathers and exculpating mothers, were a startling and inspiring means for advocating social and political reform. The best-known collection of such accounts, Louise Armstrong's *Kiss Daddy Goodnight,* was published in 1978 for mass market circulation by Hawthorne Books. Armstrong's book is not scholarly, although the first edition includes an afterword describing her research. She states that she spoke with 183 women, some referred to her by friends, and that these women were drawn from "all classes, races, and parts of the country" (232). She selected sixteen stories to highlight, largely because they would not scare readers too much. These are the stories of women "the majority of readers might think of themselves working next to" and who had an "ability to be clear in talking and in relating the specific effects of abuse on their lives" (232). This selection process reveals Armstrong's underlying concern that readers might consider her informants weird, unbelievable, not like "normal" women. Her narrative thus implicitly records the enduring constraints placed on telling by the notion that women who tell incest are depraved and abnormal.

Armstrong understands the forces that inhibit telling, even if she cannot escape them. Indeed, the main accomplishment of her book is to provide a public analysis of why women have found it difficult to tell about incest. Armstrong argues that the secrecy surrounding incest is an effect of male power. Prohibitions on speaking insure the sense of shame and isolation experienced by victims while tacitly condoning the actions of perpetrators. *Kiss Daddy Goodnight* masses together accounts of the sexual assaults suffered by ordinary women who were, as Tillie Olsen put it in her book published the same year, muzzled by culturally enforced "silences." Listening to the words of incest victims, recording them as Armstrong does, is a logical continuation of feminist practices of breaking silence that were born in small collectives and consciousness-raising groups. Rape, for example, was finally put into a social and historical context by feminist writers of this period, and, like incest victims, victims of rape also began to speak about their experiences in order to change a patriarchal culture that condoned sexual violence by defining victims as seductively "asking for it."

Women's groups and "speak-outs" were a way to make the sharing of personal experiences a strategy for uncovering shared realities of daily life and developing a new analysis of the relation between the private and public spheres. So, for example, in *Kiss Daddy Goodnight,* Armstrong features the words of individual survivors but provides a broader perspective drawn from feminist work such as the writings of Florence Rush, a social worker known for her inspiring theorizing of sexual violence: "Sexual abuse of children is permitted because it is an unspoken but prominent factor in socializing and preparing the female to accept a subordinate role; to feel guilty, ashamed, and to tolerate, through fear, the power exercised over her by men" (117). This theory of socialization lacks nuance, but it makes very tangible and familiar the dynamics of patriarchal oppression: the big against the little; men against women. Political movements need compelling metaphors, and shortcuts such as these phrases work very well to capture a truth of women's quotidian experience in the interest of a larger political critique. However, they also may become naturalized and constricting.

Telling their stories of incest within the framework of a critique of gendered and unequal power relations, individual women demonstrated a relatively new power to resist conventional views of the family as a haven. By showing how dangerous paternal power can be, they also made a strong case for more equitable gender arrangements in the family. A strong case is necessary to motivate a desire for change. Suggesting the importance of this desire as a precondition, Susan Okin asks: "How much do we care that the family, our most intimate social grouping, is often a school of day-to-day injustice? How much do we *want* the just families that will produce the kind of citizen we need if we are ever to achieve a just society?" (186). Though in this book we will chart the growing awareness—both within and outside feminism—of the incest narrative as a representational construct that can be read in competing ways, it is important to remember—remember this!—that when growing numbers of women first began to tell their memories of incest, they exposed the amnesia of a culture that had defined incest as that which did not exist in "our" families because barred by "the incest taboo."

Armstrong's book begins with an account of her relationship to her father, who raped her when she was fourteen. What follows are chapters that include sections of letters written in response to requests she placed in newspapers and magazines for first-person accounts of incest experiences. The book also includes material drawn from interviews, and Armstrong provides interspersed information about how psychiatrists had previously responded to such narratives—often by assuming these stories were fantasies, or by blaming daughters for seduction and mothers for allowing "it" to happen. The letters written by incest victims recall assaults by male family members, many of them beginning in early childhood: "Dear Louise, Don't like to talk about it—think about it— although I am now a grandmother. I was only five. My mother caught my father in the act" ("Real Incest," 17). *Kiss Daddy Goodnight* ends with an appendix listing social services that women might contact to get help. The book is thus structured to encourage its audience to acknowledge the hard truths articulated by incest victims and then get help or start giving it by working for political and social change.

Ten years later, in the introduction to the second edition of *Kiss Daddy Goodnight* (1987) Armstrong restates the political argument of her book because she feels it has been forgotten by the mental health experts now busy treating incest survivors: "our simple, homespun political analysis of the problem of incest as power abuse—one with long-standing tacit societal permission—continues to stand correct" (viii). Armstrong is talking about "power abuse" by men. Her book, focused on the suffering of girls and intent on relieving mothers and daughters of the blame traditionally meted out to them by professionals, includes only one account of a boy abused by his father and no discussion of abusive mothers. As a result, Louise Armstrong has been criticized for silencing accounts that complicate the feminist narrative of patriarchal victimization and womanly sisterhood.[2] Responding to criticisms about her focus on fathers and daughters, Armstrong has explained that she never denied that mothers could be perpetrators or that boys could be victims. Her point is simply that these less prevalent forms of abuse do not invalidate her gender-based analysis. Indeed, in her afterword to the second edition of *Kiss Daddy Goodnight*, Armstrong notes that the new "incest industry" still wants to blame mothers, though fathers are primarily the perpetrators of incest, a fact key to her feminist political analysis.[3]

The "feminist incest story," although now associated with "repressed memories," usually emphasizes long-remembered but never discussed experiences, hence its emphasis on male power as a cause of silencing. In fact, silencing is the trauma. In Armstrong's book, women catalogue effects—flashbacks, emotional numbness, problems relating to men sexually—of not telling anyone about sexual assaults that they always knew had occurred. Many of these experiences of incest are authenticated, though the pressure to validate experiences so familiar in the late 1980s and 1990s is absent in this book. For example, one woman's father was convicted of child abuse; one father said, "I really don't see anything wrong with it" (1987:45); another of Armstrong's informants, assaulted by her older brother, had been diagnosed with gonorrhea at the age of three. In several places, however, incest survivors speak the kinds of words that will later fuel the memory wars. "Jenny" explains that "until about a year ago I had no awareness that any of it had happened. I had completely removed it from any form of consciousness" (23). Jenny's memories return two years after she started talking to a college psychologist and after she began a relationship that "provoked a rush of memories." Another woman, June, tells Armstrong, "My very first memory, at my earliest age, was when I was one (but I might have been three)" (117)—ages now considered too young for the reliable storage of memories—but she does not mention having any therapy. In other words, these descriptions do not emerge from some uniform experience of therapy. When the woman with lab reports of her gonorrhea tells her psychiatrist how her brother liked to "play doctor with her," her therapist responds, "Well, it was just playing doctor" (183). There is no psychoanalytic juggernaut flattening out these women's words, words that for the most part suggest the courage and resiliency of women who dared to talk about a forbidden topic.

Armstrong's presentation of believable stories of ordinary women is meant to elicit a sympathetic response. Yet her care to be discreet is a symptom of her recognition that she might easily offend her audience. Her choice to feature informants who seem ordinary and normal is, then, an acknowledgment of a cultural tradition that frames women who tell incest stories as disturbingly exotic and seductive figures. Two early reviews of *Kiss Daddy Goodnight* demonstrate that responses to Armstrong's book encouraged both sympathy and disgust. The *Library Journal* offers this friendly account of the book: "In the scanty literature on the subject, this work provides a useful, popularly written human document as well as a brief guide to sources of help for victims. It may well give some aid and comfort to library patrons and produce in others the indignation needed to get action to correct the problem" (Sweetland, 1276). This review assumes that bringing attention to a scarcely discussed problem—incest—is a useful thing to do both to help victims and, by arousing indignation, to provoke action that might make it more difficult for children to be victimized. Notice, too, that *Kiss Daddy Goodnight* is not described as a feminist work but as a "human document," a generous description, but one that dilutes Armstrong's specific political analysis, which recommends challenging male power.

A review in the *New York Times Book Review* offers a strikingly different assessment. In the first paragraph, the reviewer, Raymond A. Solokov, begins by asserting that Armstrong is "right" to "urge a discussion of father-daughter incest so that other victims will gather courage, see that their plight is not unique and be able to do something about it . . . (and allegedly to pressure social-service agencies to drop their bias against incest victims)" (16, 20).[4] By using the word "allegedly," the *New York Times* review diverges sharply from the one in the *Library Journal*. The *Times* review proceeds to challenge Armstrong's credibility in familiar ways. As Peggy Sanday has documented, disgust and disbelief have long characterized public responses to women's accusations that they have been raped. Solokov deeply mistrusts Armstrong: "Her research was informal at best (I assume that she did not make it up entirely) and is, by professional standards, unreliable. But even by the looser standards of journalism this is a shoddy book, a string of 'true' confessions written in the coy style of pornography masquerading as science." With these words, Solokov places Armstrong in a long line of licentious "false accusers": Armstrong's complaints about incest are an excuse to provide readers with dirty talk. The review goes on to explain that the book recalls "soft-core films" that "begin in a doctor's office . . . establishing a legal claim for the film's socially redeeming value." Armstrong "covers herself with quotations from experts and a kind of feminist rhetoric, but then out comes the rough stuff." The review concludes:

> The publisher is promoting *Kiss Daddy Goodnight* as if it were a children's crusade, but the jacket illustration shows a bed frame with cute little girls' faces peeking innocently out from behind some black hearts. (20)

Solokov is clearly reading Armstrong's book through the lens of a paradigm that understands incest stories as pornographic fantasies.

Although Armstrong writes to help women and to make a larger public "indignant," the book's *cover* does market incest as a fascinating, tabooed desire.[5] The cover design thus supports the reviewer's sense that only sluts would talk about experiences of incestuous assault and only for an audience looking for titillation. This kind of argument, of course, is easily deployed to blame incest victims for seducing parents or to argue that children always like it, as some therapists and sexual liberationists do. To avoid any implication in these two familiar explanations for incest, feminists rarely mention that a daughter's reactions to a father's prolonged, invasive attentions may be informed by complex desires, which should not necessarily be considered "choices." Indeed the invocation of choice, as if desires were simply there to be claimed, is one way of making girls responsible for paternal assaults.[6] Yet if it seems that much feminist writing about incest prudishly avoids discussion of either infantile sexuality or adult fantasy, it is useful to remember the dominant discourse that invisibly regulates it. This discourse says that the desiring child or woman is "bad" and asks for violent sexual assault. Because feminist incest scholarship is explicitly an intervention into a discourse about seductive children and adolescent girls that traditionally obscures the actions of powerful adults, it dramatizes children's innocence. And in so doing, it is in a position to be aligned with polemics about threats to children, "purity" movements, that originate in the New Right.

At the end of her book Armstrong writes: "The women in this book are saying important and serious things. I believe we are raising serious questions. I hope they will lead to further serious discussion" (242). The worried repetition of the word "serious" does not forestall *The New York Times* review in which Armstrong's "speak-out," because of its frank discussion of incest, is recategorized as pulp fiction, thus undermining her authority and professionalism. Unfortunately that judgment is validated by the book's cover. If illicit sex sells books, then women who talk about incest can be seen as more manipulative and sexually profligate than the men they try to expose. This is the default view of women's excessive speech and desires that has returned with a vengeance in narratives produced by the false-memory syndrome movement.

These two reviews of *Kiss Daddy Goodnight* show that feminist writings about incest are, from the beginning, read in dramatically different ways: as moral calls to solve a human problem and as sensationalist fabrications. Does one of these perspectives have more cultural authority? Certainly *The New York Times Book Review* is a powerful medium, and the discrediting of women's accounts of abuse continues to thrive in highly visible venues. But the *Library Journal* influences library purchases: twenty years later incest is accepted as a "problem," and library shelves display an assortment of women's testimonies about sexual abuse. The increasing ferocity of the battle over the status of memories of incest undoubtedly reflects anxiety about how to respond to the burgeoning literature about sexual abuse. Do these testimonies depict real conditions, or are they sensationalist fabrications? Yet though the issue here seems to be finding a single "truth," assessments of a story's truthfulness are made through increasingly visible and layered cultural frames—feminism, psychoanalysis, family values, and so on—that create fractures within and between those who tell and hear women's incest stories. It is perhaps this very dynamic of shifting perspectives that sustains the desire for an incontestable truth.

The difficulties with telling and listening to incest stories are exacerbated within a cultural moment such as ours. Social realities are changing traditional forms of the family and economic transformations threatening not only the independent authority of the anxious wage-earning male provider but also the ability of social service agencies to provide adequate resources to women and children who need alternatives to those dangerous familial relations that defy popular rhetoric about traditional family values. Anxieties about family life reflect anxieties about the well-being of the nation, itself often portrayed as a family. Not only do political candidates appear as avuncular figures who talk about their traumatic war wounds and troubled personal lives, but they tout the traditional patriarchal family, which few of them have, as the bedrock of American life and values. Furthermore, they also insist on personal solutions for public problems. Millions of children in poverty? Tell their fathers to become patriarchal figures, a mode of reasoning that both obscures the power of economic structures—raising wages would be more helpful to both mothers and fathers—and masks any benefits to women of the decline of the traditional family structure, such as, obviously, independence from abusive men. The political does not become the personal without attendant problems for feminist analyses. Feminists, of course, have long been labeled as "antifamily," associated with the political instead of the personal, because they have analyzed the way social and economic structures have shaped and transformed behavior within the family. Clearly, if feminists are not criticized for being too personal, they can always be criticized for being too political.

As we have seen, the theoretical analysis of incest is a crucial component of the feminist critique of patriarchy as manifested in the traditional, father-dominated family. With the publication of Florence Rush's book *The Best Kept Secret* (1980), which places the sexual abuse of children within an almost universal historical frame, and, more importantly for the memory wars, Judith Herman's *Father-Daughter Incest* (1981), feminist research on incest produces an authoritative analysis of the links between patriarchy, traditional family structures, and incestuous abuse. *Father-Daughter Incest* was published by Harvard University Press, and Herman was at that time psychiatric director of a woman's mental health collective. (She is now on the faculty of the Harvard Medical School.) In her first book, Herman's analysis, like Armstrong's, centers on the power relations that silence incest victims, though her recent work emphasizes trauma and dissociation. Because it once seemed so obvious that the political (patriarchy) could explain the personal (incest), Armstrong and Herman do not invoke psychic operations to explain why incest might be difficult to tell. Instead, they describe a patriarchal taboo on girls speaking about incest, but not on fathers committing incest. *Father-Daughter Incest* offers an understanding of incest that is very compatible with Armstrong's analysis of "power abuse" by men, though Herman is even more explicit about the importance of feminism to her argument. She forthrightly asserts that a frankly feminist perspective offers the best explanation of the existing data. Without an understanding of male supremacy and female oppression, it is impossible to explain why the vast majority of incest perpetrators ... are male, and why the majority of victims ... are female. Without a feminist analysis, one is at a loss to explain why the reality of incest was for so long suppressed by supposedly responsible investigators, why public discussion of the subject awaited the women's liberation movement. (Herman and Hirschman, 3)

Herman adds, "It is no accident that incest occurs most often precisely in the relationship where the female is most powerless" (4). With these words, Herman decisively claims feminist ownership of the theoretical study of incest.

Judith Herman has more authority and institutional power than Armstrong and has exercised more influence on a range of discourses about incestuous abuse. Here is a woman institutionally positioned to tell a very believable story about incest, one that shares Armstrong's emphasis on the importance of naming oppression, though in Herman's writing therapeutic and political intervention begin to merge, as a changed psychology becomes the key to a changed, more equitable world. What is taking shape at the beginning of the Reagan years is a feminist view that revolutionary political change must follow revolutionary changes in the self; this view replaces an older notion that a political revolution would come first and lead to a changed humanity. Armstrong's book is written out of a conviction that incest victims do not need to change, they simply need to tell—and political change will follow. Herman shares Armstrong's view about patriarchy as the condition of possibility for incest but sees feminist therapy as the best place for telling incest and for beginning the arduous rebuilding of psyche, family, and society.

As was the case in Armstrong's book, *Father-Daughter Incest* crucially depends on women talking to women, this time in the form of a "semistructured interview protocol" (Herman and Hirschman, 69). Feminist discourse about abuse has begun to claim the authority of science. From their interviews of forty women conducted over four years, Herman and Hirschman developed a picture of the incestuous family that confirms Armstrong's insistence that the incestuous father "must have a sense of paternalistic prerogative to rationalize what he's doing" (*Kiss Daddy Goodnight*, 234). According to Herman, the incestuous family represents an extreme form of traditional family patterns. In incestuous families, fathers are dictatorial providers and mothers economically dependent, ill, or absent. In cases where the mother is dead, the daughter is forced to take on the mother's role—cook, cleaner, caretaker—because the father does not do "women's" work. Assenting to this division of labor and the rights it grants to fathers, women in these families, even incest victims themselves, tend to overvalue men and devalue women.

In place of the "seductive daughter" and "collusive mother" blamed for incest in earlier psychological literature, *Father-Daughter Incest* features the domineering "seductive father" who thrives within a pathologically traditional family structure. Within this structure, both men and women display extreme forms of stereotypic masculinity and femininity. Fathers are "perfect patriarchs" (71), controlling providers; mothers and daughters are helpless and deferential to men. Herman's feminist interpretation of incest makes compelling narrative and political sense as a description of privileged white families (Morrison paints a very different picture, one of paternal helplessness in *The Bluest Eye*)—and thus sets the stage for a standoff with the rival commonsense story of the virtuous middle-class family in which fathers are involved and nurturing. Indeed, in the 1980s, as Tania Modleski has pointed out, one response to the feminist demand for more male involvement in nurturing was a spate of film and television shows in which affluent white fathers happily take care of little girls—and mothers are out of the picture.[7] In the popular media, the father-daughter relationship that Herman sees as a pathological structure is presented as a heartwarming alternative to its implicit opposite, the world of impoverished and increasingly stigmatized single mothers.

In addition to a propensity to dismiss women and overvalue men, the daughter "inherits," to use Herman's term, a life marked by feelings of depression and isolation.[8] Because she possesses a dark secret, the daughter feels herself a permanently estranged outsider to normal social life. In characterizing the feelings of the victimized daughter in *Father-Daughter Incest*, Herman does not discuss forgetting, repression, dissociation, or trauma. Her focus is on those who know but cannot tell because they do not want to defy their fathers' orders. And when the victim does tell, perhaps motivated by a desire to protect younger siblings or in a desperate effort to gain an independent sexual life, Herman notes that family members tend to categorically deny the truth of the disclosure. Herman adds that even health care professionals are often uncomfortable about having to listen to stories that shock their sensibilities. These days, of course, health care professionals are assumed to be so comfortable with incest stories that they eagerly implant them in their patients.

In the last part of her book, Herman explains that the daughter's disclosure of incest is often resisted not just by fathers, who stand to lose their families, jobs, and liberty, but by powerful members of communities—judges, lawyers, ministers—who do not want to think that incest occurs in the traditional families that they so prize. The daughter who discloses will thus encounter denial, resistance, and possibly violence. Herman argues strenuously that for these reasons the father should be removed from the home and the daughter provided with support from her mother, if the bond between mother and daughter can be restored. Nancy Chodorow's *Reproduction of Mothering* was published the same year as Armstrong's book and informs Herman's understanding of how the sexual division of labor in child-rearing results in a psychological basis for male domination and female victimization of the sort she finds in incestuous families. Yet while Chodorow emphasizes the centrality of the mother-daughter bond in order to offer a critique of its role in perpetuating the sexual division of labor, Herman see this bond as something that needs to be reinstalled: "Rebuilding the family begins with restoration of the mother-daughter bond" (145).[9]

What she actually seems to mean is not a restored bond, since a mother-daughter bond does not seem to exist within the family structure she describes, but a new, utopian one formed after mothers have developed enough autonomy to protect their daughters and transform their expectations about what women can do. Herman's way of telling the feminist story thus allows mothers complete innocence but at the cost of placing an incredible burden on them for restoring a perfect relationship with their daughters. In making mothers so central, Herman again reveals the extent to which the feminist story is structured as a reversal of early psychoanalytic narratives that also made mothers key, but as actors responsible for causing incest (through their own sexual failures) rather than responsible for saving daughters.[10] Herman's reversal clearly depends upon "difference" feminism to make her case that women's special maternalized relational skills could transform familial and social relations. This idealizing of the mother exists in tandem with other assumptions that undermine this sanguine view.

Herman understands that female desires are socialized within patriarchy, but she is not able to reconcile her psychoanalytic account of female desire with her political story about the father's absolute culpability. Early in *Father-Daughter Incest*, Herman repeats the standard psychoanalytic account of female desire, merely adding that female desire for the father is a desire for power. She argues, in other words, that the daughter hopes to gain access to male power through an eroticized attachment to her father. But at the same time, Herman repeats the familiar Freudian explanation that the daughter's incestuous wishes are not suppressed by a fear of punishment because the daughter is already been castrated, made a female. This Freudian account, which explains why the daughter has insufficiently internalized the incest taboo, refuses the obvious question: isn't it the father who has not internalized the incest taboo? According to the "feminist incest story," which Herman powerfully reproduces in *Father-Daughter Incest*, for men, the incest taboo scarcely exists because "male supremacy creates the social conditions that favor the development of father-daughter incest" (Herman and Hirschman, 62). Trying to extricate herself from a tradition of mother blaming and daughter blaming, but constructing a narrative that reproduces both a psychoanalytic account of female desire and a feminist account of female victimization, Herman's narrative struggles but often fails to keep the father's desire, as well as his power, in focus. The very absolutism of Herman's depiction of the father/ offender may be an artifact of this struggle.

It is perhaps a measure of increasing feminist despair about the possibility of popular support for challenging the male monopoly of social power that Herman ultimately supports a program of changing fathers by fiat.

> Many programs . . . share common features with systems of political re-education developed in revolutionary societies. Like political re-education programs, they are designed for men who have used their power to oppress and exploit others but who are judged not to be irremediably depraved. Like political re-education programs, they are coercive, they make use of intense peer group confrontation and support, and they require confession, apology and restitution. Like political re-education programs, they attempt to create a "new man." (161)

Herman does not notice that these boot camps would be just the kind that authoritarian men might relish attending. The one specific program that Herman commends for its efforts at reeducation is Parents United, developed by Henry and Anna Giaratto, family counselors who, in the 1980s, offered national training programs for social workers and therapists. The Giarratos argued that the cause of incest was instability in the traditional nuclear family that could be rectified by reinstalling the mother in her role as "bearer and traditionally the principal caretaker" (Giaratto, 34). After this primary support is established for the daughter, the father is "invited" to rejoin this "core" (that is, if he has fully acknowledged his betrayal of the father's role in a men's group).[11] It seems, then, that Herman's "new man" would then be the unlikely product of a program with a political analysis that is based on an implicit faith in the traditional roles that have long secured paternal authority. Her advocacy of a rigid and ultimately conservative form of treatment demonstrates just how intractable and "other" she believes male perpetrators are. At the same time, it upholds her faith in the magic of therapeutic treatment to function like a political movement, though this faith in therapy seems more justified when she discusses incest victims.

The therapies Herman recommends for victims suggest great optimism about change. She argues that group therapy and self-help groups may be particularly advantageous not only in resolving survivors' feelings of shame and guilt but in developing in them a feminist analysis for challenging "patriarchal assumptions about sexuality, motherhood, and child care" (Herman and Hirschman, 215). *Father-Daughter Incest* thus demonstrates how feminist mental health professionals, convinced of the need for a revolutionary redistribution of power in order to end male violence against women, come to redefine therapy as an interaction where, even if the social order—and men—

are hard to treat, at least female victims can learn to understand that they are not to blame for their own victimage. As Herman points out, therapy can also be a place in which to rethink ideas about "normal" male and female psychology and behavior. Rape hot lines, women's groups, and health collectives make similar grassroots efforts to link individual treatment and social analysis. For Herman and many others, therapy cannot be seen as a retreat to the personal. It is a mechanism for bringing a political interpretation to women desperately in need of a larger framework for understanding personal crisis. Incest, described in Herman's book as the deepest pathology of the nuclear family, becomes an obviously important site for feminist analysis and a transformative therapeutic practice for women.

Yet Herman's expressed sense that male perpetrators are not very treatable and the growing explanatory power of "difference" feminism emphasizing women's "relational" abilities and men's lack of them constructs the symptomatic masculinity of the abuser as a foundational category even as it naturalizes women's capacity to nurture. Not only does the near essentializing of the abuser's gender create a theoretical problem (culture and history do not matter?) and a practical problem (how then should women contest violence against women?) but it sets the stage for men to notice the way in which they are being monolithically represented. Though Herman's book got favorable reviews in a variety of professional journals, predictably several reviews voice annoyance at a form of feminist analysis that looks like male-bashing. In the *Atlantic*, for example, the reviewer notes that "the author is glumly aware that incest will persist as long as the patriarchal family system produces men who cannot 'distinguish between sexuality and affection'" (Adams, 108). These words conjure up the stereotypic "humorless" feminist and her Sisyphean labors to end patriarchy. A reviewer in the *British Journal of Psychiatry* is harsher, noting that the book's subject requires "a very much more careful objective analysis than the persecuted attitude to the male" (Gallwey, 318). Notice how Herman is here linked to paranoia and unreason. A decade later, in the "false memory" writings, expressions of disdain and irritation with feminist theorizing are replaced by outrage about injuries—false accusations—supposedly suffered at the hands of male-bashing feminist therapists who are incapable of objective analysis.

It is useful to remember that before there were debates about recovered memory, the feminist incest story (almost always about *remembered* incest) had already been read as pornographic and unreasonable. Yet it is also important to acknowledge that feminists, too, now find problems with the feminist incest story. For as important as it is to condemn perpetrators and to recognize the suffering of abused women, incest is not the key to understanding the situation of women. Material and social forms of gendered inequality are not simply caused by abusive fathers, who do not all have the same kind of social and economic power. As an explanatory tool, then, the feminist incest story makes mistakes. In our view, these mistakes are small, given the energy for social analysis and reform that this narrative helped to inspire. Women's telling of prohibited stories about incest once promised to galvanize a feminist social movement that could make the world a dramatically better place. Even if a social revolution did not result from the feminist incest story, its legacy lives in an increased general awareness about violence in the family.

It is hard to admit that the revolutionary expectations associated with the feminist incest story seem dated, and not just because of the rising fortunes of conservative politics. As the number of non-father-headed households grows and the social and economic status of white men declines (despite the privilege that keeps them ahead of other workers, with black male workers a notable example), gendered models of power and change clearly need expansion and revision. Yet women who dare to tell still deserve a great deal of credit for making public a history of hidden domestic abuse. Thanks to African-American women writers and to the feminist scholarship of the 1970s and early 1980s, the interconnection between legitimized structures of patriarchal authority and occluded forms of coercive violence was, at least for a time, widely available. In other words, these women's narratives made it possible to understand incest as a familiar, not exotic, act; not only what paternal law forbids but also what it enables. The success of the feminist incest story, particularly as it has developed into a story of trauma and recovery, should not, then, simply be dismissed as evidence of a moral panic about child abuse or the self-indulgence of white, middle-class women.[12]

We are offering, then, not only a way to understand the feminist incest story, but a way to think about its relationship to what followed: narratives of recovered memories. Recovered memories became a subject of knowledge and debate as a result of a number of intersecting conditions that cannot be exhaustively catalogued but must be provisionally articulated if feminist frameworks for analyzing child sexual abuse are to be more fully understood as well as expanded. First, feminist analysts such as Louise Armstrong and Judith Herman, women whose work was inflected by a popular women's movement, had acquired enough institutional authority to shape a persuasive discourse about the links between patriarchy, incest, and women's social subjugation and psychological distress. Second, this discourse began to solidify in the early 1980s, when it found resonance with a politically powerful conservative effort to expose the evils of pornography and satanic abuse, two "problems" that were aligned with feminist concerns about patriarchal abuses of women and children.[13] This alliance obscured a crucial fact: feminists defined the traditional family as sanctioning paternal abuse of children; conservatives defined the father-headed family as a haven for children.[14] At the same time, in Reagan's first term, children were among the victims of massive cuts in social welfare, health, and educational programs, allowing child abuse to function, as Nancy Scheper-Hughes and Howard F. Stein have argued, as a metaphor for "the complicity (and collective responsibility) in the implementation of local, national, and international policies that are placing our nation's and, indeed, the world's children at great risk," a metaphor that is given tangible shape in the abuser who molests his own children (341). Last, the popular media, always looking for sensationalist human interest stories and responsive to the growth of scholarly and legal knowledge about abuse, initially supported the effort to find and punish perpetrators, while establishing itself as a moral protector of children, a stance that would eventually conflict with the cultural imperative to protect parents' rights. However, neither stance—protecting children or parents—required a public agenda of restructuring society, since parents and daughters could be understood as either active deviants or passive dupes. Added to this volatile mix, creating anxiety and fear, was an underlying sense, still familiar today, that nameless authorities were covering up more than just assaults on children.

The contemporary metaphorics of abuse and recovery contains a poignant residue of earlier feminist concerns about collective injustice that is not only masked by an emphasis on personal trauma but expressed by it as well.[15] In recent women's narratives of incest, present suffering may be displaced upon the past; the pain of the past may also be displaced upon the present. Popular accounts of sexual abuse in books like *The Courage to Heal,* for example, may be compensating for past pain levels that never were acknowledged. At the same time, women's accounts of their memories of trauma also can function to sharply reveal and criticize present social arrangements. In women's incest narratives, the recursive relation between past and present creates a circuit in which both past and present are often sites of displaced anxiety. Women's stories about sexual abuse, such as the newly canonical texts that we will discuss next, remain important as representational spaces marking past and present pain—and the consequent need for a more equitable social order. The feminist incest story always kept this goal in mind.

Chapter 4

The Canonical Incest Story

A decade after *Father-Daughter Incest,* Judith Herman published another important book: *Trauma and Recovery* (1992). The two nouns of the title largely define the discursive space occupied by the tellings of incest in the 1980s and 1990s. "Trauma," a category elaborated by researchers in medicine, psychology, and increasingly in the humanities, refers to a psychic wounding that impedes a subject's encoding of horrific experiences and creates a set of symptoms perhaps best known under the general rubric *post-traumatic stress disorder.*[1] Herman describes trauma as "an affliction of the powerless" and argues that it is the origin of the incest victim's intermittent amnesia, intrusive flashbacks, and feelings of fear, distrust, and isolation (33). "Recovery" refers to both the victim's belated reconstruction of the traumatic event and the healing associated with this process. Herman attempts to provide a balanced consideration of trauma and recovery, devoting half of her book to each topic. Yet the even division of the book belies the popularity of the concept of recovery in the 1980s and its weight in her book and many others. In the best-known books about incest—Alice Walker's *The Color Purple* (1981), Ellen Bass and Laura Davis's *The Courage to Heal* (1985), and Jane Smiley's *A Thousand Acres* (1991)—the emphasis is on recovery, in both senses of the term. So visible are these best-selling narratives that, in the cultural imaginary, they represent what the incest story is all about. This is the role of a canonical text: to provide a narrative—here one about sexually abused daughters and their recovery from trauma—that seems to speak for all.[2] The blindspots and possibilities generated by canonical texts of incest are the subject of this chapter.

For writers in the 1980s, trauma is understood to make recovery difficult, though not impossible. Herman explains that the experience of incest traumatically violates a child's basic sense of trust and order. Such a trauma is especially difficult for an isolated and vulnerable child to process as memory or story. For Herman, recovery from incest often does not take place until a victim finds a community that provides a safe place for the belated telling of incest, a telling that will allow the victim to integrate her experiences into a comprehensible story. This supportive community also has the responsibility of validating the victim's testimony, which may take the form of a written narrative about the past. Herman writes that the "survivor who has achieved commonality with others can rest from her labors. Her recovery is accomplished; all that remains before her is her life" (236). Defined in such terms, recovery holds forth the promise of a complete release from the traumatic past. The popularity of the canonical incest "recovery story" may then depend upon its reassuring message: the victim can get over "the thing."

The promise of recovery is also central to the work of feminist critics in the 1980s who wrote about the silencing of women in literary history and the need to open up the canon.[3] In 1981, Nina Baym published an influential article about canon formation called "Melodramas of Beset Manhood: How Theories of American Fiction Exclude Women Authors." Her argument is that powerful American literary critics, such as F. O. Matthiessen, Jay B. Hubbell, Lionel Trilling, and Richard Poirer, have implicitly supported the exclusion of women authors from the canon by defining canonical American fiction as literature in which a male writer manages to overcome the obstacles presented by bad women writers flooding the market with a degraded genre: the "melodrama of beset womanhood." Leslie Fiedler writes that "our best fictionists" have had to "struggle" against these melodramas to get attention for their serious writing. This writing features another gendered contest; in celebrated novels by men, the isolated American individual (male) struggles against "the socializing and domesticating woman" (73). The best American fictionists thus give women "the role of entrapper and impediment" (75) to the expression of a fully representative, and ultimately triumphant, American (male) selfhood. Perhaps these narratives could be called canonical male recovery stories.

In a witty reversal, Baym describes the ennobling effort of the male writer to tell his story as a "melodrama of beset *manhood.*" She also resurrects the initially unsuccessful attempts of women writers to produce this esteemed melodrama by positioning *men* as the entrappers and impediments to female selfhood. In the 1980s, women are more successful at turning the tables by writing a believable narrative about constraints imposed on women by men. Their recovery story is a tale of persecution and escape from male "entrappers and impediments" that also explains why women must refuse traditional domesticity. Women's canonical narratives of recovery thus implicitly rewrite literary and cultural history by placing women at the center of an earlier canonical American narrative about an individual's heroic resistance to a constrictive social order that needs to be reconstituted. Operating within this revisionary table-turning is a commonly shared assumption that the American essence is embodied in the autonomous individual who struggles to find freedom and redemption. This narrative presumption now draws upon the resources of feminist therapeutic literature but also appropriates the lineaments of the melodrama of beset manhood, which itself is indebted to Puritan spiritual autobiographies with their stages of self-recognition, suffering, regeneration, and final admission into a purified community. Our focus on what have become canonical incest texts (texts that seem to "speak for all" incest narratives) suggests the relationship of these narratives to self-help literature by including two novels and one self-help book. While there is no doubt that women's recovery stories are often utopian, or too neat and scripted in the way that consign "the thing" to the past, these narratives nonetheless provide an important challenge to earlier canonical conventions of collectivity and personhood (what we will later discuss as the "grandiose individual") that have been narrowly defined as white and male.

As we have seen, there is energy and hope informing the utopian solutions of Louise Armstrong's and Judith Herman's analyses of father-daughter incest, work that we described in the previous chapter. Alice Walker's *The Color Purple*, published in 1982, participates in the enthusiasm of this apparently revolutionary moment. As Morrison does in *The Bluest Eye*, Walker bravely depicts African-American women living with the double oppressiveness of racism and sexism. Yet unlike Toni Morrison, Walker has available to her the feminist incest story's political analysis, and perhaps more important, she also helps to shape an emergent incest narrative about recovery. Walker's novel begins with a pregnant, fourteen-year-old child's effort to write a letter about traumatic experiences of incest that her "Pa" tries to silence: "You better not never tell nobody but God. It'd kill your mammy" (1), a reworking of the threat in Stein's narrative that the father is being "killed" by the daughter who tells. Celie, the heroine and first-person narrator of the novel, suffers all the consequences of female sexual victimization that are described in Judith Herman's *Father-Daughter Incest* and that Herman will later elaborate as post-traumatic symptoms: isolation, numbness, a dogged attachment to the caretaking role. Celie is also almost illiterate and yet trying to write her story, an essential method of recovery. Writing, as Walker's novel reminds us, is also a means of gaining access to the literary achievement from which African-Americans were excluded by enforced illiteracy. Given these overwhelming obstacles to healing and witness, how does recovery occur?

Celie's recovery is made possible when Celie discovers that "Pa not pa" (183). Celie's real father, it turns out, was a man lynched by whites who were threatened by his economic success. The novel thus substitutes a narrative about deadly white economic paternalism for a tale of paternal incest within an African-American family, a transformation that recalls how, in *The Invisible Man*, Trueblood's incest story reveals the white father's exploitative paternalism. In Walker's narrative, this switch allows Celie to make a quick turn from trauma to recovery. As Lauren Berlant explains: "This complex substitution of paternal tales effectively frees Celie to reclassify her experience as a *misunder-*

standing" (840). Walker's novel needs this "misunderstanding" in order for Celie's democratic business, Folkpants, to become the vehicle for moving a profoundly traumatized African-American daughter to the center of a new, redeemed America in which the past produces no lasting traumatic effects.

There is a gap between past and present structuring the novel, but this gap is not seen as symptomatic of denial or repression. Instead, the gap is empowering. In *The Color Purple*, Celie experiences multiple forms of oppression but rises above them. She writes ever more elaborate letters, discovers a sympathetic paternal legacy, and recovers other lost parts of her family and history, talks to supportive women to get a more expansive sense of herself, and then claims a fuller, prosperous life. Indeed, she enjoys the fruits promised by therapeutic recovery—self-esteem, a satisfying lesbian sexuality, enhanced spirituality—and also finds fulfillment in work. In Walker's novel, then, African-American women are represented as both beset heroines and members of a redeemed community, a revision of the traditional white and male model of American essence that works to redress the exclusion of African-American women, both as writers and as subjects, from dominant forms of cultural representation. As Nellie McKay notes, "*The Color Purple* is important for what its popularity means in terms of the recognition it compels for the works of black women." It also compels attention to "the experiences of black women" (249). In a study of the reception of the novel, Jacqueline Bobo explains that many African-American women saw the story as powerfully affirming their lives. Commenting upon Celie, for example, one woman told Bobo: "The lady was a strong lady, like I am. And she hung in there and she overcame" (278).

The Color Purple, a best-seller and Pulitzer Prize winner, also appealed to millions of other readers by opening up space—domestic and economic—in which beset characters achieve and enjoy a miraculous prosperity within a newly harmonious social order. As a reviewer in *Newsweek* exclaimed: "Alice Walker excels at making difficulties for herself and then transcending them" (Prescott, 67). Like most utopian novels, *The Color Purple* resolves in fantasy an uneasy social contradiction. Without any sense of paradox, the novel suggests that a form of capitalism that has objectified women and racial minorities can also be the source of their redemption. In *The Color Purple*, a renewed insistence upon the economic rewards of individual enterprise (Celie mimics her father by becoming a successful businesswoman) vies with the increased visibility and vocality of those, like the angry Sofia, who is beaten and imprisoned when she insists on economic and social justice. Celie seems to have it all: the rewards of entrepreneurial individualism and a unified, redeemed African-American community. In this way, Walker's narrative temporarily elides and alleviates the continuing traumatic consequences of sexism and racism, which operate together to make "recovery" difficult. (The story's elision of present pain may also be designed to deflect charges that it is another "harangue" by an

African-American writer.) The empowerment promised by recovery—reconstructing the past and healing from it—is thus achieved at the cost of acknowledging that the victim's new and idealized identity as a healed survivor partakes in a cultural idiom of self-help whose comforts depend on looking away from continuing and collective sources of trauma.

Of course, not all readers celebrated Walker's narrative of trauma, recovery, and social transformation. Feminist critics, for example, worried about the way the novel posits "a world of perfect, immanent understanding and homogenous sisterhood" that could not admit to its own exclusions (Kaplan, 142). But these arguments among feminists about the limits of "politically correct" sisterhood were largely drowned out. The most public criticism of Walker's novel was not the feminist concern about utopian solutions as covering over differences between "sisters" (the novel is partly structured as a series of letters between two sisters) but that it was too harsh in its depictions of African-American men and of white racism. So, for example, John Simon, writing for the *National Review,* attacks the novel through the film version of it: "Miss Walker's novel—far from the literary masterpiece it has been hyped into and unable to transcend the two humanly legitimate but artistically burdensome chips on its shoulder—feminism and black militancy—is still much better than the film" (56). The columnist Courtland Milloy challenges Walker's effort to place black women at the center by reading the book as a thinly veiled attack by white men on black men, "I got tired, a long time ago, of white men publishing books by Black women about how screwed up Black men are" (B3). Another reviewer, Carol Iannone, undercuts the legitimacy of responses to the book that lend it canonical status: "The response to *The Color Purple . . .* can well be seen as a kind of literary affirmative action" (57–58). In retrospect, given the novel's celebration of individual initiative and its vision of achieved social harmony, it seems incredible that the novel was so roundly attacked for its black and feminist militancy. Though the rewards for telling an African-American woman's incest story are much greater for Walker's novel than for Morrison's, so is the punishment. The incest story that enjoys a reception as canonical fiction is also condemned as pseudo-literature by a pseudo-person, in other words, as a "melodrama of beset womanhood."

Fierce attacks on the recovery story are also directed at the "bible" (a word that suggests its canonicity) of the recovery movement: *The Courage to Heal* by Ellen Bass and Laura Davis. Before writing this key trauma and recovery book, Ellen Bass, like Louise Armstrong, had already edited an anthology of stories by survivors, *I Never Told Anyone: Writings by Women Survivors of Childhood Sexual Abuse.* From the beginning, then, Bass's work participates in the feminist incest story's assumption of the importance of telling, but it emphasizes the difficulty of disclosing incest: "I Never Told Anyone." The new recovery story's emphasis is on how a "secret trauma" (to use Diana Russell's phrase) is finally told in a safe environment and on how this telling makes recovery possible. In this formulation of the incest narrative, the nature of the promised change is not the revolutionary national transformation promised by the feminist story and that Walker's novel incorporates. Increasingly, a focus on changing the self rather than the world begins to predominate in popular books about incest—and none is more popular than *The Courage to Heal*. This new emphasis attracts charges from critics that incest tellers are self-indulgent women feeding hysterically upon fantasies of victimization and encouraging others to do so. Telling incest stories is thus again linked to sensationalism. But while claims that Louise Armstrong's anthology was deliberately provocative depended upon a reading of her book's cover, with its little girls peeping through a bed frame, there is much more than a book cover at stake in attacks on *The Courage to Heal*. We are now in the realm of the big-time incest narrative. Recovery stories dominate talk shows and media stories. For a brief moment of time, incest is *the* story to tell.

We hope to offer a more nuanced understanding of why *The Courage to Heal* was both so appealing and so appalling and became canonical, the incest book for all people, and therefore the book to attack. While its critics often describe the book, and the stories it engenders, as formulaic, attacks often seem to be just as formulaic, focusing only upon points or parts of the book previously raised by other attackers (such as the notorious "checklist of symptoms"). What gets obscured by this level of discussion are the complex social conditions and struggles that have produced this way of telling incest and how this new kind of telling opens up promising possibilities. As we have seen with *The Color Purple*, part of that novel's appeal was its ability to offer an attractive fantasy of recovery emphasizing both personal prosperity and national well-being, a fantasy that obscured the effects of a deepening economic crisis and more cuts to social programs for the poor in the 1980s. Just as Celie's recovery seems to cut off her acknowledgment of her damaging past, so too does *The Courage to Heal* offer an enormously enabling fantasy that by the same token refuses a complex analysis of the very means of recovery, writing, that it so confidently touts.

Ellen Bass is a poet who discovered by teaching creative writing that "writing itself was healing" (18). Laura Davis was a student of Bass's who felt her "healing process" would be facilitated by writing a book with her teacher. *The Courage to Heal* is thus itself a personal recovery story. Neither Bass nor Davis is an academically trained psychologist. As Bass explains, her knowledge is based on what she has "learned from the experiences of survivors" (18). *Courage to Heal* thus participates in an older form of feminist grassroots work. Bass and Davis explicitly announce that they write "in the tradition of speakouts" (13), but the focus of their consciousness-raising shifts. Unlike the earlier work of Armstrong and Herman that places women's experience in a larger theoretical frame of patriarchy, here experience alone is assumed to provide unmediated access to the truth. In *The Courage to Heal,* stories of individual experience are by definition true stories. Because no effort is thus required to understand the mediation of "experience" by social and discursive structures, Bass and Davis unself-consciously encourage the production of "recovered" incest narratives of the sort that have led to so much public controversy. This is not to disavow the appeal to real, oppressive personal experiences that is made in these stories, but to show how Bass and Davis shape the form that this testimony takes.

Teresa Ebert sums up the feminist challenge to those who believe "experience" is foundational knowledge: "While it is true that a woman, a person of color, a queer experiences oppression, this experience is by no means self-explanatory: it has to be explained in relation to other social practices" (19). But if all of us right-thinking feminists know that the personal must be theorized, do we know how to do so? In a way, Bass and Davis are writing within this gap between the older political conceptual model of the past (the feminist incest story) and present, anxious experiences that have not yet been fully theorized but that are fueling the emergence of the increasingly popular conceptual paradigm of trauma.

As with *The Color Purple,* in *The Courage to Heal* there is a rewriting of the past that de-emphasizes the legacy of trauma so as to make recovery more available. Similarly, in feminist criticism of the period the emphasis shifts from exposing the damaging effects of past constructions of femininity to celebrating the previously unacknowledged value of women's culture. New, more personable forms of feminism said less about male hegemony and instead focused on mother-daughter bonds and the nurturing, caring side of women's cultures of domesticity.[4] Of course, nurturance and care are certainly what all human beings need, especially battered and exploited women. But caring and being cared for are an understandable but limited definition of women's desire. Women's essential caring is a construction that seems merely the opposite of another naturalized essence, male violence. Furthermore, caring can become a form of control, as is shown by the quietly authoritarian voice of *The Courage to Heal.* The intrusive use of the second-person pronoun *you* has the effect of establishing the reality of the reader in an authoritarian way while seeming to provide a sensitive, caring mirror of the reader's deepest feelings: "When you were abused, your boundaries, your right to say no, your sense of control in the world were violated" (39); or "if you breeze through these chapters, you probably aren't feeling safe enough to confront these issues" (27). More widely condemned is the book's use of checklists to help "you" decide if "you" were abused: "Do you feel powerless, like a victim? Do you feel different from other people?" (39). The second-person point of view, perhaps because it can seem so relentlessly devoted to the addressee, blinds Bass and Davis to the way in which they are shaping the identity of the "you" and defining the trajectory of the victim's story. In other words they do not think about the stance of the "we" who wrote the book.

Bass and Davis are not interested in listening for what is not sayable within the structure of the trauma and recovery story, for the message relayed by the gaps and fragments that have increasingly been studied by theorists of trauma and that we will attend to in our chapter on incest memoirs. Instead, they believe that telling and recovery are fairly simple tasks. To heal, reader/victims need simply to write about abuse in what seems to be an easily accessible "safe" context. To facilitate this process, Bass and Davis provide writing assignments through which survivors are told to "define your own reality" (31). In this way, women are instructed to write themselves into health and happiness. However, this is writing without acknowledged powers of equivocation. In other words, "you" are not encouraged to exploit the insight that the past is constantly being scripted and rescripted. Nor is there an emphasis on point of view, and its relation to competing social and personal agendas: who is speaking? Who is listening? In whose interest is a particular story being told?

Courage to Heal is a massively popular text precisely because of its promise to readers that they can completely make sense of their lives—and transform them—through a simple process of writing, and thus recovering memories. In the words of one incest survivor, chosen as the epigraph for the chapter, "Effects: Recognizing the Damage":

> People have said to me, "Why are you dragging this up now?" Why? WHY? Because it has controlled every facet of my life. It has damaged me in every possible way. . . . It has prevented me from living a comfortable emotional life. . . . If I had a comfortable childhood, I could be anything today. (37)

Here incest is clearly posited as the key to everything, an originary trauma. Recovery also promises a completely comfortable future. For Bass and Davis, it is not much of a leap to assume that the cause of all adult dissatisfaction is childhood sexual abuse, and a utopian future is promised by recovery, both cause and cure thus narrowly confined to the private sphere. As Bass puts it: "I want to see us all become whole—and not stop there. As we become capable of nurturing ourselves and living rich personal lives, we are enabled to act creatively in the world so that life can continue—the eucalyptus trees, the narcissus, the sunfish, the squirrels, seals, hummingbirds, our own children" (19). This fantasy is unappealingly reminiscent of advertisements for Club Med vacations. Recovery here offers the promise that women can take an extended vacation from life.

Because Walker in *The Color Purple* and Bass and Davis in *The Courage to Heal* promise readers a fantasy recovery in which survivors enjoy life in prosperous and happy community, the trauma and recovery plot looks in some ways like an ideological fairy tale. Not that this is a reason to condemn it: the celebration of sisterhood and the possibility of a community that will work to women's benefit is understandably one that many women embrace. Indeed its attractions become more obvious when compared with the familiar counterpart to the recovery story: the false-memory story, which often features sisterhood as a coven of witches who are falsifying the past and blighting the future of men. Arthur Miller's canonical play *The Crucible* is *the* paradigmatic contemporary example of this narrative of beset manhood.[5] In her revision of the canon, *A Thousand Acres,* Jane Smiley works to expose the narrative of beset manhood as a monstrous fiction that powerful and seductive patriarchal figures tell and disseminate widely as a way of disavowing responsibility for their abuses of both real and "literary" daughters. Telling incest thus becomes a way to undercut the patriarchal cultural authority that produces and promotes the male canonical text. Smiley's novel, however, by transforming the incest victim into a tragic heroine, upsets the expectation that this process of recovering a traumatic past necessarily leads to the healing of self and community. At the same time, by insisting that the "melodrama of beset womanhood" is actually a tragedy, Smiley lends to the story the genre's seriousness and cultural prestige—and her own text makes a bid for canonical status.

In Smiley's novel, a daughter, Ginny, recovers submerged traumatic and incestuous experiences hidden within an almost mythically happy and prosperous white family. Revered texts—Shakespeare's *King Lear* and Walt Whitman's *Song of Myself*—are also disrupted and interrogated by the novel as sources of unacknowledged violence against women. Smiley's effort at canon critique closely parallels the story of canon-formation offered by Christine Froula, who draws upon Herman's *Father-Daughter Incest* to provide a theoretical basis for understanding "women's silence in literary history" (622). Froula argues that women as authors and readers are subject to violence enacted by literary fathers: "Metaphysically, the woman reader of a literary tradition that inscribes violence against women is an abused daughter. Like physical abuse, literary violence against women works to privilege the cultural father's voice and story over those of women, the cultural daughters, and indeed to silence women's voices" (633). Mirroring these ideas of canon formation as violent, gendered, and exclusionary, Smiley's novel uses recovered memories of incest to signify a woman's capacity to reconnect with deeply silenced "truths" about her personal and cultural subjugation.

As a result, the recovery plot in *A Thousand Acres* is familiar in that it partakes in the recognizable gesture of turning the tables on the melodrama of beset manhood. But Smiley knows that there are many similar stories being disseminated and that the incest recovery story can be put to a predictable use. In an interview, Smiley remarks: "There's been a lot about incest in literature in the past twenty-five years, which is inevitable as women get their voices. They'll say what really happened to them and, in many cases, it was sexual abuse or incest of some kind. But often it's used as a punch line. All these things happen in the present, then they go back and say, 'Incest! Oh, that explains it!'" (Anderson, 1). What Smiley sees, and what informs her practice in the novel, is the way in which powerful but reductive points of view struggle for dominance, to become, as it were, the "punch line."

A Thousand Acres takes on canonical texts governed by points of view so powerful that they seem simply to express universal truth. Smiley's novel, as everyone knows by now, rewrites *King Lear* from the point of view of Lear's evil daughter, Goneril. Smiley challenges *Lear's* misogyny, which makes Goneril a monster, by depicting her Goneril figure, Ginny, as bland and mild-mannered; she is the good, eldest daughter. Smiley also shifts Goneril's corrupted sexuality from the daughter's body to the father's as Lear becomes Larry Cook, an abusive father. As Ginny gains narrative authority, her sister, Rose, describes her never forgotten experience of abuse, and Ginny herself overcomes an internalized prohibition against remembering that she, too, has been sexually abused by her father. In the novel, the daughter's recovered memory of incest reveals the depredations of the sovereign power of the father and so argues for his repudiation. However, this memory does not provide either catharsis or an utopian alternative to the corrupted present. *Lear,* for example, is a kind of past, a locus of cultural authority structuring the novel, that can be powerfully reinterpreted but not easily shed.

Smiley's rewriting of *Lear* hopes to excavate the misogyny of the patriarchal bard by exposing the play's violently unsympathetic portrayal of unruly women. The novel's acknowledged—and rebuked—literary heritage also extends to American canonical literature and American constructions of the individual and his—we use the pronoun advisedly—relationship to the land. The phrase "a thousand acres" comes from Walt Whitman's *Song of Myself:*

> Have you reckoned a thousand acres much? Have you reckoned the earth much?
> Have you practiced so long to learn to read?
> Have you felt so proud to get at the meaning of poems?
>
> Stop this day and night with me and you shall possess the origin of all poems,
> You shall possess the good of the earth and sun . . . there are millions of suns left,
> You shall no longer take things at second or third hand. . . . nor look through the eyes of the dead . . . nor feed on the specters in books,

You shall not look through my eyes either, nor take things from me,
You shall listen to all sides and filter them from yourself.

(26)

These stanzas introduce a number of concerns addressed in the novel. Whitman contrasts the reader to those who take things "at second or third hand," who are, in other words, burdened by their relationship to the past. Americans are promised an unmediated, full present. By criticizing the idea of the full plenitude of the present, Smiley is also offering a critique of the recovery story's participation in the celebration of present possibilities that seem to be disconnected from any sense of the past. Her novel thus suggests that recovery *of* a traumatic past does not ensure a complete recovery *from* it.

"Reckoning" a thousand acres might, it seems, limit the fullness of the present moment. The language of reckoning is that of the accountant, the counting house, of ledgers and bankers. Yet reckoning "the earth," though it seems an impossible task, is perhaps a more noble one since the reckoning allows an inclusive stock-taking that the poem seems to approve of as it moves toward a celebration of possession: "you shall possess the origin of all poems, / You shall possess the good of the earth and sun." This form of possession attempts to transcend the material acquisitiveness of the possessive individual by requiring so much acquisition that the territorial boundaries reckoned by the accountant disappear. But at the same time, the grandiosity of this project is linked to a grandiose individual and an imagined American community in which everyone is accommodated. This universalizing narrative is one that Smiley challenges.

Whitman's grandiose individual is embodied in Larry Cook, whose name links him to America's imperialist beginnings through the allusion to Captain Cook. His middle daughter, Rose, calls him "the great I AM" (211). Discussing the patriarchal base of American agriculture, Deborah Fink explains: "By controlling the land, wealth, and social services, men were in position to have their wishes heeded" (208). A web of moralized power relations promotes respect for asymmetric and gendered power relations on the farm. Ginny says, "Trying to understand my father had always felt something like going to church . . . and listening to the minister we had . . . marshall the evidence for God's goodness. . . . Finally . . . the failure of our understandings was their greatest proof of all, not of goodness or omniscience or whatever the subject of the day was, but of power" (20). Because Larry Cook is presented as a center of authority, status, and wealth, the focus of the novel is initially on his ownership of the land and the legitimating structures that both naturalize his violence to his daughters and silence alternative perspectives on this behavior.

Yet the novel ultimately shows that as long as members of the family farm, including the farmer himself, believe in the absolute power of the father-landowner, they cannot see the social and economic changes that are shifting power to new places. Indeed, what undermines the family is not simply allegations of abuse stemming from recovered memories of incest but the unacknowledged power of unseen economic forces, a point that is completely missed by critics who want to position recovered memories as the cause of all evil and the novel as a dangerous support for the recovered-memory movement.[6] In the novel, Larry Cook's loss of authority is more closely linked to his economic decisions than to his daughter's allegations. Cook amasses a thousand acres, a size too large for single-family farming, by appropriating the land of his neighbors. He needs these increasingly large tracks of unfenced land in order to make possible the use of ever larger machines, such as the "new bigger tractors [that] meant greater speed and a wider turning radius" (206). Farmers are themselves thus implicated in the process of concentrating land in ever fewer hands to the point that they are themselves "industrial farmers" who rely on the labor of others (Vogeler, 30). Larry Cook decides to pass on this farm to his daughters and their husbands as a "corporation" (18).

There is a perilous moment of balance in this dream of something for everyone. But this fantasy of family harmony is already being undone at the moment of its conception. The family corporation is not even Larry Cook's own idea but Marv Carson's, whose name recalls several talk show hosts. The very insubstantiality of Carson, a faddish loan officer, allows Smiley to show that power is already shifting to places that are less palpable than the older form of patriarchal authority incarnated in Larry Cook. Ginny's husband, Ty, the "good" son-in-law, likes the idea of the corporation because he wants a hog confinement system or "Boar Boutique," but this form of livestock production leads him into debt—and a future with a corporate hog operation. Ginny and Rose carefully seal off from their youngest sister, Caroline (the Cordelia figure), the violence and drudgery on the farm so that she has no knowledge of her own past. As a result, though she is the one who has gotten away, she is also the one who wants things to stay as she imagines they must have been on the mythic American farm, a powerful cultural fantasy. Indeed, the emphasis on a romanticized notion of independent farmers working family farms obscures not only the oppression of agrarian women but also the economic transformations that have led to the triumph of agribusiness over family farmers. Caroline's investment in the myth of the family farm aligns her with her father, who does not understand challenges to his independence as effects of his own aggressive capital investments. He, too, has memory problems. And so it goes.

In Smiley's novel, the destruction of the family is, then, clearly the work of larger forces and so cannot be blamed solely upon Ginny's recovered memories. Before Rose tells Ginny about their abuse as teenagers, Larry Cook has already moved out; he has blamed his daughters for all his problems and rushed out into the storm, the act that leads Caroline to initiate her lawsuit;

and the farm is falling into increased debt because of Ty's investment in a hog confinement building. It is at this point that Ginny recovers memories of incest. Her recovered memories, validated by Rose's corroborating and never forgotten memories, are a sign that Ginny's own point of view is finally consolidating.

As is the case for many women who recover memories, Ginny's memories signify the emergence of a new point of view from which to take self-interested action. Indeed, the vantage point of the novel is her first-person reconstruction of the past. Her narrative authority requires, as we learn from the novel, that she not only challenge the naturalness of her subordinate position in her family but that she break strong ties of loyalty with her father, her husband, and her sister. Her point of view thus depends upon a radical autonomy that recalls heroic figures of "beset manhood" but is unlike the forms of new identity offered to incest survivors in feminist literature in which survivors claim a place within nurturing women's communities. Indeed, Ginny's sister Rose, the angry feminist who cannot forget her abuse, is shown to be too selfish and vindictive, too like her father, to be a reliable ally. Furthermore, while Rose is preoccupied with defeating her father, she has arguably suffered more deadly harm from the chemical residue that causes her cancer (and leads to the loss of the future through Ginny's miscarriages). In *A Thousand Acres*, the pervasive toxicity of the Cook farm is described through a metaphorics of "treacherous undercurrents" in which the polluted water flowing under the seemingly solid ground, a serious problem in the corn belt, is linked to both horrific repressed memories and unexamined economic pressures.

Ginny does not make a career of her role as a victim, though she remains angry about the "family values" of the farm, which are dependent on the subjugation of women and children to the will of the farmer. Her recovered memories of incest are an important way for her to clarify not only how much violence she has endured but how numb she has become to it. Here is where the feminist discourse about trauma and dissociation is especially useful to Smiley. Ginny's physical numbness, her passivity, and her amnesia are not only available as telling symptoms of the abuse victim but of "the private, secret traumas to which a feminist analysis draws attention . . . those events in which the dominant culture and its forms and institutions are expressed and perpetrated" (Brown, 102). These words offered by feminist therapist Laura Brown are part of an argument, a manifesto really, for the need to expand the range of experiences that are interpreted as traumatic: "a feminist perspective, which draws our attention to the lives of girls and women, to the secret, private hidden experiences of everyday pain, reminds us that traumatic events do lie within the range of normal human experience" (110). Incest, when linked to trauma, may then function as a key that renders visible the many invisible shocks associated with the experience of "everyday" femininity.

But not everything that Ginny and her family suffer can be attributed to her sexual abuse as a child, or, for that matter to her retrieving memories of that particular abuse which is shown to be part and parcel of a social, economic, and cultural "package." Indeed, Smiley is all too aware of how incest can become the "punch line"—the origin of all damage. Rather than recovering a punch line, Ginny's recovered memories of incest enable her to shift her point of view and her conceptual framework. She informs her husband Ty:

> The thing is, I can remember when I saw it all your way! The proud progress from Grandpa Davis to Grandpa Cook to Daddy. When "we" bought the first tractor in the county, when "we" built the big house, when "we" had the crops sprayed from the air, when "we" got a car, when "we" drained Mel's corner, when "we" got a hundred and seventy-two bushels an acre. I can remember all of that like prayers or like being married. You know. It's good to remember and repeat. You feel good to be a part of that. But then I saw what my part really was. . . . You see this grand history, but I see the blows. I see taking what you want because you want it, then making something up that justified what you did. I see getting others to pay the price, then covering up and forgetting what the price was. Do I think Daddy came up with beating and fucking us on his own? . . . . No, I think he had lessons, and those lessons were part of the package, along with the land and the lust to run things exactly the way he wanted to no matter what. (342–44)

This speech, located near the end of the novel, sums up how Ginny's memories of incest allow her to challenge foundational myths of American collectivity by showing her what her part "really was." As Michael Lambek and Paul Antze explain, "traumas offer a way of inserting a radical, often transformative break in the flow of a life [we could say "cultural"] narrative" (xvii). But in Smiley's novel this break, though transformative, is not redemptive.

Smiley structures her novel with great care to make the point that the structure of the past involves a "package" or hegemonic ensemble that includes canonical texts that ennoble patriarchy and misogyny while obscuring the exploitation of women and the land, itself often understood as feminine (a point that Baym makes in "Melodramas of Beset Manhood"). The "package" also makes it hard to see that agribusiness has subjected the farmer-father to violent disruptions, sometimes in the form of "opportunities" that are rendering the one-man farm nearly obsolete. Incest, in other words, is only one of many vehicles for representing forms of systematic oppression and exploitation. Given the richness of her analysis of this "package," it is surprising that *A Thousand Acres* has been selected by both its fans and its detractors as *the* paradigmatic novel about recovered memories of incest. Janice Haaken, for example, sees Ginny as "like the prototypical daughter in contemporary incest narratives" who moves from "an unenlightened to an enlightened state of mind" (*Pillar of Salt*, 20), and Elaine Showalter uses *A Thousand Acres* as her example of "the many novels and movies" that "continue to reproduce recovered-memory plots" (158).

Smiley's insight that Ginny's act of recovering memories can result in a new conceptual framework, one that might take American story of the "beset" individual in new directions, is obscured by those who respond to the novel by making incest into the "punch line." Critics of the novel such as Elaine Showalter and Mark Pendergrast worry that the novel legitimates a feminist analysis that "incest" is the key and the father is to blame for the family's breakdown and his daughter's misery. But what the novel shows instead is that all of the characters are caught in a larger web of forces and discourses. Indeed, Smiley's layered allusions to other texts challenges the ease with which "recovery" simply entails or equals writing, as it seems to in Walker's novel. Ginny becomes self-conscious enough to better understand her positioning in cultural nets, and to a certain extent free herself, but she is not greatly rewarded; Smiley's tragic point is that there is no outside to escape to. By the end of the novel, the dispersal of the family farm gives Ginny the freedom to become a low-paid service worker who lives on processed foods—and who occasionally takes psychology classes. Ex-farmwomen do not really have much going for them in a postindustrial economy.

A Thousand Acres acknowledges that the incest recovery story offers a belated, displaced encounter with the past. This novel, then, is not sanguine about the power of literature to mirror the past. Instead, it suggests that unitary, universalizing gestures of canonizing American history, including the belief in its inevitable repetition, may become a serious blind spot. The novel's expansive vision of women's historical experience, like Ginny's, is thus purchased by understanding and breaking a repetitive cycle. And yet Smiley herself still has her fist clenched, still relies upon repetition to make her point, even her point that repetition is the point. And perhaps this is why the last paragraph of the novel continues to insist that recovered memories of incest constitute a hard truth—and a weapon, a "punch line":

> I can't say that I forgive my father, but now I can imagine what he probably chose never to remember—the goal of an unthinkable urge, pricking him, pressing him, wrapping him in an impenetrable fog of self that must have seemed, when he wandered around the house late at night after working and drinking, like the very darkness. This is the gleaming obsidian shard I safeguard above all the others. (370–71)

The "gleaming obsidian shard" is not a quite a memory of incest, though it is linked to, and confirms, the act of incest. Ginny's fictional reconstruction of incest is her hard shard of the past. This new view allows her to understand her father's urges as blanketed in a selfhood—made foggier by drink—that acknowledges little outside of itself. And so the novel ends by staging the impossibility of a father's remembering in order to demonstrate the necessity of a daughter's act of revisionary memory.

Is it wrong or mistaken to use a daughter's reconstruction of incest as if it were hard evidence? Smiley understands the difficulty of this question. In her novel, the too-good-to-be-true quality of the recovery plot begins to be commented upon within the recovery story itself. *A Thousand Acres* does offer a fairy tale, most obviously in its borrowing and reversing of *King Lear* in order to allegorize—and canonize—the recovery story, which dramatizes how a heroine is beset by the burdensome power of the father. But as we have shown, Smiley's novel also insists that what needs to be recovered is a past connected to and responsible for forgotten incest, but not defined by it. The recovery story, here working against its own embrace of a clear and linear chain of cause and effect, is thus capable of providing a nuanced understanding of memory, recovery, and the claims of individualism. Smiley's novel, in other words, questions the recovery story's positing of a simple cause—the father, the male entrapper—from whom the beset heroine manages a heroic and satisfying escape. Curiously, such an awareness of the complexity of the project of telling and remembering incest is not always so available in narratives of false memory, in which a sophisticated understanding of memory's malleability is expected to fuel a powerful challenge to the knowledge provided by women who tell. It is to false-memory stories that we will now turn.

Chapter 5

The Science of Memory
False-Memory Stories

False Memory Syndrome Foundation members, largely those who have been accused of child abuse and expert witnesses on their behalf, have compelling reasons to insist that repressed memories of abuse be verified by clear and convincing empirical evidence, precisely the kind of evidence often lacking in incestuous abuse cases.[1] While there are cases where a child with venereal disease or a bleeding vagina is admitted to an emergency room and evidence obtained of abuse, signs of molestation may not be at all obvious. Adults have been mistakenly charged with abuse as a result of misreadings of physical evidence, resulting, for example, from incorrect assumptions about what "normal" genitals and hymens are supposed to look like (Nathan and Snedeker, 180–81). And children enjoined to silence may long delay reports of abuse, with the result that physical marks of molestation, should they exist, would be healed by the time accusations are made. Without damning physical evidence, charges of incestuous abuse are hard to prove. If the memory wars reflect deep ambivalence about the declining fortunes of patriarchal authority, they are sustained by problems with collecting incontrovertible evidence of sexual abuse, whether to vindicate accusers or the accused. What is debated are less tangible archives of the past. As we have seen, proponents of recovered memory focus on psychological processes, such as repression and dissociation, that long impede the recollection of sexual abuse. Their antagonists, false-memory writers, proffer "scientific" evidence that demonstrates how easily memories are distorted. In particular, they discuss the nature of memory itself, aligning themselves with recent thinking about the reconstructive nature of memory. Recovered memories cannot be reliable, accurate, or objective, they argue, because those who study memory have demonstrated that memories are fallible, constantly shifting, and influenced by our present circumstances.

Because their arguments are tied to the findings of psychological researchers on memory, false-memory syndrome advocates at first seem more sophisticated than those naive therapists and clients who apparently share a deluded, outdated view that recovered memories of long-buried abuse can be taken as the raw truth of the past. Yet paradoxically, because false-memory proponents are allied with those who stress memory's unreliability, some of these writers find themselves in the difficult position of being both delighted and devastated by the "scientific" descriptions of memorial processes that they are dependent upon. They are happy to insist that memory has a very uncertain relation to the past, which allows them to argue that recovered memories of abuse must be understood as impermanent confabulations of the present. Yet this view of memory is also potentially devastating because false-memory proponents want to be truth-tellers, and new views of the malleability of memory put into question their own ability to offer an unbiased view of events. The tension between new views of memory and traditional ideas about memory's unproblematic access to the past structures the peculiar nature of the anxiety that false-memory writers must try to manage in book after book attacking the recovered-memory writers. This chapter studies a narrative war in which commentators fight over territory: who owns the master plot for trusting or dismissing a story about recovering memories of incest? False-memory writers want their stories to convey historical truth, but their dependence upon narrative and their insistence on memory's shiftiness make it hard to elude the forms of fabrication that they so decry. They, too, are storytellers.

Though a dependence upon contemporary notions of memory is to a degree present in the arguments of every major writer in the false-memory movement, Richard Ofshe and Ethan Watters in *Making Monsters: False Memories, Psychotherapy, and Sexual Hysteria* (1994) have most scrupulously explained the relevance of these notions of memory to the false-memory argument. To demonstrate how fabrication is linked to memory, and thus explain the formation of false memories, Ofshe and Watters appeal to Donald Spence's *Narrative Truth and Historical Truth* (1982).[2] Spence's book is influenced by the interpretive turn, in the late 1970s and early 1980s, toward emphasizing the role of narrative in the psychotherapeutic process. Spence points out that therapists have shifted from Freud's belief in the historical "core" of each patient's memory, from believing analysis is a form of archaeology, toward a recognition of the importance of the patient's linguistic constructions of the past in providing an effective means of therapy.

Drawing upon Proust's novel as an aid to understanding the difference between "historical truths" and "narrative truths," Spence explains that "narrative truth" is articulated in the French title, *A la recherche du temps perdu,* which means "in search of lost time." This title places an emphasis upon the process of discovery and the author's evolving realization that "the same event can take on different meanings depending on the conditions under which it is remembered" (31). The French title, suggests Spence, conjures up a malleable and usefully literary view of memory. Opposed to this understanding of the past are "historic" ideas of memory, neatly summed up by the English title, *Remembrance of Things Past,* which emphasizes not the search for a time that has been lost, but remembered things. The English title, says Spence, promises a record of "concrete objects and events that happened at some earlier period and that can be brought forward to the present. The focus is on the act of remembering, which, when properly carried out, provides an accurate, concrete encounter with 'things past'" (31). Spence argues that while therapists should keep accurate transcriptions of the data that are the foundation for interpretation, these data should function as a reminder not to assume the adequacy of any one interpretation too quickly. "Historical truth," then, is the stuff from which "narrative truths" are made. Spence legitimizes the psychoanalytic emphasis on narrative truth, on understanding the past as continuously being constructed, by demonstrating that it is congruent with experimental research on memory conducted by Elizabeth Loftus (now a key participant in the memory wars) suggesting the ease with which memories become distorted (93).

Ofshe and Watters import these ideas about the malleability of memory into their book on false memories in order to criticize narratives of the recovered-memory movement for displaying a misleading faith in memory as capable of providing an authoritative account of the past. Bass, Davis, Herman, and other feminist therapists, according to Ofshe and Watters, cling to an old-fashioned belief that memories house the past intact, crystalline, if temporally hidden by defense mechanisms such as repression and dissociation. Ofshe and Watters, like many other false-memory writers, explain that the persistence of this view of memory is shown in the way recovered-memory advocates describe memory as like a videotape or computer disc, metaphors suggesting that what is replayed is exactly what was recorded. So, for example, therapists may insist that repression hides past events in "storage" and therapy restores them to view. Quoting extensively from Spence's work, Ofshe and Watters explain that therapy cannot provide patients with this kind of access to the truth of the past. Instead, information offered by the patient to the therapist actually "passes through several lenses each of which has the ability to magnify, diffuse or distort the actual events of a person's life" (51). One lens is used, for example, when "the patient attempts to translate thoughts, feelings, and memories into words," shaping a life history, a process filtered by other lenses such as "the patients' understanding of what sort of language and topics are appropriate to a given therapeutic setting—and a given therapist" (51). Finally, we have the assumptions of the therapist, which give authoritative significance to what is being said. Spence notes that therapists "are, in effect, constructing an interpretation that supports our private theory or collection of paradigms. . . . Interpretations are persuasive, not because of their evidential value but because of their rhetorical appeal" (qtd. in Ofshe and Watters, 52). Spence here comes close to describing the process involved in what is called the "false-memory syndrome," the consequence of a therapist leading a patient to believe that she has been sexually abused.

While Spence's theory of narrative and memory provides Ofshe and Watters with a way to undermine the authority and truth of recovered memories, his endorsement of a mediated and indeterminant narrative reality rattles their own confidence about what can be known about the past. There is a price to be paid for adopting new views of memory. According to Ofshe and Watters, Spence is left without a way to condemn "psychotherapy for its ability to create a believable but fundamentally untrue narrative" (52). And they report that they feel narrative creation in therapy is "disturbing" (53) and "distressing" (54). Without a definitive past as an anchor, Ofshe and Watters feel unmoored, sailing upon uncharted, choppy seas. Most devastating is the idea that without the ability to recover real events that carry inherent and unilateral meaning, patients are completely open to whichever winds of fashion their own therapists sail by: "Psychotherapeutic fashions, not being based on science, are formed by the culture and what groups of therapists decide among themselves. Because directions are determined by loose consensus, psychotherapy is extremely susceptible to the winds of the current zeitgeist" (59–60). Having appealed to what might be called a postmodern paradigm of memory that insists upon its shifting, constructive properties so as to discredit recovered memories, Ofshe and Watters try to dig their way out of the "pitfalls" associated with the doctrine of "narrative truth" by appealing to "historical truth," the same elusive, archaeological nugget that recovered-memory advocates so prize: "Surely, the information provided by clients about their own histories cannot be totally distorted by the lenses it must travel through in therapy" (54).

Ofshe and Watters offer a very developed example of how this idea of lenses works when they discuss the case history of "F.T.," first published in Robert Langs's influential *Techniques of Psychoanalytic Psychotherapy* and reinterpreted by Charlotte Krause Prozan in *Feminist Psychoanalytic Psychotherapy*. According to Langs, his patient, Miss F.T., reported dreams, symptoms, and memories that Lang interpreted as stemming from penis envy and from his patient's having witnessed a primal scene between her parents. Apparently, as a result of this analysis, the patient experienced quite a bit of relief from her initial symptoms of "acting out," and her functioning improved. In her book, Prozan reanalyzes the case of F.T., proposing, as Ofshe and Watters put it, "that penis envy may have been an inappropriate diagnosis and that the patient had found the diagnosis meaningful only because she desired to please Langs" (57). Prozan notices that F.T.'s symptoms might now be read as clear signs of repressed sexual abuse, a diagnosis that she admits may be linked to therapeutic fashion:

In 1973 and before, analysts were looking for penis envy. In 1990, we are looking for sexual abuse. . . . Patient and analyst are living in the same culture, and are being formed by similar trends. They may collude in what they believe is an accurate diagnosis of the patient's problems. But because they are both culture-bound, the truth may elude them both. (59)

Here Prozan simply reiterates what has become a relatively standard understanding that the cultural narratives available for organizing experience into a diagnosis may not be isomorphic with the truth of experience itself.

Prozan's statement about narrative frameworks is, Ofshe and Watters conclude, "a rather devastating admission" (59). This harsh judgment is a bit puzzling since the idea that memorial pasts are malleable was initially proposed by them as an enlightened one: "While it's comforting to believe that all our experiences . . . are stored somewhere in our minds, this model of memory runs directly counter to almost all scientific studies and experiments on the topic" (38). And Ofshe and Watters laud the work of Loftus and Spence because it offers an alternative, presumably more defensible view that memory work is constructive, precisely the view that seems to inform Prozan's writing. Yet Ofshe and Watters now find this view "devastating" and lash out at Prozan (though she might be seen as simply putting theory into practice) rather than at Langs or even Spence, who first helps them make the case for the centrality of memorial reconstruction and interpretation.

Prozan, a self-identified feminist therapist, becomes Ofshe and Watters's target because they assume she is one of those dangerous, politicized therapists who implant false memories. The proof? First, after demonstrating that Langs's interpretation is governed by normative views of femininity and suggesting alternative readings of F.T.'s case, Prozan offers "the possibility that F.T. was sexually molested as a child" (206). Next, she admits that this new interpretation reflects a shift from a male-centered Freudian view to a feminist view that now has widespread cultural authority. This admission is itself a threat to the integrity of the past—the Freudian past in which women's stories of incest could be understood as fantasies, expressions of desire for the father. But Prozan goes further. Because Prozan explicitly says that the "truth may elude" both the Freudian and the feminist paradigms, Ofshe and Watters see her analysis as offering a damaging acknowledgment of the role of social forces in shaping analytical paradigms.

Oddly, Ofshe and Watters also try to suggest that Prozan's work is an example of the therapist's unwavering belief that stories of abuse are always true stories. Prozan, they assert, does not acknowledge the "pressure within therapy circles to *never* question the reality" of abuse narratives (60). However, it is Ofshe and Watters's own unwavering belief in her credulity that is exposed in their reading of Prozan's text. Their interpretation is a defense, perhaps, against the anxiety created by her claim that feminism has altered readings of the past. Prozan explicitly recognizes that the abuse narrative she offers is only one possible interpretation of F.T.'s dreams and memories, though she also argues that her feminist analysis is able to account for features of the patient's narrative that Lang must ignore in offering his analysis. For example, she notices that Lang ignores the power that the father may wield.

Ofshe and Watters are increasingly agitated about the apparent chaos generated by the possibilities of reconstruction and reinterpretation offered by Prozan, imagining that suddenly there will be an infinite number of equally efficacious (or damaging) therapeutic interpretations about what really happened in the past. "By offering a history of abuse along with several other imaginative interpretations, Prozan seems to suggest that any number of narratives might have engendered confirming memories and proved equally effective in F.T.'s treatment" (61). Their worry about wildly proliferating interpretive solutions suggests that they have not fully acknowledged that social arrangements change very slowly, at least those that give rise to truly different, authoritative interpretations. The shift from diagnoses of penis envy to diagnoses of sexual abuse only took place after decades of feminist challenges to psychoanalytic views of femininity—and to the authority of a privileged male vantage point.

Indeed, the problem seems to be not that there are too many convincing therapeutic interpretations of women's experience but that there are not enough. The centrality of abuse narratives that Prozan comments upon, and sees vaguely linked to social forces and the media, has been made possible by an adherence to a single story line, now so familiar that it comes to seem natural rather than constructed. In fact, Spence's contribution, which has been valuably underscored by the false-memory argument, is to remind people of how naturalized the constructed narratives of therapy may become. Therapists forget that when diagnosing incest they are looking through several lenses. Yet Spence's way of addressing this problem also suggests ignorance about the power of cultural constraints: he imagines that the patient's free associations are rife with possibilities. Our point is that at any given historical moment most of these possibilities cannot be heard or articulated. The reductive scripts of both false-memory and recovered-memory testimonies are proof of this. As Janice Haaken has pointed out, both types of story often deny the "the diversity and nuances of injurious experiences within the family" ("Sexual Abuse," 121).

Despite their insistence on the malign influence of psychotherapy, Ofshe and Watters nonetheless offer the beginnings of a more broadly conceived analysis of the memory wars. Because of their careful attention to issues of interpretation that ultimately threaten them, they open up a space for a consideration of gender, power relations, ambiguity, and rhetoric as crucial components of the recovered-memory/false-memory debate.

Ofshe and Watters's anxiety about the difficulty of establishing the truth should not be construed simply as evidence that they are caught up in the vestiges of a dying system of belief in the past's accessibility. Like Spence, who also offers a place for verifiable historical data, they have a responsible concern with accountability, and its fate within very complex discourses about memory. Because of cases involving million-dollar lawsuits and the health of elderly parents, Ofshe and Watters have an understandable attachment to verifiable truths. Going to a therapist for comfort drawn from the able recasting of the past is one thing; going to court and using revisionary memories as evidence to sue a parent is quite another. Of course, narratives produced by the false-memory syndrome movement are dangerous too. False-memory advocates who serve as expert defense witnesses provide "scientific" narratives about memory that have a damaging power to rationalize the view that women are hysterical and unreliable witnesses. In this way the narrative truths of false-memory experts may work to suggest that there is no reason to listen to women's accounts of sexual abuse.

Whereas the desire of women to validate recovered memories produces appeals to child abuse statistics and to a recognition of the trauma found in domestic life, false-memory proponents use "science" to attack what they conceive of as a popular mode of irrationality, the belief in stories produced in therapy. In the background of false-memory arguments is the saving power of science as a grounding truth, one that also upholds the sanctity of the family. Frederick Crews, though not a scientist himself, has become the key false-memory spokesman for empiricism. In his attacks on recovered memories, Crews insists, first and foremost, upon the necessity for scientific, "empirical" criteria as a way of differentiating between real and false memories. Armed by an insistence upon "controlled studies," and "demonstrable proof," Crews cuts a rather ruthless swath through what he believes is the deplorable legacy of psychoanalysis as it is dramatized in recovered-memory therapy. According to Crews, Freud was a quack whose ideas about the mind have never been proven. Today Freud's blinded followers still find an intellectual home—in a morass of logically contradictory practices and beliefs that they perpetrate on helpless, vulnerable patients who are rarely helped and often harmed.

Crews's certainty, and his accompanying arrogance, are fueled by an idealistic faith in the "rational-empirical ethos." What false-memory and recovered-memory writers often share in common is an insistence on the existence of an unproblematic reality, "true stories," as Lenore Terr puts it in the subtitle of *Unchained Memories*. In practice, what this means is that both sides must downplay the complexity and ambiguity of the supposedly true stories they are telling, while holding their opponents to impossibly high standards for establishing the unvarnished truth. As a result, each gets to dismiss the other side while also making itself vulnerable to further attack. Crews, for example, claims to offer the truth of science against the falsehood of hysterical opponents. But, of course, it is possible to conduct an analysis of empirical arguments that would look like Prozan's analysis of therapy, which reminds us how culture-bound these arguments are. Raw observations made by scientists are processed through different lenses because scientific work stands within traditions that offer different perspectives. This is not to say that there are no facts, but that the factual world is not devoid of ambiguity because there are different frameworks for making sense of data and scientists must construct narratives to convey their findings.

The writings of Crews make clear yet another problem with the idealistic attachment to a simplified version of the truth. Because Crews has a mission to defend truth from falsehood, there is no room for compromise. Eventually nothing, it seems, will satisfy him or achieve his aim to defend the truth other than the utter destruction of psychoanalysis and every related school of therapy. Not for him the "seeming rationality" of "moderate" positions. Responding to a therapist who in fact agrees with him that some memories are true and some are false, Crews accuses her of a lack of rigor and "middle of the road extremism" (249).

Crews's "exchange" with therapists in the *New York Review of Books* vividly highlights this polarizing dynamic. To exemplify its vituperative and unproductive nature, we can look at the "dialogue" between Crews and Prozan (a familiar cast of characters appears regularly in all of these writings). As we have seen, Prozan is particularly disturbing to false-memory writers because she acknowledges that diagnostic tools are culture-bound, which is not a controversial claim in many contemporary conversations about the production of knowledge. Crews uses a snippet of the quote from Prozan's book that Ofshe and Watters cite at greater length. In a paragraph devoted to "young [Freudian] fanatics" who believe that memories can be recovered, even back to the womb, he concludes with this sentence: "And in *Feminist Psychoanalytic Psychotherapy*, Charlotte Krause Prozan, who sensed which way the wind was blowing long ago, reports that whereas analysts used to be watchful for penis envy in women patients, today 'we are looking for sexual abuse'" (221).

Crews is unfair in two ways here. First, he suggests Prozan's guilt (and these therapists are criminal, according to Crews) by association. Her practices, as he views them, can be adequately represented by categorizing her with the more extreme and bizarre practices of recovered-memory therapy. Second, he quotes her out of context so that her acknowledgment of the cultural reinforcement for "looking for sexual abuse" becomes an unqualified endorsement of the practice. Crews is crafting a uniformly hostile argument designed to win unquestioning support for his view that there is no point to listening to therapists discuss the psychoanalytic process because, well, they are narrow-minded fanatics.

Understandably provoked, Prozan responds in a similar vein. Characterizing his critique as a "hit piece," Prozan represents Crews as irrational, "polarizing the topic by vindictive, bitter, and emotional attacks against those who disagree" with him (235). But Crews has the last word in this exchange, and his response, of course, is not meant to seek common ground but rather to demolish her integrity as a therapist. He mocks her feminist analysis as based on the reading of only one feminist article about recovered memories of abuse, though her book actually includes a wide range of references to feminist scholarship that has informed her thinking. He also asserts that she takes her direction from ill-digested readings of incest survivor handbooks. Then, adding injury to insult, he draws from her case notes to insinuate that she has harmed a patient. To Prozan's simple charge that she has been quoted out of context, he responds, "To be sure, that phrase was plucked from a paragraph in which Prozan displayed a momentary realization that diagnoses are subject to fashion. . . . the quotation accurately reflects her policy" (255). His sarcasm transforms her into an unreflective therapist who bullies her patients into illusory and destructive memories of child abuse.

Because Prozan is characterized as a faux feminist, she can be used to make "fashionable" feminism a target. This strategy is employed again in another of his contributions to the memory wars when he attacks two other feminist therapists, Adrienne Harris and Judy Messler Davies: "With their less than deferential reference to Freud, their portentous hints about the need . . . for altering 'power within the family,' and their scorn for the 'magisterial' (male) analysts' 'evenly hovering attention, neutrality and capacity to stand aside and objectify,' Harris and Davies are mounting an unapologetic feminist assault on the traditionally masculine ethos of Freudianism" (245). Because Crews is a self-confessed "Freud-basher," it is stunning that he here stands with Freud against feminists on the grounds that they are assaulting the "masculine ethos of Freudianism." At this moment, his expressions of commitment to the "rational empirical ethos" and the "capacity to stand aside and objectify" can be seen to function as one rhetorical strategy of a male backlash against feminism and the feminizing of the profession of therapy.

Crews's use of the Ross Cheit case reveals how tortured the logic of this backlash can become. Cheit, a professor at Brown University, recovered memories of being abused by the administrator of a summer camp who eventually confessed to the abuse. Given the way false-memory partisans have cast doubt on the veracity of women's memories, it makes sense that only a male victim of nonincestuous abuse could provide for Crews a convincing example of a "true story" of recovered memory. The case is tricky, but Crews valiantly attempts to enlist Cheit's substantiated memories of abuse for Crews's "side." First, Crews asserts that Ross Cheit's memories of sexual abuse were "proved beyond question." Though elsewhere Crews acknowledges the prevalence of sexual abuse,

this is the only time he firmly credits the truth of a story about recovered memories of abuse—and it puts him in an awkward position. Because he believes
Cheit, Crews wants to prove that Cheit never really forgot his abuse. This way,
Cheit's true story of abuse will prove the truth of Crews's position: only quacks
believe in repression, and so recovered memories are quackery. Cheit's uncertainty about what happened to his memories helps a little; Cheit tells Crews in
a phone conversation that he is "inclined to doubt that he abruptly and completely consigned his experience to oblivion" (165). In his original essay for the
New York Review of Books, Crews had concocted a firm story to shore up
Cheit's tentative words: "the adult Cheit *refocused* his faded but unrepressed
experiences after he had read a book about pedophilia (as he did) and became
morally exercised about it" (55).

This ringing conclusion is revised when Crews is informed by Cheit that he
had read the book at the suggestion of his psychotherapist *after* his memories
came back. Crews rewrites and comes up with this: "The possibility—indeed,
the likelihood—that Cheit lost track of the incident at issue through an ordinary process of atrophy renders the example of his restored memory useless as
proof of repression" (166). While it would seem that Cheit's story—he experienced anguish as an adult, went to see a therapist, recalled forgotten memories
of abuse—serves to strengthen the validity of therapeutic accounts about long-
occluded traumatic events that belatedly and painfully intrude into the present,
Crews waves away these features of Cheit's story by turning the "possibility" of
memory atrophy into a "likelihood" (165–66). In an "exchange" with Crews,
Michael Erdelyi writes: "Ignoring for the moment the question of repression,
which is a vast red herring in Crews's article, Cheit's recovered memory suggests that memories do not invariably decay over time. Even if, for the sake of
argument, we chose to deny the existence of repression as Freud defined it—
the exclusion of some memory or impulse from consciousness—inaccessible
or forgotten memories *for whatever reason,* are still subject to recovery" (269).[3]
In Crews's response to Erdelyi, he makes no mention of Cheit, a "real-world
case" (and Crews likes practical examples) that ultimately calls for too much
openness to what would be called a "survivor story" if a woman told it.[4]

Crews's polemical tactics seem far removed from the presumed ethos of
science as characterized by dispassionate, reasoned inquiry. Passionate rhetoric
on the part of advocates on both sides makes difficult a productive discussion—productive of doubt as well as assent—of the issue of child sexual abuse
and its representation. However, there are feminists among the false-memory
movement who are genuinely interested in finding common ground with
recovered-memory advocates because they understand that women's experiences of sexual abuse were long rendered invisible and silent. While a number
of false-memory writers tend, like Crews, to make feminist therapy seem a
monolithic and almost criminal practice, these writers complicate that story by

their very existence.[5] Two writers who have been particularly important in this regard are Elizabeth Loftus and Carol Tavris.

Elizabeth Loftus is highly visible both as a memory researcher and as an expert witness for defendants in recovered-memory cases. In addition to numerous academic publications, she has coauthored two first-person popular books that recount "true stories" (*Witness for the Defense,* xiii) of her personal and professional experiences. In the most recent of these, *The Myth of Repressed Memory* (1994), she labels those who believe in repressed memories "True Believers" and those who challenge them as "The Skeptics," a way of categorizing each side that makes clear which side she is on.

> My research into the malleability of memory aligns me with the Skeptics, but I am also sympathetic to the True Believers' concerns. I do not want to see a return of those days, not so very long ago, when a victim's cries for help went unheard and accusations of sexual abuse were automatically dismissed as fantasy or wish-fulfillment and shunted away into the backwaters of public conscience. Nor can I automatically accept the idea that significant numbers of therapists are carelessly implanting memories in their client's minds. I don't believe the world is so purely black and white. (32)

And so she answers all letters, talks to both sides, and tries to remember that the debate is "not about sexual abuse or the hard-won gains of the women's movement," not about "ideology" but about memory (213). Only because Loftus does not see her research on memory as situated within political and discursive contexts, or on a terrain where a narrative war is taking place, can she claim that her work is above the fray.

Loftus's research on the shiftiness of memory is put to a number of polemical, if not ideological, purposes. Spence uses Loftus's work to legitimize his view that "narrative truth" emerges in the therapeutic process. For Spence, her work explains why it is no longer "scientific" to believe that undistorted, foundational truths of the past are easy to retrieve. Though this challenge to "historical truth" is disturbing to Ofshe and Watters, they also use Loftus, but to attack a particular set of narratives that have emerged in therapy. Ofshe and Watters, like Loftus herself, thus can retain a conviction about the unquestionable truthfulness of their own stories about incest and memory while challenging the truth of narratives about recovered memories. In recovered-memory arguments, however, Loftus's research is criticized for downplaying studies that show the accuracy of long-term memory and for overgeneralizing her own findings, which do not focus on adult memories of abuse. Feminist proponents of recovered memory, because of their insistent focus on the relation between knowledge and power, are particularly disturbed that Loftus's work on the manipulability of memory abets those who would like past sufferings to "go unheard." Bending over backward to demonstrate her awareness of this problem, Loftus actually cites concerns about her own work expressed by Judith Herman. Herman says that it offers a "new way to challenge the authenticity of child abuse and invalidate women's testimony about child abuse" (qtd. in *Myth of Repressed Memory*, 213). Loftus's research, as she admits here, functions in multiple ways as it is appropriated for different polemics. Indeed the anxiety created when reading this literature is caused by the effect on the reader of becoming invested in the truth of certain stories—those of recovered-memory proponents or those of false-memory proponents—only to have that faith betrayed. If, as Freud says, anxiety is the anticipation of danger, reading the opposing texts on recovered memory is likely to create anxious readers.

Loftus's work seems less partisan than the work of those who both defend and attack her research. She is more open and counts herself a feminist who wants to acknowledge the frightening consequences of false accusations without denying the frequency of child sexual abuse. Yet her work straddles both sides of the memory wars not only because of her explicit desire to establish a middle ground but also because of an implicit structuring tension that exists between the stories she tells about her personal life and her research on memory.[6] For example, Loftus's first mass-market book, *Witness for the Defense,* contains a "true story" about an event that occurred when she was on the witness stand explaining how two mothers might have used leading questions to distort their children's memories of being abused at a summer camp. Loftus was asked to be an expert witness because the idea of memories as formed through a manipulable process of rehearsal is important to new views of memory and to her own research. In the course of her testimony, the prosecutor skeptically asked: "You really don't know anything about five-year old children who have been sexually abused do you?" At that moment a "memory flew out at me, out of the blackness of the past, hitting me full force." She answers the prosecutor, "I do know something about this subject because I was abused when I was six years old" (149).

With the force of a blow, a forgotten and apparently unrehearsed memory of being abused by a baby-sitter suddenly emerges after many years, its truth uneasily opposed to the falsehood of children's "rehearsed" memories or the "contaminated" memories that she produces in her laboratory to show memories are but "mist" (4). Nonetheless, in her second popular book, *The Myth of Repressed Memory,* she argues against the existence of "repressed" memories because they depend upon belief in an invisible, unproven mental operation, repression. In narrating her own abuse story, Loftus almost admits that her memory is governed by an unseen force: the unconscious? To the defense lawyer who thanks her for sharing her memory, she responds: "I'm not sure I had any choice" (151). At this moment, Loftus sounds remarkably like a woman recovering a traumatic memory. Recovered-memory proponents have seized on Loftus's story to argue persuasively that she has not been able to integrate her own experience into her research; her straddling of two "sides" is then a manifestation of her split response to the issue of recovered memory.

Another interpretation is possible. If Loftus's doubt that she "had any choice" supports belief in spontaneous, recovered memories, Loftus perhaps includes her story about her abuse because it strengthens her credibility as an expert witness against the validity of recovery memory. Precisely because she has recovered memories of her own abuse, Loftus can be seen as unbiased when she disputes other women's testimony about recovered memories. After all, her traumatic memory (it hits her "full force") is a response to a question about her credentials: "You really don't know anything about five-year-old children who have been sexually abused, do you?" Oh yes I do, she tells him. I am an expert here too. This is a strange kind of credentializing, which depends upon Loftus's commitment to two very different narratives about sexual abuse and memory.

When she narrates another personal memory in *The Myth of Repressed Memory,* she chooses one that easily supports the thesis that memories are reconstructions. In this story, Loftus tells us about her mother's death, an event she also draws upon to demonstrate "motivated forgetting," a concept she finds more acceptable than repression because it is consciously willed: "When I think about my mother's death, for example, the images and emotions are so painful that I immediately push them away out of mind" (214–15). To depict a memorial truth "that never happened," she begins by describing what *did* happen one summer when she was fourteen: "one bright morning I woke up and my mother was dead, drowned in a swimming pool" (39). That, she says is the "happening truth," or what Spence might call the "historical truth." She also had adopted a narrative truth about these events, one that was suddenly revised, many years after her mother died, when her uncle informed her that she was the one who found her mother in the pool. Until this moment, she had believed that her aunt had found the body. For three days, Loftus developed ever more detailed memories of finding her mother until her brother called to tell her that her uncle had checked the facts and found that his memory was wrong. With a sense of loss and grief, she had to give up her newly minted memories, more coherent than her old fragmented ones.

Loftus's personal story of an invented memory is much more vivid than the ones developed in her laboratory in which subjects are led to believe that as children they were lost in a mall. While Loftus's story certainly depicts the malleability of memory, it does something more. Like the story about the baby-sitter who abused her, the narratives of her mother's death evoke our sympathy—and hence belief. It does not seem surprising that Elizabeth Loftus, a haunted woman, would continue to be concerned about "victims' cries" or why she would dedicate herself to exploring the way memories shift, separating us, protecting us from pasts that may be more ambiguous and disturbing than even the horrible stories we devise to represent them. Stories about false memories, like stories about recovered memories, are conditioned not only by ideological ends—which side are you on?—but also by their ability to shape the potential meanings found in our mundane but deeply felt pasts. Certainly Loftus tells us about the "new" story of her mother's death as part of a power play; it provides compelling evidence for her argument about memory's malleability. At the same time, her account of rescripting the past demonstrates that the "new" story of her mother's death allowed her access to unmanageable material that her first story could not reach. Because the "new" story, awful as it was, gave her consolation, Loftus found it hard to give up.

Like Loftus, the feminist sociopsychologist Carol Tavris has become a public witness against recovered memories, though initially she was more interested in arguing that the early political feminist incest story about abuse is better for women than the feminist recovery story. By comparing her discussion of "survivor" narratives in her *Mismeasure of Woman* (1992) with an essay of hers published a year later in the *New York Times Book Review,* we can see how her analysis of recovery narratives changes and consolidates as it is retold in a different venue and at time when media skepticism dominates reports about recovered memories. Tavris, like many others in the debate, is ultimately pulled into the role of an arbiter between truth and falsehood. Her initial feminist analysis of how political and institutional pressures shape narratives of abuse becomes something quite different when redesigned for a more general audience. Her *Times* piece is a lecture about incest stories that largely consigns "recovery stories" to the realm of error. In return, those feminists who want to marginalize her political analysis are able to denounce Tavris as part of the backlash against feminism.

In a small section of *The Mismeasure of Woman* titled "Choosing a Story: Victims, Survivors, and the Problem of Blame," Tavris probes the "misty intersection between political analysis and psychological trauma" (313) in an effort to answer the question: how did we get from Louise Armstrong's political analysis of incest to a reliance on the highly individualizing narratives of psychotherapy? To some extent we have already told this story ourselves, but Tavris's contributions are especially trenchant because of her keen appreciation of the cultural reinforcements for abuse narratives. Drawing on the work of Nancy Matthews, who has analyzed how, in the evolution of the antirape movement in Los Angeles, grassroots work incorporating feminist patriarchy theory was gradually replaced with state-supported and apolitical therapeutic programs, Tavris explains that decisions of funding agencies helped to define rape in the 1980s as an individual rather than a political problem. At the same time, the proliferation of public horror stories about child abuse deflected attention from Reagan's cutbacks in funding for children's programs, prenatal care, and other forms of welfare to women, children, and families. The proliferating and increasingly personal narratives of "past" incest abuse were thus ever more at odds with the present social reality in which large numbers of children were (and are) being maltreated because of their growing impoverishment. With few resources supporting the grassroots feminist work that provided a broad political critique, therapy provided the context for personal stories about abuse and provided the place where anxieties about the changing role of women, expanded definitions of normative sexuality, and economic insecurity could be represented—and somewhat contained. Within the individualized and constrained discursive community of "survivors," women talk about their difficulties and find an explanation for their problems: they were victims of abuse. Tavris notes that this story tells women that their problems stem from past events; their current realities, however difficult, are not the key issue. And by telling abuse narratives, women gain the support of other victims who offer them the comfort of shared understanding.[7]

Yet though the abuse story appeals to many women and decreases their isolation, Tavris argues that it does not work to challenge a system that provides ever less to those who have least. As she points out, middle-class survivors do better than working-class survivors because they have more options. Tavris's expressed belief that survivor groups can make women feel better is mitigated by her political analyses of a narrative that focuses on "past reasons for current problems": "It overlooks the current realities that entrap survivors, and, by assuming that all survivors share economic opportunities as well as psychological suffering, it blurs the different prospects that people have to recover from trauma and to make abiding changes in their lives" (321). Tavris does not deny that women are traumatized; instead, she challenges the political efficacy of conventional, highly individualized narratives of traumatic abuse. "Nothing changes."

Tavris's irritation with the success of what she calls "the sexual-survivor ideology" became more public as a result of an essay she wrote for the *New York Times Book Review*, "Beware the Incest-Survivor Machine." The title, despite its jocular reference to Lewis Carroll's "Jabberwocky," suggests a paranoia about mechanically produced incest survivor stories that was absent from her book. Not surprisingly, the article contains very little of the powerful feminist political analysis that fueled her book's critique of sexual abuse stories. Instead, she focuses on much-attacked books on incest, the best known, of course, being Bass and Davis's *Courage to Heal*. Though Tavris mentions the social anxieties crystallized in abuse narratives, her review is primarily devoted to making the case that recovered-memory horror stories express a popular but outdated view of memory. Loftus's work (not mentioned in *Mismeasure of Women*) and other accounts of memory are extensively discussed and complex views of memory contrasted with the simplistic stories about the past found in abuse-survivor books. "Beware the Incest-Survivor Machine" contains no discussion of the economic resources of survivors or of federal cutbacks. In the last three paragraphs of her essay, Tavris finally does return to her book's concern about the depoliticization of women's victimization, but because feminist scholarship has been marginalized, her conclusion simply functions to add to the guilt of foolish "survivors." Not only do abuse "survivors" tell misguided stories about the past but they impede social change.

Tavris's patronizing account was bound to elicit angry responses that could ignore her now reduced political analysis. The *New York Times Book Review* printed two full pages of letters generated in response to "Beware the Incest-Survivor Machine." The first letter is from Judith Herman, who begins, "As a professional authority on incest and one of the few writers whom Carol Tavris cites with respect, I must protest her mean-spirited and completely gratuitous attack on incest survivors," and ends, "If Ms. Tavris is really so tired of hearing about incest, she should stop trashing other women and join with us to try to end the epidemic of sexual violence" ("Real Incest," 3). The next letter reminds her that "child abuse and sexual abuse are not rare phenomena" ("Real Incest," 3). Another tells Tavris that the crime of incest is often unseen and unprosecuted and asks her what she thinks victims should do. There is only one letter, written by a member of "a family in which one member . . . declared herself to be an 'incest victim'" that applauds Tavris essay in an unqualified way ("Real Incest," 27). Of course the nearly univocal quality of the responses to Tavris is a problem too. This "exchange," much like the Crews "exchange," is highly moralized and adversarial.[8]

In Tavris's response to these letters, she reiterates her concern about real abuse and defends her feminism. To raise concerns about stories of abuse "does not make me antifeminist, any more than criticizing some policies of my government makes me anti-American" (27). Of course, in her review she never does criticize policies. This difference between the analysis in her book and the one provided in her review is significant because it means that Tavris's essay in the *Times* does not do the kind of feminist critical work that she both practices and commends in her book. For her article in the *New York Times Book Review,* Tavris more narrowly, and predictably, focuses on survivors and therapists as causing sexual hysteria by manufacturing memories. Not surprisingly she, like Loftus, is now on the board of the False Memory Syndrome Foundation, whose profound influence on media coverage has been criticized by Mike Staunton in the *Columbia Journalism Review* as actively blocking the publication of stories that either challenge the phenomenon of false memory or try to investigate the FMS Foundation itself.

Also missing from the *NYTBR* exchange between Tavris and her detractors is any further analysis of the enormous market for "survivor" books, one of the explicit causes of Tavris's alarm. She notes in her opening paragraph that more than five hundred thousand copies of *Courage to Heal* had been sold by early 1993. The exploding market for survivor books and survivor groups worries writers on both sides of the debate. For example, an accused parent, Mark Pendergrast in *Victims of Memory,* and a victim of incest, Louise Armstrong in *Rocking the Cradle,* demonstrate a surprising congruence of opinion about the need to criticize the immense appeal of survivor experiences and cures as consumer products. Louise Armstrong, whose important early work we have already discussed, surveys with disgust the recent incest "scene" in her *Rocking the Cradle:* "More and more, breaking the silence—having come to be an end in itself—had come to seem bankrupt. Amazingly at the same time, it was obviously increasingly bankable" (206). Incest, she points out, is always on the menu of talk shows, and most magazines and newspapers have published numerous articles on the recovered-memory/false-memory syndrome. Offering and contesting incest therapy, writing and buying books about incest, constitutes a lively market for largely middle-class consumers. For Armstrong and Tavris, women who tell incest are, like Trueblood, interfering with uplift, but here the uplift of women. These tellers represent women in the worst possible way, that is, as stereotypic, passive victims, and make money while doing so.

Arguably, in the absence of political (public policy does not support the domestic work of women), social (women remain more tied to the private sphere than are men), or legal solutions (rape and child abuse remain difficult to prosecute), many women use the sphere of consumption, long a feminized domain, in an attempt to solve their complex problems. Shopping at a bookstore, a woman can buy a form of therapy. This product will also offer her advice about how to exercise her agency by choosing a therapist. (Indeed, a section on selecting a therapist is now a standard addendum to psychology books about incest). Through an act of consumption, then, such women can place themselves within the discourse of survivorship and satisfy their desire for an identity—often that of an innocent victim—that releases them from guilt about their ambivalent and anxious participation in family life. There are paradoxes, of course, in finding freedom in an identity linked to past victimization; but despite the passivity involved in the victim's role, it is one that does provide opportunities for self-expression and feelings of change, "recovery."

Those who join groups like the False Memory Syndrome Foundation also find comfort from an identification with other victims. Their individual lives become amplified and validated as members of a different kind of survivor group. The FMSF newsletter publishes letters, often from "dads," who express their sense of betrayal by daughters and vent their rage at manipulative therapists. These are the kinds of stories found in all false-memory literature. In *The Myth of Repressed Memory,* for example, Loftus tells a representative false-memory story, the story of "Doug," in a chapter entitled "The Family Destroyed." (She does not seem aware that this title presumes that the family was once happily unified—Doug's view only.) Doug represents himself as an honest, caring, concerned father who cannot understand, and strongly denies, the accusations of his wife and daughters that he has sexually abused his daughters. Doug's story, like many survivor stories, is told entirely from his point of view and emphasizes his victimization and slow recovery from the trauma he experienced as an accused father: "He is learning how to reconstruct his memories ["scientific" therapy?] by pushing the accusations, therapy, sessions, and trial scenes from his mind. While the recent, painful memories continue to intrude, he is becoming more skillful at fixing the earlier, happier memories in his mind, and calling them forth when he needs to remind himself that his family was together and happy, once upon a time" (138). By using the words "once upon a time," Loftus inadvertently suggests that Doug is creating a fairy tale, one in which the father, like the father in Stein's vignette, creates himself as a traumatized victim. That the false-memory movement is also participating in the construction and consumption of survivor identities and myths about the family has been masked because false-memory narratives are linked to a discourse of science and reason. For this reason, the survivor identities of "dads" may be more convincing, ultimately more viable than those of daughters. In our culture, it is women, not men, who are usually designated the prototypical, irrational, excessive consumers of trendy, psychologized identities.

The problem is that at the very moment that consumers, whether male or female, choose familiar plots of recovered or false memory to embody their experiences, the individuality of that experience becomes regulated. Yet that regulation allows enhanced representation. There is an evolution from a nearly formless telling such as Gertrude Stein's barely intelligible vignette to the widely disseminated and recognized plots of narratives about recovered memories or about false-memory syndrome. The very availability of these genres has made them seem to be faddish products. In the America of the 1980s and 1990s, consumption and self-expression are intertwined. As Anne Norton remarks: "Consumption offers a mode of discourse, and an immanent symbolic lexicon, to those who lack access to the press, to publishing, to those political and economic institutions in which some speak and write authoritatively" (65). And we could add, consumption may increase access to these realms of authority. There is a certain cultural status and visibility attached to telling stories of abuse, whether by daughters or fathers like Doug. Yet as a result of an emerging middle-class consensus about the dangerous power of female psychologists, their emancipatory potential for women has been reduced.

Belief that accounts of male victimage are more real than women's stories of their victimization is reflected in fears about a supposed cultural disorder—feminist hostility to the father—that recalls the Moynihan report's concerns about the matriarchal black family as spawning a culture of pathology. In false-memory literature, a powerful, male-hating, feminist community is accused of making men into marginalized victims. Though it has largely been women patients who have been accused of hysteria in the memory wars, there is an hysterical tone to some of these pronouncements, whether by men or women. A web site designed to provide legal help for men accused of incest, for example, provides a bizarre form of testimony to women's scary efforts to appropriate male authority. In a futuristic fable, Kenneth R. Pangborn explains:

> The plan devised by the old elders of Female supremacy was one built on the philosophy of slowly boiling the frog to death. Cleverly devised sexual harassment laws made just about any act on the part of men actionable. Women used this to advance in the economic world, to seize power by inches.[9]

The imagery of the boiled frog in the aged, female supremacist's cauldron draws on the metaphorics of the sexual abuse "witch hunt." That this rhetoric of the witch hunt is assumed to be disinterested by even a feminist such as Elaine Showalter is a sign of its broad popular acceptance. One consequence of this view is that it has become easy to think that women's narratives about recovered memories of incest are crazy, predictable, and reductive in their accounts of the past. Our next chapter, on memoirs about incest, will show how these narratives belie such expectations.

Chapter 6

The Incest Survivor Memoir

Memoirs about recovered memories of incest share in the new possibilities for expressing experiences of incest, but their reception has been influenced by the shift from media coverage largely supportive of recovered-memory stories in the late 1980s to coverage largely supportive of false-memory stories in the early 1990s. Prominent feminists have been among those voicing concerns about women's autobiographical tales of recovering memories of child abuse. Louise Armstrong, for example, followed her feminist anthology of incest narratives *Kiss Daddy Goodnight* (1978) with another book, *Rocking the Cradle of Sexual Politics* (1994), that scathingly indicts the recovery movement as betraying earlier feminist political analyses of incest as about power. How, Armstrong asks in this book, did we "go from total silence" (7) to so much mainstream media "noise," from a "feminist literature [that] boldly addressed the need for social change" (11) to a language of "personal pathology and recovery" promulgated by therapists? (39). As we have seen, other feminist writers such as Elaine Showalter, Carol Tavris, and Janice Haaken have raised similar concerns about incest stories as exploiting and making formulaic women's varied experiences of distress. Echoing Louise Armstrong's fears that incest literature is now a consumer fad, they suggest that the "incest industry" is feeding upon a victim culture that has encouraged women to write self-pitying tales about their fantasized woes. Incest, such critics tell us, is too hot a topic, the only one that sells. So much is this now the voice of common sense that it seems undeniable that there are too many incest memoirs. As it turns out, incest survivor memoirs are less available and heavily marketed than these commentators fear.

In this chapter, we will analyze incest survivor memoirs as a way of telling incest that, importantly, is distinct from those stories included in abbreviated form in anthologies and self-help books, fictionalized in novels and movies, or bandied about on many a talk show. By *incest survivor memoirs* we mean American and Canadian book-length autobiographical accounts about recovering memories of incest. These full-length incest survivor memoirs are far from readily available in huge numbers. A dedicated search of large and small bookstores, as well as several databases, yielded—with much more difficulty than we had anticipated—twenty-one memoirs.[1] From this set of twenty-one available books, we have chosen to discuss seven: *My Father's House* by Sylvia Fraser (1987), *Don't* by Elly Danica (1988), *Dancing with Daddy* by Betsy Petersen (1992), *The Bat Had Blue Eyes* by Betsy Warland (1993), *The Laid Daughter* by Helen Bonner (1995), *The Architect of Desire* by Suzannah Lessard (1996), and *Memory Slips* by Linda Cutting (1997).

When we began to read incest survivor memoirs we not only assumed that there were too many of them, but we also expected that they would have a predictable narrative pattern. The master narrative, so familiar that it almost goes without saying, would have the following plot line: the author—a woman in distress over her contemporary dilemmas—suffers from flashbacks and bodily symptoms that she cannot explain. Operating like a detective, with the assistance of a supportive therapist, she begins to understand the forgotten origin of these symptoms—incest. Then, through a process of reconstruction, she discovers that her father was an evil perpetrator and she a silenced victim. Healing takes a narrative form, a coherent story about the past that gives the narrator a new identity as a survivor. Of this master narrative, Paul Antze, agreeing explicitly with feminist psychotherapist and writer Janice Haaken, has written that it comes at the "price of inducting survivors into an illness idiom that excludes fantasy, moral ambiguity, a sense of agency, and the kind of remembering that can offer openings to the future" (11). In short, this narrative is seen to sacrifice a sense of the glorious complexity of human subjectivity and put in its place a reductive sense of self.

Our review of incest survivor memoirs suggests that critics of the genre have themselves told too simple a story. Indeed, incest survivor memoirs may be less formulaic than the two dominant narratives of incest that they challenge: the mainstream critique that says it is now all too easy to recover and tell memories of incest, and an older, yet related, narrative that insists that incest does not happen in middle-class homes. To our surprise, the memoirs that we read do offer a feminist political analysis, and contrary to feminist worries about incest survivor memoirs, they are not self-pitying victim stories. Furthermore, in their acknowledgment of paradox and contradiction, they demonstrate a surprising stylistic and formal subversion in their ways of telling about traumatic pasts. These memoirs bring an analysis of middle-class ideology to this formal experimentation, in which an "official" story of a protective and nurturing middle-class family is brought into dynamic conflict with the horror of something unspoken and finally unresolvable as experience, memory, or representation. In other words, as an emerging genre of autobiographical "telling," these memoirs do not insist that they represent the past as a certainty or foundational truth.[2] As a result, the narrative "I" is situated less firmly as a type—the victim or survivor—than as a mobile effect of contexts past and present. We hope to show how the incest survivor memoir thus differs from the recovery story, both in its challenges to the ease of achieving agency and identity and in the way it inscribes the intrusiveness and elusiveness of the past as two impediments to the construction of a coherent story.

These memoirs are written by middle-class women, which may explain why there seem to be too many of them. As these women narrate their pasts, their consciously remembered childhoods seem the very apogee of middle-class upbringings. They remember homes that range from Fraser's "three story frame house on a shady street" (3) in Hamilton, Ontario, to Petersen's comfortable home in northern California's most prosperous neighborhood, Hillsborough, to Lessard's life on an estate, "The Place" on Long Island. Their parents are often hardworking and dutiful, keeping the lawn trimmed, the "house smell[ing] like furniture polish," and "everything ironed, even the sheets, even the underwear" (Bonner, 37). So what's to complain about? These memoir writers take a considerable risk with their readers' patience. Some reviewers of these memoirs suggest that, given such comfortable lives, these women should not harp on their unhappy pasts. Further, the received story enforces the view that incest does not really happen in the middle class.

In an article in the *New Yorker*, Joan Acocella repeats this story, insisting that "as for poverty, study after study has shown its high correlation with child abuse" (78).[3] After Acocella locates incest as a problem of the poor, she goes on to suggest that recovered memories and multiple personality disorder primarily appeal to women supposedly left behind by the feminist movement, "notably a large number of working-class women" who apparently go into therapy to get "something that they could not get from society: an interesting job" (69). Acocella thus reinforces dominant sociological myths not only about the shiftless poor, but about incest as a working-class problem. These myths are comfortable to a middle class, always fearful, as Barbara Ehrenreich reminds us, of "falling" and anxious to maintain its sense of virtue by scapegoating other classes. Given the evidence that indicates "incest is in fact more prevalent in the white middle class than it is willing to admit," Elizabeth Wilson points out that "all the hostile suspicion being raised about repressed memories seems like an instance of class consolidation against an internal threat to its moral self-representation (and eventually to its class power based on that self-representation)" ("Not in This House," 52–53). Thus it is not surprising that survivor memoirs written by middle-class women are met with incredulity and charges of self-indulgence.

It is feminine self-indulgence that is highlighted in critiques of the incest survivor narrative as too formulaic. Carol Tavris, in her controversial *New York Times* review of women's writing on incest, uses Betsy Petersen's memoir, *Dancing with Daddy*, as a way to point out this problem of the incest survivor memoir in more detail: "Betsy Petersen seems to have completely shut out 'the world outside my skin,' and ultimately this is the problem and appeal of the survivor narrative. It places responsibility for the common problems in women's lives on a single clear villain, someone safely in the woman's past. The victim doesn't have to do anything except understand the origins of her problems. . . . And she gets a love bath from her friends and supporters. Who could resist?" (17). Tavris thus insists on the seductions of what she calls the survivor narrative; the survivor simply needs to rely upon a formulaic script with clear villains and victims; armed with this formula, she then "doesn't have to do anything but understand the origins of her problems." Likewise, the victim experiences no resistance to telling her story, given the promising reward of a "love bath."

Tavris's own desire to find polarized victims and victimizers in the survivor narrative makes it an easy target and masks the extent to which memoirs like those we are analyzing are structured by a paralyzing ambivalence, by the daughter's respect for and anger at her father—and her sense of guilt as well as her feelings of victimization. The father in many incest survivor memoirs, for example, is anything but a "single clear villain." Indeed, while the 1980s memoirs emphasize the terrifying power of fathers to silence their daughters by explicit threats, many 1990s memoirs render the father and the daughter's situation differently. So, for example, survivor memoirs such as Elly Danica's *Don't* and Sylvia Fraser's *My Father's House* represent the perpetrator-father as making specific threats and as dominating and intimidating their families. But in later memoirs, daughters rarely seem to be silenced by fathers who threaten violence. They instead write about self-silencing: the internalization of the perpetrator's voice and covert family "rules" about keeping up appearances based upon an understandable desire to remain ensconced in the security of a middle-class family life that is both real and fantasized.

Many of the daughters who write incest survivor memoirs describe themselves as girls who adored their fathers, represented as idealized figures of protection and generosity. Fathers are educated, often successful, and not infrequently respected by the outside world as compassionate, intelligent, and gentle. Betsy Petersen goes so far as to include in her memoir letters of appreciation from the patients of her father, who was a successful surgeon, patients who viewed him as no less than a saint. And, of course, fathers desire to be idealized—exaggerating their own role as providers—while also feeling insecure about their own power, a mixture of fear and strength that makes vulnerable adoring daughters a likely target for the mixture of violence and love that is expressed in incestuous assaults. Both the perpetrator and the victim attempt to live up to a cultural ideal of virtuous middle-classness—and the fear of falling from this ideal fuels compulsive efforts to make "good." Much work is involved in such facades, work that usefully makes reflection and remembering difficult. To remember would not only challenge a revered way of life, but would also indict the rememberer as crazy, as madly unable to appreciate and be grateful for such an existence. Obeying rules of middle-class discourse—the demand to keep things sanitized and polite—makes it hard to rehearse and thus remember events that are so transgressive of the "official story" about how things are.

The "official story" is a discourse that reinforces middle-class ideology and is reproduced both in a family's private attempts to keep up appearances (efforts described in most incest survivor memoirs) and in celebrations of middle-class family life by the media, church, and state. This discourse promotes a sense of the middle-class family as benevolent and orderly, governed by parental figures who are protective and in control. In a sense, trauma theory requires recognition of the power of dominant stories, such as this one, so as to understand why certain traumatic experiences might not be representable within them. According to theorists of trauma, a traumatic event is an experience that is violent and unpredictable and overwhelms an individual's ability to integrate or accommodate it within an existing framework—a framework such as the discourse that we are calling the "official story."

The issue of representability comes up in the very definition of trauma itself. As Cathy Caruth puts it, the traumatic wound is "the breach in the mind's experience of time, self, and the world. . . . an event experienced too soon, too unexpectedly to be fully known" (*Unclaimed Experience,* 4). As most writers on trauma point out, a trauma is not necessarily defined by the nature of an event alone, since violent events do not traumatize everyone equally. Similarly, an early definition of traumatic events in the 1987 American Psychiatric Association's *Diagnostic and Statistical Manual* as "outside the range of ordinary human experience" has been contested as neglecting the impact of repeated traumas within everyday life, with special reference to women's daily experiences of violence. This way of rethinking the definition of trauma might be seen as making the definition too broad, but "trauma" need not stand for all women's troubling experiences of daily life. It may usefully refer to a portion of them.

The debate about the validity of trauma theory, however, has less to do with the definition of a traumatic event than with what happens in the mental processing of it. That such an event might be "stored" in memory and return "absolutely true to the event" has, as we have already seen, been met with skepticism. Skeptics, such as Elizabeth Loftus and Frederick Crews, point to the inevitable erosion and distortions to which memory is subject over time. Responding to such criticisms, contemporary trauma theorists make a distinction between nontraumatized and traumatized memory, often relying upon the growing field of cognitive science that posits different memory systems and different functions for the brain in storing and accessing memory, processes that take place outside of conscious awareness.[4] These writers also build upon the work of Janet and Ferenczi, claiming that classical Freudian psychoanalysis overemphasizes internal psychic conflict and repression and neglects the impact of actual events. As Cathy Caruth points out, however, Freud himself returned to a notion of trauma that is in keeping with current trauma theory in his study of the "war neuroses" of World War I. Unable to account for the nightmares of traumatized soldiers within his own framework of wish fulfillment and unconscious meaning, he was astonished to find that these nightmares represented "purely and inexplicably, the literal return of the event against the will of the one it inhabits" (Caruth, *Trauma*, 5).

Skepticism about the "literal return" of any memory often leads critics of trauma theory to point out that it seems to neglect the importance of conflictual wishes and of fantasy in the reporting of memorial events.[5] To give one example, Janice Haaken, a careful critic, emphasizes what she feels is Freud's main contribution to the understanding of mental life, namely the child's active agency in the creation of meaning, a form of agency that seems to be obscured in trauma theory's emphasis on dissociative states. Freud's "repression model," she writes, "posits that events with affect-laden, personal meaning are never passively registered in memory but filtered through motivational states and psychic structures" (*Pillar of Salt*, 74). In contrast, the concept of traumatic memory, which requires a notion of what Haaken calls "split-off areas of mind," seems to posit an unacceptable and threatening passivity in the adult who is represented in this theory as "possessed" by memories. When the "possessed" are women, women haunted by memories of incest, they appear to be cast in a stereotypic role as both morally innocent and lacking in aggression and desire.

Yet precisely because critics of trauma theory tend to play up the rememberer's capacity for fantasy, they often play down the importance of physical reality in the child's life. Further, the perpetrator's own capacity for fantasy may disappear from the picture, as it does in many false-memory proponents' tellings of the father's story. In other words, challenges to trauma theory may minimize the extent to which a traumatized child may be processing both an actual overwhelming, terrifying event and a perpetrator's definition of that event, a definition that is a product of the perpetrator's own fantasy ("we shared something special") and that may also be internalized by the victim, who is often told she is responsible for what is happening to her.[6] Incest survivor memoirs suggest the struggle of the memoir writer to represent and to account for disturbing, returning fragments of memories that are at odds with a fantasized self-image that is, itself, in part built upon the idealized notion that middle-class families are a safe haven from familial violence. It is precisely this gap between the sanitized picture of middle-class life and unspoken and barely remembered horrors that is an expressed source of great pain for writers of incest survivor memoirs. In *The Architect of Desire,* Suzannah Lessard captures the consequences of denying experiences of familial violence:

In the beautiful environment of the family past, there was a magnificent figure who had gone out of control, in ways destructive to those in his course—including his family—and ultimately to himself. Behind my memories of a blissful childhood in a beautiful place, there were also destructive forces that were blind and out of control, but unacknowledged. Yet to this inner truth and all its ramifications I had no access. (4–5)

The child in such an environment loses "access" to what everyone around her also denies, the irrational and often violent behavior of adults. Fathers, in the sacrosanct privacy of their well-kept middle-class homes, are further protected by an ideology of success that garners the admiration of the outside world. Given this level of denial, it is not surprising that these memoirs are shaped by a sense of something hidden, forgotten, a "secret." Feelings about the past as both idyllic and violent are perhaps best summed up in Lessard's oxymoronic phrasing: the past, she writes, was for her, a site of "serene catastrophe" (56).

The conventional view of incest, namely that it is found only among "other" families, makes it especially plausible that incest within the middle-class family would be experienced as traumatic by the victim and understood as confabulation by many others. Incest survivor memoirs, describing a gap between an experience of incest and conventional paradigms for understanding it, reflect and shape new understandings of trauma and its expression. Indeed, reading middle-class incest survivor memoirs helped us to appreciate the usefulness of efforts in psychiatry and critical theory to understand trauma, especially the pressure put on narrative by what is not fully narratable. Trauma theory's basic insight is that trauma is produced by just the sort of gap between a discourse of benign normality and a lived reality of abuse as that experienced by middle-class daughters. Indeed, trauma is defined by the inability of victims to integrate experiences of violence into a culturally dominant paradigm about how everyday, mainstream reality is understood. So, for example, the internalization of a domestic ideology that exalts middle-class morality and material success makes experiences of incest inexplicable to the child victim and perhaps to her victimizer as well. The experiences are a content without a language or a form of knowledge to speak them.

Far from feeling that they have a story that is easy to tell, these writers report, as Helen Bonner does in her memoir, "No one ever worked harder to discredit my own memories than I did. They emerged despite enormous resistance" (243). As Bonner puts it in the beginning of her memoir, "What if something even did happen back there. It was so many years ago, what did it matter? I was fine. I had a good job. I did it well. I had good friends. Leave it alone" (15). Here, again, middle-class prosperity argues against unnamed and unnameable experiences. Elly Danica also describes "*enormous* resistance" to remembering. Her memoir, *Don't,* "took so long to write, through so much denial, through so many false starts, so many pages of pain. Thirteen years and 2,100 pages later the book is published" (Afterword, 97). The finished book is only one hundred pages long. The media's commonsense view of incest stories is that they are all too easy to tell. What these memoir writers reveal instead are the powerful social, economic, and psychological forces that constrain both remembering and telling.

These women are constrained not only by their internalized sense of, and desire to maintain, middle-class order and safety within the family, but also by their internalized commonsense view that such horrifying experiences could never have been forgotten. Because they also share mainstream doubts about the credibility of memories of incest, victims feel that flashbacks and fragmentary memories could be proof of their own craziness. Betsy Petersen portrays that part of herself as an internalized "red-faced prosecutor" who says to her, "I am willing to believe . . . that you have not deliberately lied. But isn't it possible, just remotely possible, that you might be mistaken? How in the world can you expect us to believe that you *forgot* something of such importance?" (158). One reviewer of Sylvia Fraser's *My Father's House* gives voice to these concerns: "What form of repression could have Fraser disavowing incidents that recurred over the first 17 years of her life, while leaving her to function as well as she did? How are we to understand the status of her memories?" (Hamilton, 33). The issue here is both how she could forget and, again, how she could be so successfully functional and yet have suffered so much.

In our view, the severity of the problems narrated in survivor memoirs—memoirists recount an overwhelming sense of fragmentation and a loss of connection with their sexuality, their past, and their sense of worth—convincingly suggests past violations by a trusted and loved figure. Jennifer Freyd argues, for example, that any child, dependent upon caretakers for its survival, might be uncertain about, or unwilling to understand, experiences that suggest a radical disregard for the child's needs and desires.[7] As Freyd and other trauma theorists argue, a child is not simply silenced by threats but is motivated to dissociate experiences of betrayal, motivated to "not know" in order to preserve and protect a sense of order in the world and of a caretaker's goodness. Forgetting, or rather an effort at forgetting, may be the child's strategy for coping with an intermittently terrifying situation and ensuring her survival. Furthermore, these memoirs record the growing acknowledgment that a family culture of denial also reinforces the child's motivation to forget. When those around her act as though nothing has happened, the child learns to minimize the experience of abusive behavior.

If we say that incest survivor memoirs are *plausible,* especially if read through the lens of studies about trauma, dare we say that they are historically *true?* Sylvia Fraser announces at the beginning of her memoir that she has found corroboration for her recovered memories, and Suzannah Lessard writes that three of her sisters had the same memories of sexual abuse. But for many of these memoirists and their readers, it is simply impossible to know for certain. Our point is not to emphasize the historical truth of these accounts, though trauma theory asks us to consider the significance of actual events, but rather to understand the way in which the very impossibility of knowing for sure shapes these narratives. The writers of these memoirs, from this perspective, have the daunting task of making real—for themselves and their readers— a past life that is not ever fully known to themselves.

To dramatize her own experience of dissociation, for example, Fraser writes that as child she split into two personalities, which she refers to as the Girl Who Knows and the Girl Who Doesn't Know. Fraser's neat story of how she packaged what she could not allow herself to know or to remember is belied by her memoir, in which refused knowledge cannot be so easily managed. In telling her story of growing up, the narrative is repeatedly interrupted by fragments, printed in italics, of her reconstructed memories of incest. Rather than being completely banished, then, it might be more accurate to understand the experience of incest as occupying a site of contradiction and paradox. Survivor memoirs attempt to tell a story about experiences that have never been fully accessible to memory but that continue to haunt and hound the victim. When traumatic experiences are never consciously articulated, rehearsed, or narrated, these historical experiences are not, as Cathy Caruth points out in her writings about trauma, "a possessed knowledge, but itself possesses, at will, the one it inhabits . . . [and] often produces a deep uncertainty as to its very truth" (*Trauma*, 6). So, for example, not ever having been fully known, the experience of incest announces itself in muted, repetitive symptoms that intrude, belatedly, to mark traumatic moments of the disconnected past. These symptoms create other forms of disconnection: in all the memoirs, writers talk about feeling cut off from self and others.

The traumatic event, in other words, can only be known in its aftereffects. Elly Danica, for example, says that she was motivated to remember when she found herself "unable to function on any level in the real world, to hold a job, to handle a relationship" (qtd. in Gzowski, ix). Sylvia Fraser could not find a reasonable explanation for a seemingly irrational hatred for her father, a terror of her own home, a driving anxiety that accompanied roller coaster changes in mood, and an almost compulsive need to write novels full of sexual violence, even as she never set out to tell such stories. Betsy Petersen writes that her inexplicable rage at the demands of her sons prevented her from, as she puts it, "being the mother I wanted to be" (4). Linda Cutting, a concert pianist, stopped being able to perform because she suffered memory slips. Suzannah Lessard writes of early promiscuity, a broken marriage, and finally a writing block that was only lifted when a conversation with her sisters began to make public her family's hushed-up history. In all of these accounts, the unbearable symptoms that motivate these victims to tell their story mark a loss of connection, not only with significant others in their lives but with themselves and their sense of the past.

The writers of incest survivor memoirs, then, must contend with a set of conflicts and paradoxes that not only fuel their need to remember and tell, but also challenge the very conventions of the memoir that is their chosen vehicle of telling. In popular understandings of the genre, the memoir, as autobiographical project, lays claim to authenticity and facticity and makes a contract with its reader to record "what really happened." Yet these writers have access to their pasts and what happened only through elusive memories and intrusive symptoms. The plausibility and credibility of what they narrate both contributes to and depends upon an explanatory, conceptual framework of trauma that directly challenges assumptions about memory as a reliable archive. The conventional memoir would seem to promise a coherent self that can be referentially captured, and yet these memoir writers feel that they are fragmented and must convey that experience of fragmentation to their readers. On the other hand, these writers would also seem to be out of tune with postmodern critiques of representation and unitary subjectivity because they choose to tell their stories in a genre whose assumptions and conventions are so aligned with realism. What is interesting from the point of view of narrative is that these writers have found a way to challenge conventions of realism while giving shape to the felt reality of their experience.

Though all of the memoirs aim to end numbing self-censorship and to challenge family and social denial, each memoir writer deploys a somewhat different set of terms to record the impact of this experience. Two of these writers, for instance, choose metaphors that have personal meaning, yet resonate on a mythically collective level. In this way, these memoirs both adopt and challenge heroic feminist models of "beset womanhood" and triumph similar to forms of feminist canon-formation that we have already discussed. Elly Danica's interest in archaeology, for instance, led her to the myth of the goddess Innana who makes a descent into the underworld. The allusion to Innana's journey structures Danica's narrative of her memories as a journey through successive gates of hell, each gate marking entry into another more terrifying memory. Danica also chose Innana's story as one, like the story of incest, that has been, as she puts it, "either hidden or retold from a masculine perspective where we are erased or marginalised" (qtd. in Williamson, 84). Helen Bonner, too, connects her personal story with stories of legendary women who have been silenced, by playing on her name and Helen of Troy's, a reminder that women must reclaim their past or repeat it.

Though now some feminists challenge, as a representational strategy, the appeal to legendary heroines, this strategy speaks poignantly to the traumatized narrator's feelings of worthlessness and powerlessness, feelings compensated for by identification with idealized figures of strength or beauty. The reliance on legendary stories that seem to lend historical weight to these memoirs may also reveal the difficulty of finding a language for telling. Given the way these stories work inward, rather than outward as they would for the typical (male) hero, they record how hard it is to move on and out when so much—trauma, memory, gendered places in the family—pulls them back and in. Invoking patriarchal myth is repetition, as well as a plan of escape.

Other writers turn to structural metaphors of more personal significance. Linda Cutting shapes her narrative using the metaphor of "memory slips" and also by alternating between two narratives, set ten years apart, that reflect the way "time is experienced in the first movement of Beethoven's Sonata, op. 109. One narrative spans a year, the other, one month. In the 1982–83 sections, time is moving quickly, even rushing by. In the 1992 sections, time slows down, almost to a standstill" (12). Suzannah Lessard is not only writing about architecture to tell the story of her great-grandfather, the famous architect Stanford White, but uses architecture as a metaphor to render the family legacy of denying the impact of White's secret life of sexual promiscuity with young girls. She had long realized, Lessard says, that there was a "correlation between the architecture of my family history and my inner life . . . in both, something was hidden" (4). And even in a metaphor that would seem to have only private meaning—Betsy Warland's bat that had blue eyes—the creature speaks to a personal memory of a bat in the house that was caught and buried alive still squealing, and also to broader cultural links of this creature in the popular imagination with the terrifying blood-sucking vampire, and, in other cultures, with shamanism, rites of initiation, and healing. These chosen metaphors, then, are integral both to the life being narrated and to the shaping of the life, and are a reminder of the memoir's artful selection and design.

In addition to these familiar conventions of ordering are more challenging violations of a linear sense of time (such as those suggested by Cutting's use of the Beethoven sonata). The more experimental memoirs incorporate violations of conventions of space in terms of both narrative distancing (that is, the space between narrator and reader) and the arrangement of words on the page. Perhaps the most experimental narrative, *The Bat Had Blue Eyes*, forsakes, as Warland puts it, "nostalgia for narrative" and renders her experience of incest in fragments of prose and poems that are not explicitly connected for the reader, even on the page. In an effort to explain how "in grade 3 i lost faith in words / At 43 I understood why" (35), Warland's project is to place language in the foreground, not only deconstructing the part it plays in perpetuating and silencing abuse but the blindness involved in trusting its neutrality and transparency: "The reason that shook my faith in the written word far more profoundly. I was being sexually abused . . . as is often the case, my abusers' words placed the blame on me" (34). Her experimental narrative, self-conscious in its use of feminist and deconstructive practices and published by a small press, is unlikely to reach a large audience and challenge mainstream views of what the discourse for telling incest sounds like.

Elly Danica, in her memoir *Don't,* makes a more considered effort to challenge expectations that incest is easy to tell, while also creating a text accessible to a wider public. In an interview, Danica reflects upon her attempt to achieve this difficult balance: "I had to find a structure that would function on more than one level because I did not want to eliminate a whole group of readers who weren't interested in experimental writing. I had to make it clear enough for that group, but interesting enough for women who read it on more than one level" (Williamson, 81). Though the metaphor of a journey to hell anchors and guides the reader, the journey is presented in short prose fragments with no explicit transitions. The effect she aimed to achieve is, as she puts it, "to present on paper the pain of this experience with no space between the text and the reader. No distance" (qtd. in Williamson, 79). In this respect, the prose fragments both reflect and embody the narrator's sense of her self as "The woman made of potshards. Pieces. Not herself. Never herself. Who is herself? Only broken pieces" (*Don't,* 14). The voice of her father, a voice Danica has internalized, dominates some of the fragments and becomes intermingled with the narrator's own injunctions to herself: "Don't tell. Don't think" (7). By closing the distance between her father and herself, herself and the reader, Danica attempts a form that will help the reader understand the child-victim's experience of incest as a violation of boundaries. It is a narrative structure that "inscribes the dynamics of abuse at the level of reading" (Winter, 188).

Even memoirs that are more apparently reliant upon a realistic narrative line, such as Betsy Petersen's *Dancing with Daddy* and Helen Bonner's *Laid Daughter,* are not the predictable teleological fables of recovery that the mainstream press has led us to expect. Both of these memoirs, for example, announce the writer's recovery of incest memories immediately in their opening pages. Recovering more details of this experience and insisting upon its historical accuracy in every detail is not the point. Given the elusiveness, if not the inaccessibility of memories of past traumatic experience, "what happened" is deliberately and necessarily represented as a sequence of reconstructions that are shaped by fragments of dreams, associations, fictions, and journal entries. Bonner's memoir also undercuts the expectation of a straightforward journey from blindness to insight by narrating a repetitive process that leads her to ceaselessly reinvent herself; so much so that the reader can lose track of Bonner's many different jobs and relationships. Her repetitive reinventions of herself suggest an insatiable need to rupture intimate relationships. This repetitive rupturing is the point, serving as both symptom and clue to the childhood shattering of a trusted relationship. An acknowledgment of her past does not lead to recovering a coherent self; instead it gives recognition to her many selves, with whom she "checks in" from time to time, an offhand comment meant to convey her sense that a composite self is quite ordinary (Bonner, 245). Linda Cutting's memoir explicitly and self-consciously plays with the terrifying deep freeze of repetitious behavior that cannot be accounted for, a legacy of harboring a traumatic secret. Entitling a chapter "Fugue," she uses this term both as metaphor and as shaping device. Musically, a fugue is a complicated piece ceaselessly inventing variations on a single theme. In psychoanalysis, a fugue state can refer to the experience of dissociation and the terrifying inability to remember that fuels repetitive behavior. Both in shape and in content, these memoirs reveal that the more the child "forgot," the more she fell prey to the psychological paralysis associated with repetition. The repetitions of these memoirs, then, take shape from the traumatic experience they attempt to convey and, in doing so, challenge the conventions of realism by reminding us of the self as composite and invented. The story of achieving a sense of self, or "a whole that I could live with," as Danica puts it, is also held up as the product of conscious design and selection. In *Beyond Don't*, her second book, she reminds readers that her memoir is not the sum total of her identity. There are other stories that she could tell.

Recovery and healing for these writers, then, is bound up in an act of authoring, of trying to *own* memories, through a conscious reenactment, that seemed to own and control them. The narrative practice of acknowledging previously buried selves and memories and producing a story dependent upon reconstructions that make sense or feel real is less a claim to an essential unified self than a bid for a sense of agency and authority. Unlike recovery stories, memoirs of incest remind their readers of both the psychic and the political necessity of achieved coherence and identity, and the artificiality of this achievement. The selfhood and traumatic past of these memoirists are explicitly acknowledged to be reconstructed upon the base of bodily symptoms and fragmentary memories—something really happened—and yet dependent upon a language that enacts gaps and discontinuities and interrogates foundational truths offered by the victim and her class. As with narratives of the recovery movement that we discussed in chapter 4, the practice of writing is important to healing, but healing is interrogated by giving far more space and attention to the experience of trauma, the damaging legacy of the past, and the difficulty of telling it.[8]

These memoirs are haunted by the unsaid and unknown—and all of them are maddening because they both do and don't recover from the past. In an odd way, these memoirs make the reader want what critics say they actually are: a life story written as a linear narrative in which the "I" achieves a new and triumphant identity as a survivor. Although Linda Cutting returns to her concert career, Fraser writes successful novels, and Lessard achieves family harmony and writes her best-selling book, their memoirs record something else; they teach that stories about triumphs often mask pain. How is the reader to distinguish a false start from a genuine one? The incest survivor memoir is a narrative of self-understanding that reveals self knowledge to be a labored production that is both constraining (for it is a facile middle-class imperative to say everything is fine) and transformative, for the memoir revises and critiques that story even as it enacts it. Given this troubling of middle-class waters, it is not surprising that even feminists might feel that there are too many incest survivor memoirs, though perhaps there are too few.

Chapter 7

On the Borders of the Real

In the 1990s two popular novels, Dorothy Allison's *Bastard out of Carolina* (1992) and Sapphire's *Push* (1996), recenter the incest story in the homes of the poor. Allison's novel, set in the rural South, features the culture of "poor, white trash" and a narrator named Bone who is physically and sexually abused by her stepfather. Sapphire's narrator and protagonist, Precious, is a black, unwed teenage mother who lives in Harlem on welfare. She is sexually abused by her father and brutally exploited by her mother. Neither Bone nor Precious has forgotten that she was raped by her father, a fact that lends authority to their accounts of abuse. Yet telling these stories would also seem to confirm the middle-class expectation that incest is primarily found among the lazy and immoral poor. In an effort to revise this expectation, Allison and Sapphire combine the strategies of other incest narratives to "tell" incest in a new way. Like Ellison, they contend with the hunger for stories of incest told by exotic others. Like Walker, they offer a compensatory story about a plucky heroine capable of rising above abusive circumstances, but they also challenge the "recovery story" by insisting upon the long-lasting and fragmenting effects of trauma. The changes in the telling that we have documented in this book have made possible a self-consciously hybrid construction of subjectivity, sexuality, and memories of incest.

As do most narratives, incest narratives exist on a boundary between fact and story, and this doubleness is explicitly acknowledged by Allison and Sapphire. Allison, for example, describes her work as "not biography and yet not lies" (*Trash*, 12). This border genre claims authenticity and truth—but only to a point. Certainly, Allison and Sapphire attempt to remain true to their own experiences of incest. In a memoir written after *Bastard out of Carolina*, Allison writes: "The man [her stepfather] raped me. It's the truth. It's a fact. I was five and he was eight months married to my mother" (*Two or Three Things*, 39). Similarly, Sapphire has, in therapy, "'recovered' memories of being sexually abused by her father when she was three or four years old" (Powers, B2). And both writers draw heavily upon their direct experiences of life among the underclass; Allison grew up in a "poor white trash" family, and Sapphire taught in Harlem, finding in one of her classes a direct model for Precious, a student who was a "single mother . . . overweight, HIV-positive," who had a "Down Syndrome baby by her father" (Powers, B2). These direct experiences further buttress the authority and "truth" of accounts that are also "not biography" or, better, not just autobiography.

Yet linking their novels to autobiographical experience lends them credibility and thus gains them a special hearing, as reviews of both novels indicate. A commentator in the *New Yorker* notes wryly that Sapphire's grim portrait of Precious "can make writers who think they've been truthful feel extremely jealous" (Rose, 48). And while a review of *Bastard out of Carolina* in the *New York Times* praises the artistry of Allison's novel, both the title of the review—"No Wonder People Got Crazy as They Grew Up" and a prominently featured sidebar about Allison's childhood—assure readers that this terrible story is based upon Allison's real-life experiences. Allison is a major new talent, claims the reviewer, who writes "in a manner as authentic as that of any credible autobiographer" (Garrett, 3). Yet Allison says in the same review that her story is not fully autobiographical: "I made her, Bone, a stronger child than I was—and more important—I gave her a way out . . . if the book had been autobiographical it would have been a lot meaner" (3). This admission that her novel mutes her life's meanness suggests that *Bastard out of Carolina* offers some of the comforts of the "recovery story."

As we have already seen, a "recovery" novel such as *The Color Purple* is structured to offer recovery and empowerment to beset, traumatized characters. This narrative model continues to appeal to writers and readers, and it is not surprising that Allison and Sapphire appropriate some of its drive to "heal." More interesting is how their novels both deploy and rupture the promise, conventionally made by autobiography as well as the recovery story, to tell a real and true story. Feminists have developed a compelling critique of realism that by now operates as a form of conventional wisdom.[1] At least since the early 1980s, when Catherine Belsey published her insightful book *Critical Practice,* realism has been understood as a system of representation that does not so much reflect the world as construct it. This constructed "real" world seems complex, true, and familiar precisely because it reflects a shared body of understanding that is called "the dominant ideology." The literary tradition of realism is one in which characters are represented as individuals implicated in, but often successful at rising above, their familial, social, and economic circumstances, and thus it reinforces the dominant ideology of individualism through an emphasis on the exceptional individual. So, for example, in *Bastard out of Carolina* and *Push,* reliable first-person narrators demonstrate how a female child, immersed in an abusive environment that is personal and social, comes to understand and provisionally transcend that environment. The advocacy of realism by and on behalf of culturally marginal subjects, which is a serious plea for greater inclusiveness "in the real world," thus also risks embracing the values of an individualistic society that has crushed such people.

The constitutive tensions in *Push* and *Bastard out of Carolina* are related to this problem of individualism as portrayed in the realist novel. In both novels, the protagonist is featured as having a resourceful, autonomous "self" and, at the same time, as having been shattered by implacable external forces. Neither Bone nor Precious stands outside or fully escapes the forces that threaten to crush her. At the same time, neither is represented as absent of agency and desire. Indeed the child victim's intense desires and provocative modes of representation disrupt familiar expectations about the recovery novel and the autonomous individual at its center. The power to fragment is depicted as both a weapon employed by the protagonist (it is displayed in Bone's meanness and in Precious's use of poetry) and a weapon wielded by intrusive victimizers. This doubleness leads to the production of a subject who is not an "innocent," passive victim.

The active and "knowing" female subject is usually constructed in opposition to the innocent, good girl. We have already discussed why feminist scholarship about incest often dramatizes children's innocence: it hopes to challenge an oppressively gendered discourse about seductive children and adolescent girls that traditionally obscures the actions of powerful men. Yet the result is "monster talk" about monstrous adults and innocent children, talk that is open to the charge, recently reiterated by James Kincaid, that this discourse denies all sexual feeling to the child (3). And if children and adults both have sexual feelings, should we not talk about power because such explanation is "hostile to desire," as Kincaid also argues? (33). Clearly here is the familiar double bind: admitting to children's sexuality becomes a demand to forget that adult-child relationships are structured by asymmetries in power. The feminist incest story, whose central focus was on power imbalances within the family, insisted upon the innocence of the abused child in response to a dominant narrative that blamed incest on seductive girls. Allison and Sapphire create an alternative story that acknowledges asymmetries of power without sentimentalizing or desexualizing the female child. Indeed the refusal of innocence operates as a claim for agency.

Allison's victimized protagonist, Bone, is not an "innocent" child, although neither is she to blame for what happens to her. Belief in the child as essentially pure implicitly works to censor a child's sexuality as deviant and provocative; it also supports the emotional logic of good/bad used to maintain class hierarchy. Either the poor are naturalized—as being "always with us"—and in this guise understood to be innocently noble and hardworking, clean but unlucky. Or the poor deserve what they get because they have been bad: lazy and morally depraved. "I understood that we were the bad poor. . . . We were not noble, not grateful, not even hopeful" (*Skin*, 18). Allison knows that by this logic: "My cousins and I were never virgins even when we were" (*Two or Three Things*, 36). For the poor, female child there is a double motive to expose the oppressive way in which notions of innocence operate. As Jenny Kitzinger points out, "Implicit in the presentation of sexual abuse as the 'violation of childhood' is an assertion of what childhood 'really' is, or should be. The experience of abuse is contrasted with the 'authentic experience of childhood': a carefree time of play; an asexual and peaceful existence within the bosom of the family. The quality of childhood that is most surely 'stolen' by abuse is 'innocence.'" This view "stigmatizes the 'knowing' child," whose world does not conform to the ideal (157–58).

In Bone's world, children have sexual desires, and adults talk frankly about sex. The bosom of her family is hardly peaceful, and nobody is carefree. As does Toni Morrison in *The Bluest Eye*, Allison depicts a world that hardly meets idealized white middle-class norms. But Pecola and her family are trapped in a world where their feelings of helplessness and rage turn in upon themselves. By contrast, Bone appreciates her white trash family's social class as the source of her dissident perspective: "We're smarter than you think we are. I felt mean and powerful and proud of all of us, all the Boatwrights who had ever gone to jail, fought back when they hadn't a chance, and still held on to their pride" (*Bastard*, 217). The social and economic forces that create the Boatwrights' poverty also fuel them with the rage to fight back and resist. Yet Morrison may not make the same claim for the Breedloves or the McTeers because she is aware that African-American "meanness" is too threatening to white readers. The Boatwrights' "meanness" may be more permissible, for the white poor are expected to be "mean" but not genuinely threatening to the status quo.

Allison claims to write in a spirit of revenge: "I am the meanest writer I know how to be. Because, to change people, you have to crack them, and at the core of that is breaking their hearts" (Jetter, 57). To perform this kind of "breaking," she must be more than permissibly mean—and so her novel must challenge the benign assumptions of the recovery story. One way to do this is to draw upon the resources of the earlier "feminist story," which dramatizes male violence against women and children. Allison's embrace of violence in the telling of the incest story disrupts those feminist practices that assume violence is always bad and male. Much feminist antiviolence rhetoric has focused upon how violence has been directed at women, and how responding in kind perpetuates a cycle. And in difference feminism, the very identity of women is posited as more therapeutically nurturing than an opposed and essentially violent male identity. Yet as Pamela Haag writes in her overview of the feminist debates about violence and victimhood, "while most thoughtful feminists within the academy—and many without—have sensed that identity politics and a therapeutically absorbed feminism are irksome and ideologically inadequate, the alternative seems to offer either an obliteration of the victim at the hands of a delusional, rugged-individualist discourse of 'free creatures' or an abstract directive to denaturalize the concept of sex difference that historically has organized the feminist critique of social relations" (24). For the feminist novelist aware of these issues, the task is to contextualize violence without losing track of gender and to create a victim neither innocent nor blamable, neither passive nor free.[2]

For Allison to want to crack the hard hearts of her readers in need of changing might at first sound like what the perpetrator of her story, Daddy Glen, does to the young victim, Bone. But admitting to both the desire and the pleasure, as Allison's novel does (and as she has in interviews), of being mean, aggressive, and angrily vindictive acknowledges and makes use of these hostile feelings to build a different story about women, violence, and sexual abuse. The feminist story, however, is still structuring Allison's novel insofar as it blames patriarchy for what happens to Bone. The "meanness" of Bone's world comes not only from its grinding poverty and hunger and limited horizons, but from the attitude of its male inhabitants. Physical meanness is gendered, figured in the uncles who are described as "invariably gentle and affectionate" with Bone and her cousins. But

> half the county went in terror of them. . . . Only when they were drunk or fighting with each other did they seem as dangerous as they were supposed to be. . . . My aunts treated my uncles like over-grown boys—rambunctious teenagers whose antics were more to be joked about than worried over—and they seemed to think of themselves that way too. . . . Men could do anything, and everything they did, no matter how violent or mistaken, was viewed with humor and understanding. (22–23)

Yet no matter how much the uncles terrorize other adults in the county, they never terrorize children.

This particular form of meanness is left to Daddy Glen, who comes from a prosperous middle-class family, and whom Bone's mother Anney marries, ironically, to gain respectability. White trash men may be mean and vicious, but it is the terrifying aggression of white middle-class men directed toward those weaker that is the cruelest. And Daddy Glen's "meanness" is mirrored in other white middle-class institutions, such as the bureaucrats at the county courthouse who refuse to correct Bone's birth certificate and the "meanness" of the sheriff who, though he intends to help Bone, only manages to badger her for information about her abuser. Bone has already absorbed the lesson that the law does not serve white trash; it only fines, harasses, and imprisons them.

There is a double sense of meanness in the novel. Meanness is linked to love and resistance but also to cruelty and destruction. Bone learns from her aunts that women love men who are mean, another lesson that challenges the feminist story about women's innocence. As Aunt Ruth puts it, "that's what Earle is, a hurt little boy with just enough meanness in him to keep a woman interested" (25). Part of the appeal of the mean boy is indeed that he himself is "a hurt little boy." Not only is Earle hurt, but Glen too is hurt (and mean because of it) by *his* father, who rejects him and makes him feel less competent than his successful brothers. Bone's mother, Anney, explains her attraction to him in precisely these terms: "Anybody can see how Glen got bent, what his daddy's done to him. I an't never seen a boy wanted his daddy's love so much and had so little of it" (132). She adds, "It was like looking at a little boy, a desperate hurt little boy. That's when I knew I loved him" (133). Women in this configuration of relationships are the mothers and nursemaids to their mean little boy-men.

While it looks like the Boatwright women are the sympathizers and nurturers, they too are mean, even in the desire to love. In the intense focus on their love these mean but hurt little boys, there is a familial pattern of neglect of girls. Granny favors her boys, neglecting her girls. Aunt Ruth has driven away her daughter DeeDee, who is sick of picking up after her brothers and taking care of her debilitated mother. Women's love for their partners has another kind of meanness, in that it often comes at the expense of children's needs. Aunt Alma destroys her house and furniture and terrifies her children and claims she wants to kill her husband Wade only because she loves him; and even Aunt Raylene, who loves a woman, nearly brings herself and her lover to destruction by making her lover choose between her child and Raylene. Most important to Bone, her mother's love for Glen almost always takes precedence over her desire to protect her daughter.

The cycle of neglected women-girls loving their hurt men-boys rather than their children who grow up to be hurt men-boys or abused, neglected girls has its emotional fulcrum in deprivation, which is compounded by the hunger and economic distress of the characters. In one vignette, Bone and her sister, with only soda crackers and ketchup to eat, dream of pretend meals. In another scene, Bone, forced by her mother to return stolen candy to a bloat-bellied store manager at Woolworths, feels a hunger and rage in the back of her throat that reminds her of a similar hunger that "would throb and swell behind [her] tongue" (98). This hunger makes Bone want "to hurt somebody back" (98). She pulls roses off the bushes at Daddy Glen's father's house, and she gets her revenge on the manager of Woolworths by using a trawling hook, trash found in the river, to break into the store, not stealing from it but smashing counters and leaving it to be looted. It is no wonder, then, that one of Bone's own masturbatory fantasies has to do with a raging fire, an apocalyptic, destructive symbolic vehicle that conveys both her own terrible anger at her abuse and lack of protection from those who should love her, as well as her triumphant escape.

By showing that this form of destructive love is both a familial pattern and a dimension of the family's economic circumstances, Allison lifts the novel away from blaming individuals, while still refusing to make these individuals innocent and desexualized.

The representations of sexuality, meanness, and rage in the novel humanize the characters. And given that white trash culture is often made to seem less than fully human, this appeal to human nature is strategic. *Bastard out of Carolina* suggests that sexuality is human primarily in its excessiveness. Like a fire, it is that which always threatens to rage out of the characters' control. And in its very excessiveness, it addresses, though it never resolves, the characters' immense sense of deprivation. Daddy Glen, the black sheep son of a middle-class family, is emotionally suffering from rejection by his father. Glen is so angry that he loses job after job, losses that exacerbate his sense of economic distress; he is so angry over his failure and inability to provide that he punishes Bone by beating her. That Glen, from a solid, prosperous middle-class family, gets caught in a cycle of deprivation and rage aligns him with the white trash family that he marries into. The uncles grant him some respect, as does the grandmother, when they discover that the "berserker rage that would come on him was just a shade off the power of the Boatwrights' famous binges" (100).

This identification of Glen with the uncles also extends to Bone, a child suffering from both economic and emotional deprivation similar to his own. His sexual abuse of her punishes her as his father punished him and is for him a source of pleasurable authority. The story he tells himself and others to rationalize this punishment is that he is keeping Bone in line: "Someone has to love her enough to care how she turns out" (107). Minor infractions, often imagined, serve as triggers. Though the actual beatings and abuse are nothing but terrifying and painful, Bone creates a masturbatory fantasy that allows her to re-create the punishment so that not only is she pleasurably reliving the event but controlling it. She fantasizes that as she is being beaten, she is proud and defiant and that people are watching her: "I was wonderful in their eyes" (112). In these scenarios, she is in control and special.

In fantasy, then, Bone finds a way to express her anger, make up for a sense of deprivation, and gain control. Danger and sexuality are linked for her, but she is not hurting anyone the way Daddy Glen does. As Ann Cvetkovich points out, Bone masters the trauma of sexual abuse by repeating it in fantasy, with the difference of creating authority and agency for herself. Thus Bone's fantasies become a way to manage and control, without disowning the violence and aggression that have constituted her as a sexual subject. But what cannot be fully recuperated is her sense of self-worth. "I was ashamed of myself for the things I thought about when I put my hands between my legs, more ashamed for masturbating to the fantasy of being beaten than for being beaten in the first place. I lived in a world of shame" (112–13). Her sense of shame exceeds the pleasure of the fantasy, ultimately making her feel guiltier about the fantasy than about the abuse.

Bone's shame over her fantasies helps to insure her silence about her abuse, but other factors contribute to her unwillingness to speak, even to a sympathetic listener. After offering Bone an explanation for Glen's hatred of her: "There's a way he's just a little boy himself, wanting more of your mama than you, wanting to be her baby more than her husband" (123), Aunt Ruth gently invites Bone to confide in her by asking Bone if "Daddy Glen ever . . . well . . . touched you? . . . ever hurt you, messed with you?" (124). Bone knows perfectly well what Aunt Ruth is referring to, "that thing men did to women. I knew what the act was supposed to be, I'd read about it, heard the joke. 'What's a South Carolina virgin? 'At's a ten-year-old can run fast'"[3] and commands herself, "Tell her . . . Tell her all of it. Tell her" (124). But she cannot bring herself to say anything more than that Glen scares her by the way he looks at her. It is not simply shame that silences Bone; she has been given her cues from Aunt Ruth as well. Ruth's face grows increasingly pink with embarrassment even as she sympathetically persists in questioning Bone. Ruth's embarrassment, Bone's shame, and her association of rape with a "joke" reinforce her reluctance and, finally, her inability, to tell.

As Allison herself has pointed out about *Bastard out of Carolina,* the story's emotional center is the damaging failures to protect Bone rather than the abusive acts themselves (Strong, 96). As the scene with Ruth reveals, however, the individual "failures" of the adult women in this particular culture are so intertwined with unquestioned beliefs about their men and the rightness of expected patterns of behavior that there is no "outside" for any one individual to appeal to. Neither does the violent vindictive beating that the uncles administer to Glen as both punishment and warning serve its purpose; rather, it seems to backfire in the even more horrifying rape of Bone at the end of the novel.

Although Bone is not protected by the adults in the novel, she does take it upon herself to protect her mother, and her protective impulse is another reinforcement for Bone's shamed silence. Even her final departure from her mother reflects an adultlike and still protective recognition that her mother needs Glen. Bone, then, never really tells her story. Nowhere in the novel does Bone ever say that Glen beats or rapes her. Physical signs and acts must speak for her: An x-ray shows that her coccyx is broken; her Aunt Raylene sees her bloodied legs; her mother discovers Glen raping Bone. In what she has described as an effort to make sure that her novel was not pornographic, Allison is careful not to graphically represent Glen's sexual abuse of Bone, especially because it is Bone's emotions that she wants to place in the foreground (Jetter). But at the same time, Bone's silence, meant to protect her mother, is also Allison's silence. Allison's need to protect her family and her class, while also refusing to make her characters "innocent," constructs a gap within the novel. On the one hand her story reveals the secrets of "white trash," the neediness, anger, and meanness, and on the other hand it conceals and protects.

By making Glen the villain, Allison uses the abuser to blame middle-class patriarchy and capitalism as the source of white trash misery. Because white trash have little power in this world, they can, in a way, be mean, drunken, and enraged without having much impact. Their destructive acts are figured as a series of childish pranks. One impulse behind the novel's muting of meanness may be a form of class loyalty that emerges in a lyricism that celebrates the landscape, the food, the gospel singing, and the strength and endurance of the women, all of which are conventional literary ploys for representing the "authentic" southern poor. But because of Allison's own rage at her family's and her mother's inability to protect her or themselves, and because she does want revenge, the novel torques on the counterimpulse to reveal as well as conceal the helplessness of these impoverished, blind adults. Bone never can tell her mother about the abuse because her mother, as well as the other women in her family, cannot hear what she is saying. Perhaps they do not need to hear this story: her hurt is not, for them, the primary one. Their paradigm for understanding their men as hurt and wounded boys, and their function of saving them, precludes any ability to save Bone. Bone will die if she does not save herself by escaping.

Bone, then, is not simply a survivor of sexual abuse. She also survives growing up in poverty, a culture she depicts as a trap in which helpless and mean adults neglect and abuse children who perpetuate the cycle. There are no options *within* this culture for, as Bone puts it:

> Growing up was like falling into a hole. The boys would quit school and sooner or later go to jail for something silly. I might not quit school, not while Mama had any say in the matter, but what difference would that make? What was I going to do in five years? Work in the textile mill? Join Mama at the diner? It all looked bleak to me. No wonder people got crazy as they grew up. (*Bastard*, 178)

To say that a child's options only point to the dead-end road of craziness is to dramatize the terrible constraints of her class—the same class that Allison wants to celebrate. Given this contradiction, it is not surprising that Allison does not enthusiastically endorse Bone's success at surviving her experiences. Bone's shame and guilt are not simply a sexual guilt, but a more complex form of survivor's guilt.

In an interview, Allison points out that her own "escape" from her family created an excruciating double bind.

Survivor guilt is so deep. I'm convinced that to be worthy of having sur-
vived when all these people I loved didn't survive, there's got to be something huge that I'm supposed to do. . . . The world would like us to believe
that if you do well, if you do anything successful, you are proof that every-
body else in your family is worthless. (Strong, 97)

The celebration of survivorship in therapeutic feminist culture does not
acknowledge the dark side of survivorship or that it can have more than one
origin. The popular recovery narrative extols the importance of a community
of nurturing women who empower incest victims and provide "safe" places,
but Allison, who figures just such a comforting and healing community in the
Boatwright aunts, shows its investment in passive constructions of femininity
and oppressive forms of heterosexuality that are inimical to Bone's safety.

Lesbianism certainly might offer an alternative to this traumatized and
traumatizing form of femininity. In the novel, Aunt Raylene seems to suggest
this way out. Late in the novel, Bone learns that Aunt Raylene ran away to the
carnival where she worked like a man, "cutting off her hair and dressing in
overalls" and calling herself Ray (179). And in the novel's last chapter, Aunt
Raylene tells Bone that she "made the woman I loved" choose between Raylene
and her child (300). Because Allison is herself a "cross-eyed, working-class, lesbian" who has explicitly discussed how her lesbianism saved her, the links
between Allison and the fictional Raylene and Bone are easy to forge (Jetter,
54).[4] Ann Cvetkovich argues that Bone finds in her "queer childhood sexuality" a form of agency that is both a fantasized and a real way of acquiring power
(369–70) and that Aunt Raylene is a "displaced marker of Bone's queer sexuality, if not her incipient lesbianism" (371).

The idea that "incest makes you queer" is a powerful and dangerous one.
One of the strengths of Cvetkovich's article is that she is willing to discuss the
limitations and possibilities of this idea. Because, as Rosaria Champagne has
shown, false-memory syndrome proponents use a family values rhetoric and
have engaged in lesbian-baiting, they have created a climate in which admitting
to a link between survivorship and lesbianism might fuel homophobic attacks
on survivors, whose legitimacy as truth-tellers is already precarious (167–92).
And, of course, positing sexual abuse as a "cause" of lesbianism is also a way of
pathologizing it, though as Allison has remarked: "if people really believed that
rape made lesbians, and brutal fathers made dykes, wouldn't they be more
eager to do something about it?" (*Two or Three Things*, 46). Cvetkovich's own
smart way of breaking the silence is to register her surprise and dismay at the
recovery movement's timid disavowal of the connection between coming out
as a survivor and coming out as a lesbian: "As someone who would go so far as
to claim lesbianism as one of the *welcome* effects of sexual abuse, I am happy to
contemplate the therapeutic process by which sexual abuse turns girls queer"

(357).[5] She uses the word "queer" to emphasize the unpredictability of the outcome of this object choice, yet her revealing exploration of *Bastard out of Carolina* creates a trajectory that consolidates Bone's sexual identity ("incipient lesbianism") as Allison does not. Cvetkovich knows she is looking for something that is not quite there: "Allison stops short of the autobiographical connection that would explore lesbianism's presence in Bone's queer sexuality, perhaps out of fear of the dangers of linking incest and lesbianism" (371). The problem with this explanation is that it emphasizes Allison's "fear," when Allison may have other reasons for refusing to make sexual identity a key.

What is also queer about Bone is her anger. Anger, abuse, poverty, brokenness, and raging need are what Allison writes about, and they represent the most potent danger to the comforts of the recovery story and its creation of imaginary "safe" havens. As she has written, "It was my anger that my aunts thought queer, my wild raging anger. Temper they respected in a boy and discouraged in a girl. That I slept with girls was curious, not dangerous" (*Trash*, 100). Allison's anger is "queer" to her aunts because the women Allison knows best take "damage until they tell themselves they can feel no pain at all" (*Two or Three Things*, 8). Allison crosses conventional gender lines not in terms of whom she sleeps with but by allowing herself to appropriate the energy of "wild" and boyish temper. The implication is that without exceptionally queer anger, bone-true stories about sexuality, racism, poverty, and violence cannot be told by women, much less believed. To get her story told, Allison must "pour blood on the floor to convince anyone that every word I say is true" (*Two or Three Things*, 51).

Yet the novel's ending does not "pour blood on the floor," is not that "mean." Where is Bone's anger in the concluding sentences of the novel? "I was who I was going to be, someone like her, like Mama, a Boatwright woman. I wrapped my fingers in Raylene's and watched the night close in around us" (309). But if Allison relies upon the narrative trajectory of recovery, she also reveals the darker side of its creation of the mythically strong and exceptional woman. Without undermining the necessity for such strength (a source, after all, of survival), she reveals, first, that her mother's and aunts' strength unwittingly perpetuates a cycle of infantilizing men, and that Bone's strength and identity have been seriously compromised by the trauma of her experience. As a result, at the end of *Bastard out of Carolina*, there is no clear consolidation of Bone's identity within a harmonious context such as the one provided for Celie at the end of *The Color Purple*. Allison herself reveals that while she had the strength to break out of this cycle, her ability to do so relied as much upon her enormous anger as upon a supportive sisterhood, and that a legacy of trauma, survivor's guilt, will always be with her. Allison's novel might serve as a cautionary tale for feminists caught up in the heated exchange about incest that so often seems to position strong women and reasonable feminists against hysterical victims and their gullible supporters, a positioning that never seems to inspect what women's "strength" relies upon or perpetrates.

In *Push* Sapphire also constructs a story of affirmation and survival, but in doing so, she self-consciously makes explicit, and a matter of some debate, the writing choices an author must make to attract an audience and gain its sympathy. Basing her protagonist upon a real person and her gritty urban life, Sapphire departs from *The Color Purple*'s (and to a lesser extent, Allison's) rural nostalgia. Precious makes the point that

> one of the critizisms of *The Color Purple* is it have fairy tale ending. I would say, well shit like that can be true. Life can work out for the best sometimes. Ms Rain [the teacher quite obviously based upon Sapphire herself] love *Color Purple* too but say realism has its virtues too. (85)

Push reveals the conflicting desires behind this dialogue: an optimistic desire that life work out for the best for deserving people vies with an equally strong insistence upon the "virtues of realism," cynicism about a social order that is hard to push against. In opting for the "virtues of realism," in however qualified a way, *Push* seeks to put before its readers a dark vision of "REAL-ITY," which is, as Precious puts it, "a 'motherfucker, leeme tell you" (85).

Precious "know what REALITY is" and is impatient with Ms. Rain's "IZM stuff" (85). The power of this vision resides in the conviction that raw experience can be represented. Like Precious, Sapphire draws upon the authority of her own experience to validate and shape her novel, especially her own recovered memories of being sexually abused by her father. Yet the "raw" experience of recovering memories is a highly mediated "source," given that her memories came to her in therapy and that she admits to doubting them. Moreover, her story is written as a novel that emphasizes the place of writing in healing. In *Push*, the protagonist's writing draws both upon the recovery story's narrative of self-determination and growth and upon the trauma memoir's insistence on the authority of the fragment. This doubleness allows Sapphire to explore the tension between a view of the individual's essential capacity for growth and one that emphasizes the individual as traumatically and productively fragmented. In *Push*, poetry offers a form of fragmentation that provides an alternative to the constraints of a realist narrative.

Both Sapphire and Allison first wrote about their experiences of sexual abuse in poetry. "To the Bone," a poem in Allison's *The Women Who Hate Me*, is a source of *Bastard out of Carolina*. It concludes with these words: "That summer I did not go crazy / but I wore / very close / very close / to the bone" (28). The "I" who suffers this abrading process makes retention of a tenuous rationality a kind of victory. But this is a victory whose truth is perhaps best understood by those who know how hard it is to resist the forces making poor women into something hard and senseless. The power of the bone as sign of victimage and source of authority is also figured in Sapphire's first book of poetry, *American Dreams*. In Sapphire's poem, "poem for jennifer, marla, tawana& me" the speaker is shattered, yet her "bones" become both weapons and tools for changing the patriarchal world.

American Dreams is dedicated to "the child within us all," a dedication meant to embrace all readers. Inner child therapies, as Marilyn Ivy observes, assume that many people are adult survivors of childhood violence who need to be reparented and healed so that they can experience "growth." Ivy agrees that inner child therapies are an "index of widespread pain in the United States" caused by a violent "American capitalism that fosters compulsive gratifications in an all-too-real foreclosure of childhood." But she also worries about a logic that assumes the dysfunctional family to be a "cross-cultural" verity, a belief that forecloses any attention to race or class or social history (243). The end result of these therapies, she argues, is to shift awareness from an analysis of historical contexts and economic conditions, in which race, gender, and class inform the mistreatment of children in specific ways, to the inner core of bourgeois individuals. Since the incest novel is a way of entering into the life of an abused child, imagined from the point of view of the adult who is writing, Ivy's worries are a useful way of thinking about the challenges faced by Allison, who wants to contextualize the abused child, and by Sapphire, who wants to engage the sympathy of her readers for children who are not just "inside" but who suffer sexual abuse, racism, and poverty "outside." To get readers to identify with children vilified in mainstream culture, it may be strategic to ask readers to identify with "inner children" so as to facilitate sympathetic identification with "inner city children." But this form of identification, as Ivy points out, may also function to displace the social/political with a universalized personal sphere.

Sapphire develops the humanity of Precious so that the reader fully appreciates the waste of her life and potential and understands that child members of the black urban poor fully deserve resources and opportunities to grow, imagining these resources as primarily educational. As does Allison, Sapphire humanizes her narrator to make the case that threatened poor children should be listened to and given the resources to help them achieve their dreams of educational attainment—and of escape. Although this is an innocuous plea for sharing opportunity that does not even explicitly attack institutionalized pressures to deny simple human need, Sapphire's writing is scandalizing because it features luridly brutal and brutalized subjects. As Vaughn Carney scathingly put it in his *Wall Street Journal* review of *Push* and its marketers:

> Why does the publishing industry have this morbid fascination with the most depraved, violent, misogynist, vulgar, low-life element in the African-

American experience? . . . I resent having my people defined by the lowest elements among us. To see the majority of African-Americans as shards of a degraded and dysfunctional monolith is hugely insulting and unfair. (A14)

Carney is responding to a problem that Ellison and Morrison also had to face: the tendency to associate depictions of black poverty and sexual violence with "authentic" black life. Pointing to Sapphire's five-hundred-thousand-dollar advance for her novel, a reviewer in *Newsweek* notes the "tremendous appetite for minority voices" that publishers feed with novels like *Push,* a process of "feeding" that Susan Willis has linked to the consuming audience of a dominant white culture that "seems to have an insatiable need for the ethnic and new," a need related to the demand that "marginal groups be authentic" (180–82).

Of course, her hostile reviewers do not think that Sapphire takes any risks to tell the black incest victim's story. Instead, they believe that she gives the dominant culture exactly what it wants. This view of Sapphire's *Push* echoes the fears of the black college administrators about Trueblood telling his story to a voyeuristic white audience that rewards him with money. But the lesson of *Push*'s publication history could be understood in a different way. Certainly, Sapphire has much more support for breaking the incest victim's silence and shaping her narrative than Morrison did in 1970. The marketable promise of authenticity, the evolution of the incest novel into a popular genre, the recovery movement, all work to provide Sapphire with a sympathetic, affluent audience (even before the novel was published, an excerpt had appeared in the *New Yorker*). Yet despite her large advance, Sapphire has refused to negotiate with Hollywood for the film rights. She has not, then, encouraged the further mass commodification of her novel in a form where she would lose authorial control: "To have a child sitting in the audience look up and feel shame . . . that could really happen. . . . At some point I do have control" (Powers, B2). Here, the author asserts control by presenting her story only to a smaller, more privileged group of adult readers who, to judge by the attention her novel received, as well as many positive reviews, have acceded to the novel's demand that they value the abused child as "precious."

Further, in her novel itself, Sapphire challenges those who would see the "majority of African-Americans as a . . . dysfunctional monolith" by using a realist focus on individuals, all of whom manage both to use the system and to find the loopholes of benefit to themselves. Yet even in doing so, Sapphire does not shy away from the destructive consequences of the individualist credo, depicted in the opportunism of adults like Precious's parents. When the book opens, Precious is sixteen and pregnant for the second time by her exploitative father. Precious's mother is figured as an obese woman who force-feeds Precious and devours food herself, while also verbally and physically abusing her daughter and stealing the money that should be used to provide for Precious's first child. Although it is possible to see these parents as themselves victims of a greedy and narcissistic society, their brutality is so unqualified in the novel that they simply seem evil rather than socially and economically deprived.

Precisely because Precious's parents, unlike the Boatwrights in *Bastard out of Carolina,* lack any self-awareness or redeeming moments of self-reflection, anger at them is a more available response. Their brutality thus works to create more sympathy for their victim, who, like Bone, is not to blame and yet not innocent. Precious is overweight, self-hating, rebellious, and totally illiterate, though she goes to school every day and has been promoted to the ninth grade. She admits that she continues to live only because "Ain' no plug to pull out" (35). The risks Sapphire takes in focusing upon Precious's trauma and recovery are those that we have already seen are associated with the recovery model itself. False-memory advocates might see in *Push's* depiction of Precious's parents clear evidence that "monsters" are being created here. And to emphasize Precious's resourcefulness is to appear to participate in the all-American ethic of individualism and its celebration of the will to "push." Yet if Sapphire's novel is implicated in oppressive ideological formulations, her invention of Precious also implicitly argues that culturally prized ideas about self-determination can be a resource for a disenfranchised, nearly invisible teenager.

To construct, as Sapphire does, welfare parents as wicked, lazy, and greedy is also to take the risk of confirming the cultural deficiency model: underclass parents cause their children to suffer. Sapphire makes it difficult to blame anyone but Precious's monstrous parents for her victimization. Giving voice to the victim, Sapphire follows Walker's lead in *The Color Purple,* but she does not share her strategy for letting the perpetrator—"Pa not Pa"—off the hook. Instead, Sapphire immerses the reader in Precious's point of view and language and welcomes the reader's anger on Precious's behalf. Anger about Precious's victimization is undoubtedly intensified by Sapphire's depiction of the social and economic conditions that both create the dehumanizing situation in which the narrator lives and are integral to her consciousness and language. But the contexts in which incest takes place and that are defined as a cause for anger in *Bastard out of Carolina* and in Ellison's and Morrison's novels are less of a target in *Push.* Unlike Pecola, who is annihilated by her circumstances, Precious always finds some lifesaving crumb within her experience to nurture a growing healthy sense of self. She also finds an "angel" in every situation, in keeping with *Push's* epigraph from *The Talmud:* "Every blade of grass has its Angel that bends over it and whispers, 'Grow, grow.'" Like Morrison, Sapphire makes use of a natural metaphor to suggest that there is something outside the social and economic, a life force that in Morrison's novel is utterly destroyed and in Sapphire's novel is irrepressible. But in some ways there is more to be optimistic about in 1996. Clearly incest is not the big secret in either the black or the white communities that it once was—and it is no longer understood as the problem of one class. Hundreds of books have been written discussing the effects of trauma and suggesting the means of recovery. And even the socially marginal Precious ends up going to several recovery groups. Sapphire is assured of an audience who, far from being offended by the topic, want to see it explored.

In *Push,* not only does the incest victim tell her own story, but the story is almost exclusively about her coming into language and the development of her self and of her growth as an authority. Sapphire borrows freely from, but also implicitly criticizes, the central therapeutic technique for incest survivors: journal writing. As we have already seen, Bass and Davis's *The Courage to Heal* features many samples of journal entries, always articulate, that reveal as much about the class of these writers as about their past experiences—and the conventions for narrating them. If memory is linked to a process of rehearsal, then some people have greater access than others to visible, powerful means of rehearsal. Precious cannot even write prayer letters, as Celie does. When her lesbian feminist teacher, Ms. Rain, announces that students in her pre-G.E.D. class have a daily assignment to "write in our notebooks," Precious responds, "How we gonna write if we can't read? Shit, how we gonna write if we can't write!" (51). Precious has to start with the alphabet. Through oral testimony and some third-person narration, Sapphire somewhat awkwardly holds the novel at the edge of literacy until Precious acquires enough pieces of the alphabet to write to her teacher, who offers Standard English translations in parenthesis: "Dr Miz Ms Rain, all yr I sit cls I nevr lren (all years I sit in class I never learn) bt I gt babe agn Babe bi my favr (but I got baby again Babe by my father)" (71).

Recovery, in texts like *The Courage to Heal,* means not only healing from incest through journal writing and groups, but recovering memories of it. But in *Push,* as in *Bastard out of Carolina,* forgetting abuse is not an option: "what i got to rmember i nevr dun forgit" (102). What Precious *does* recover is the ability to live in the present and to hope for a future. But the novel so vividly renders the effect of trauma upon Precious's ability to construct a coherent account of what has happened and is happening to her that she fits the model of women who dissociate—and forget—their abuse. Precious, then, is an amalgam of the survivor who forgets and the survivor who remembers. Precious "spaces out" so frequently that she loses track of where she is and what people are saying to her. In these lost moments of time, she is "remembering," but this is hardly a straightforward process. Early in the novel, Precious describes her memories as a process that continually whirls the past into the present "like clothes in the washing machine at laundry mat—round 'n round, up 'n down" (23). Rather than the popular "camcorder" or "computer" metaphors that lend a much debated "truth" to recovered memories, Precious's memories are shifting and agitated by what she has seen and absorbed from television—its happy families and prosperous middle-class citizens—as well as by her own dreams and nightmares. Memory is imagined as a set of displacements—and subject to the power of a machine, which is at once a figure for the mind and for the social order that may leave Precious homeless at any time.

Part of the courage of the novel is its refusal to relinquish to a straightforward narrative line its complicated sense of memory and of the difficulties of gaining a voice. As Precious's life story is shaped into a familiar—because linked to stories of recovery—narrative order, Precious's writing becomes more and more like poetry than a coherent prose story with a beginning, middle, and happy ending. Poetry, then, energizes a disruption to a more blandly predictable narrative structure. The page literally opens up, with small lines of Precious's poetry surrounded by much white space and followed, in smaller italicized print, by Ms. Rain's translations. After Precious narrates her discovery that she is HIV-positive, Precious's journal entries, untranslated by Ms. Rain, begin to predominate. Ironically, as Precious's voice grows stronger and her literacy skills increase, the text seems to graphically fall apart—words are crossed out; drawings and arrows are included.

What does poetry offer that a prose narrative cannot? Poetry speaks a different language, in Precious's case, the language of an illiterate and impoverished child who has experienced traumatic abuse and whose subjectivity has been constituted within experiences of fragmentation. Through poetry, the linear recovery tale of growth and recovery is disrupted by a discourse of circling and shattering that has resonance with work on the long-term effects of violence on traumatized subjects. The textual fragmentation that marks Precious's poetry brings experiences of subordination, of psychological and social trauma, into view. Because of her illiteracy, Precious writes in fragments. She cannot write prayer letters as Celie does in *The Color Purple* (how did Celie gain access to writing and, without much difficulty, to middle-class discourse?). Yet if Precious's poetry demonstrates her distance from such language practices, it also proves that she is "somebody" despite her inability to express herself in Standard English (35).

Poetry, a learned form of articulation, allows Precious to bypass rules of syntax (poetic license), giving her access to a lyric subjectivity that her illiteracy denies her. Indeed, illiteracy, when transformed though education into poetry, becomes a sign of enhanced creativity and resistance. The open spaces surrounding the poems, whose lines are often only one word, correspond to the opening of Precious's own mind and vistas, but also encourage, as poetry does, the reader's own active participation in creating meaning. In this way, *Push* breaks and refashions silence in a new way. Fragmentation, then, is a sign of agency even as it marks Precious's vulnerability.

By formally opening up the text to many possible interpretations, Sapphire insures that a triumphant ending is no longer the necessary one. *Push* contains two endings. The first ending makes *Push* into a recovery story. Precious sits in a place called the Advancement House. Sun is coming in the window and shining on her son, "an angel child" (142). Her thoughts about the future are optimistic. Maybe there will be a cure for AIDS. Maybe it is enough to appreciate the beauty of the moment, her son's beauty, and her own. And yet the reader gets a choice. It is possible to stop there, but *Push* also includes an appendix, Ms. Rain's class book, written by her students, and called, "Life Stories." This section is in a different typeface, and it is not paginated.

The violence in these stories makes the point that, feminist teachers and recovery stories notwithstanding, female students are not free from the violent imposition of patriarchal power. The stories depict a world in which fathers abuse daughters; sons are favored; girls are punished for queer sexuality. Ms. Rain has nurtured her students' sense of self and taught them to refuse being declared deviant, but they have not become survivors for whom "reality" is no longer a "motherfucker." The appendix begins and ends with poetry, but now poetry pulls the reins in on an utopian ending by insisting that what Precious has to say is no fairy tale: it is not a familiar Mary-had-a-little-lamb story that leads to laughing and playing at school. Precious writes, "marY had a little lamb / but I got a kid / and HIV / that follow me / to school / one day." After this poem, prose narratives by her classmates suggest that what follows them to school is also a history of violence.

Sapphire allows Precious to push about as far as she can. The community of nurturing women Precious discovers are all clients and employees of a welfare system that is itself threatened. Yet compassionate and well-intentioned individuals use its resources to push for alternatives that suggest a different, more communal and cooperative social order. *Push*, then, struggles with and pushes against forces of economic and social disenfranchisement by a forceful emphasis upon the determination and subversive resourcefulness of individuals, who succeed in opening up at least some new space. Yet Precious's final poem, and the final words of the novel—"tick / tock"—remind the reader that there is not much time for Precious left, that even the most courageous and resourceful individuals are flattened by the bone-crushing momentum of a system that depends on the regular wastage of human resources.

Bastard out of Carolina and *Push* work to crack open the more linear recovery story even as both novels draw upon its conventions. As we have seen, the contradictory impulses fueling Allison's novel, the silences and gaps that these create, are not explicitly highlighted in the telling of the tale. Nonetheless, Bone's anger and meanness challenge expectations about both the guilt *and* the innocence of the victim, her mother, and her class while also exposing the limits of the virtues of the middle class. In *Push*, Sapphire makes gaps in the story more visible—and more linked to traumatic experience—by formally opening up her text. However, like Allison, she draws upon the resources of the recovery story, especially its claims for the full humanity of a character who, if she does not completely triumph over adversity, has a seemingly innate desire to push. Why uphold conventions of the recovery narrative if they make it impossible to express "the thing" or its difficulty? The answer is that a novel's promise of "reality" and of recovery encourages both belief in true stories of incest and identification with victims, understandable goals given the public debates about the truth and falsehood of incest stories and their tellers. These novels insist that incest really happens to people you could care about, and reader, if you believe that, you might also believe that whole peoples are dominated and abused.

Yet, as we have already seen, racial and class "others" are often associated with the "real" or the "authentic" and thus made objects of voyeuristic interest, already a danger given the possible voyeuristic appeal of incest narratives. Self-conscious about this danger, Allison refuses to fully embody scenes of incest, and Sapphire emphasizes Precious's seemingly universal selfhood so as to link "realism" to humanism as well as the miseries of poverty and sexual abuse. But the effort to create a "real" document of an individual life, crucial as it is for witnessing, for validating experiences that have remained marginalized and therefore occluded, can also put into the margins a different "they" whose economic and social powers remain invisible and difficult to recover through individual processes of memorial reconstruction. And this particular difficulty, the difficulty of locating forms of power that are neither local nor familial, points to the limitations of a story that feminists have long felt offers clear links between the personal and the political. Yet if incest cannot be the enormity that speaks for all the crimes of the powerful, the work of Allison and Sapphire shows that the autobiographical incest novel does compellingly speak, on the border between what is real and rupturing, autobiographical and fictional, about women's complex experiences of subjugation and hope.

Notes

Introduction

1. The most famous of these trials was based on Eileen Franklin Lipster's recovered memories of her father raping and killing her friend, Susan Neason. The trial, which took place in 1990, employed expert witnesses Lenore Terr, for the prosecution, and Elizabeth Loftus, for the defense, both of whom later wrote popular books about recovered memory. In her book, *Unchained Memories,* Terr tells the stories of eight people who recovered memories of traumatic childhood experiences and explores why and how such memories return. Loftus, in her work, *The Myth of Repressed Memory,* consistently links repressed memory to falsification of the past. We will discuss the debate about the validity of recovered memories in more detail later. What is important to acknowledge here is that well-publicized trials have shaped the audience for recovered-memory narratives as a kind of jury.

2. I am grateful to Michelle Massé for her conversations with me about this practice of cultural projection.—DH

3. The problems with emphasizing fantasy and also with denying fantasy any role will be discussed in more detail later.

4. We chose not to analyze films about incest, for example, because (like the narratives we discuss) films are part of a genre with its own complex history. The best-known films about incest include *Lolita* and *Chinatown* (more recently, *The Sweet Hereafter* and *Eve's Bayou*), but beginning in the 1980s with *Something About Amelia,* television also becomes an important venue for telling incest. More recently, talk shows and documentaries have also focused on the issue of recovered memories of incest. (There exists feminist scholarship on this development; Alcoff and Gray's "Survivor Discourse: Transgression or Recuperation" is a notable example.) In addition, feminist film theory has explicitly debated the significance of cinematic representations of violence to the female body and it has also analyzed the spectacular visibility of women's bodies in the medium of film. This extensive archive suggests to us that a consideration of filmic tellings of incest deserves its own separate, substantial consideration.

5. When he describes this "epidemic" in his book, *The Memory Wars,* Crews refers specifically to memories that emerge in therapy.

6. Diana Russell, in *The Secret Trauma* (1986), writes: "it is clear that further research on racial and ethnic differences in the prevalence of incestuous abuse as

well as most other aspects of the incest experience is urgently needed. This has been a seriously neglected area in the field" (112). Ten years later, Kali Tal echoes Russell's concern by pointing out the way in which anthologies of incest stories, such as *Voices in the Night* and *I Never Told Anyone,* universalize the experience of incest by ignoring racial and ethnic differences, or rather, by ignoring the specific social and economic conditions that complicate telling and perpetuate "the myth that 'womanhood' is white middle-class womanhood, and that black or brown womanhood is merely a variation on the theme, rather than a kind of womanhood in its own right" (179). Yet, as we do, Kali Tal focuses on African-American and white women's tellings (save for one example of a narrative by a Native American). Like Tal, we have found far fewer representations of incest in writings by Latinas and Asian-American women. Perhaps these writers have initially fought other battles in their writings, and so lack the tradition for telling incest that African-American women writers—and white women who draw upon their work—can now rely upon for help in writing about incest within their communities.

7. The temptation to use the term *recovery* in a playful way—in recovering memories, victims re-cover the past—is hard to resist. However, given that *recovery* already has a double meaning as retrieval and healing, we have decided not to make our use of the term any more complicated than it already is.

8. Despite the media emphasis upon false accusation in the mid-1990s, those who challenge the recovered-memory movement often position themselves as bravely disputing mainstream belief in the validity of recovered memories of abuse. In part, the stance of these critics reflects shifts in media coverage, which earlier provided many sympathetic stories about recovered memories. In chapters 4 and 5, we offer a more detailed account of this shifting terrain of representation.

9. Elizabeth A. Waites, in *Trauma and Survival,* writes that "Although there is no evidence that endogenous fantasy produces the characteristic biological and psychological patterns associated with inescapable shock, a body of literature dating from the early work of Maier (1949) indicates that there are certain reliably observable negative effects of actual traumas and that these are not confined to humans with their complex capacities for fantasy" (34). Waites goes on to discuss the way in which trauma affects fantasy; "ironically" it initially impoverishes fantasy—flashbacks and nightmares simply "reproduce" the traumatic event, and "when this occurs, the victim is deprived of the adaptive uses of the imagination, a deprivation that can leave her trapped in painful literalities. Eventually the fantasy usually modifies such literal responses. . ." (35). Waites's analysis suggests that the impact of the traumatizing event is liminal, both biologically and psychologically significant.

In *Soul Murder,* Leonard Shengold writes, "I assume that actual overwhelming *experiences* [his emphasis] in a child's development of seduction, rape, and beatings by parents have a different, more profound destructive and pathogenic effect than do the fantasies of such experiences that inevitably arise in the psychic elaboration of the child's sexual and aggressive impulses. . . . There ought not to be disagreement that experiences have greater pathogenicity than do fantasies" (16).

The "real" versus "fantasy" debate is a subject of much interest in work on trauma. Here, we only want to suggest that trauma theory represents the trauma/memory/fantasy triad in such a way as to preserve a place for actual events in causing trauma, even as fantasy shapes the experience of those events.

Chapter 1

1. The idea that denial of abuse is itself a form of abuse is drawn from Deborah E. Lipstadt's *Denying the Holocaust*. Lipstadt uses the "Holocaust" metaphor to equate Holocaust revisionism with the Holocaust itself: "On some level it [Holocaust denial] is as unbelievable as the Holocaust itself, and though no one is being killed as a result of the deniers' lies, it constitutes abuse of the survivors" (3). Lest it be assumed that the Holocaust metaphor is necessarily linked with progressive critiques of conservative political agendas, it should be noted the right-to-life movement employs the Holocaust metaphor to describe the "mass killing" of babies.

2. D. S. Lindsay and J. Read provide a good overview of debates about the prevalence of childhood sexual abuse. They note that Bass and Davis, in *The Courage to Heal* (1988), believe that prevalence rates are very high: one in three girls is abused by the age of eighteen. What would an accurate prevalent rate look like? The major source of widely differing results in retroactive surveys of childhood sexual abuse is variability in how sexual abuse is defined, from verbal solicitations to rape. If broadly defined, prevalence rates might look like those cited by Bass and Davis. However, because evidence suggests that adult problems are closely linked to incestuous contact abuse, especially forced contact by fathers, and because this kind of abuse is the primary focus of recovered-memory therapists, the base rate of incestuous contact abuse by fathers is something that Bass and Davis need to think more about. In their review, Lindsay and Read describe studies that provide base rates of this kind of abuse as ranging from a high of 12 percent to a low of 0.25 percent. Lindsey and Read cite a number of studies that do not support the view "that a large percentage of clients are completely amnesiac for actual childhood sexual abuse" (312).

Because it is easy to be skeptical about claims that clients are amnesiac before coming into therapy, it is also easy to unfairly dismiss claims made by recovered-memory therapists about the prevalence of incestuous contact abuse and its long-term effects. Mike Males has argued that the media now gives short shrift to confirmed victims of sexual abuse, though because he does not define terms, it is unclear how much of this abuse should be understood as incestuous abuse. To emphasize his point about media "escapism," he also attacks media silence on "other violent abuse of children," asking why the media seem more interested in crimes by youth rather than crimes done to them. "Ideally, journalists can serve as a counter force when politicians embark on their all-too-predictable crusades to blame powerless scapegoats for vexing national problems. But no sign of media courage is evident in today's expedient political attack on adolescents, nor in exposing the official silence on epidemic rape, violence, and impoverishment adults inflict on the young" (10–11).

3. James Twitchell makes a similar argument: "One of the most frightening aspects of our new interest in, and knowledge of, intrafamilial sex is that the incidence of incest *seems* to be increasing exponentially as information becomes available. . . . For if incestuous behavior is a learned process, a communicable disease, as some social scientists now assert with reference to the undeniable explosions in statistics, then this may well turn out to be a major public health problem for which the only cure may be, ironically, its return to obscurity and silence" (39). Clearly Twitchell decided that someone else should begin the nontalking cure after *he*

finished talking. In our view, those with the least visibility and social power are those who should be granted the longest lease on discourse about abuse. And it should be emphasized that there is also no evidence that incest was less prevalent when it was not talked about.

4. Standard definitions of sexual harassment describe it as any unwelcome sexual advance, request for sexual favors or other verbal, nonverbal, or physical conduct that interferes with work, is made a condition of employment or evaluation, or creates an intimidating environment.

5. Analyzing forms of resistance to existing power relations, Michel Foucault concludes: "Finally, all of these struggles revolve around the question: 'Who are we?'" (Afterword, 212).

6. In a recent book, *The Social Construction of What?* Hacking offers a reconsideration of his claims in *Rewriting the Soul,* labeling himself as a "sinner" who has carelessly confused the "object [child abuse]" and "the idea [the concept of child abuse]." After making this confession, he adds, "We analytic philosophers should be humble, and acknowledge that what is confused is sometimes more useful than what is clarified" (29).

7. Feminists are well aware that Foucault's work on sexuality can support both sides of the debate about whether "talking incest" harms or benefits women. Survivor discourse is linked with the confession, with the production of women's sexuality as a danger that must first be elicited so that it can be regulated. The confession does not enhance the power of the person confessing but of regulatory apparatuses of the state.

Yet Foucault also insists that speech is an arena in which power is contested. The feminist discussion of incest offers a critique of powerful knowledges that have constructed and disciplined women's sexuality. Feminists "talking back" have educated women about the possibility of resistance and interrupted the demand for acquiescence in sexual practices defined solely by naturalized male desires. This is not to say, of course, that survivor discourse can speak for all women or that it always functions in progressive ways (see Alcoff and Gray; and also Bell). Hacking's book relies on Foucault's early *Archeology of Knowledge,* in which Foucault attempted to explain the rules that govern speech acts within expert, discursive formations. In his later work, Foucault moved away from this approach to an interest in relationships among power, knowledge, and discourse—especially the limitations of discourse: "Silence is less the absolute limit of discourse, the other side from which it is separated by a strict boundary, than an element that functions along side things said, with them and in relation to them within overall strategies" (*History of Sexuality,* 27). By considering the production of incest stories over time, it is possible to see how the boundaries between the said and the unsaid transform as feminist analyses develop increasing authority. It should be noted, however, that feminism's institutional power is limited.

8. "Hanging in" may be a good strategy in some situations but it is not self-evidently the best way to respond to an evolving understanding about the past, one that comes to include memories of sexual abuse.

9. Rosaria Champagne points out that false-memory literature regularly suggests the link between victim politics and feminism in newsletter pronouncements such as the following: "Emerging political movements almost always exaggerate their 'oppression' and attack the powerful and rich. That is par for the course. In

the FMS phenomenon, victimization has become the ideal, the preferred state" (168). Such rhetoric obviously hides debates within feminism about survivor discourse. Feminists like Carol Tavris and Wendy Kaminer have raised useful questions about the commodification of victimization and the popularity of psychologized identity politics. However, as we will show in chapter 6, these feminist critics have also covered over the interesting differences between survivor narratives.

10. Leonard Shengold writes that *soul murder* is "a dramatic term for circumstances that eventuate in crime—the deliberate attempt to eradicate or compromise the separate identity of another person" (2). This crime is "most often committed by psychotic or psychopathic parents who treat the child as an extension of themselves or as an object with which to satisfy their desires" (3). It is, he adds, an abuse of power.

11. There is a tradition of gothic narratives that includes incest motifs, but this conventionalized idiom, often featuring sibling incest, is quite different from emerging stories in which a female narrator attempts to describe incest in the context of mundane family life. In the gothic, aristocratic characters and their "exceptional" transgressions are posed against the morality of the middle class, justifying its ideological dominance. Elizabeth Wilson has written about another way of protecting middle-class morality: defining incest as a problem of the poor.

Hacking does not focus on the gothic or on specific narrations of incest. In line with Foucault's early work, Hacking's interest is in expert narratives, especially those that incorporate the idea of trauma. In "Narrative Structures and the Analysis of Incest," Wendy Evans and David R. Maines provide an excellent analysis of the supports for a narrative about incest that encourage what they call the "taboo story" that incest is rare.

12. While Linda Gordon notes the economic benefits of prostitution as a way for a daughter to become less dependent upon her father, there may be other benefits as well. In an interview, Denise Turner, an incest survivor and former sex worker, explains: "It kind of brought me into reality about dealing with men. Particularly adult men who were as old as my stepfather, and were being sexual toward me. I felt that I could take charge of my situation, and I could handle it. I could speak for myself. I wasn't silent, and I could take control. It was really positive for me in that way" (qtd. in MacCowan, 236–37). (My thanks to Natalie Josef for bringing this interview to my attention.—DH.) Clinical literature discusses prostitution and sexual promiscuity as familiar symptoms of traumatic early sexual experiences but does not consider the possibly liberatory effects of sex work. See, for example, Finkelhor and Browne.

13. "Confessions" were mandatory in Magdalen houses in which "fallen" women were required to tell their tales. Rodney Hessinger writes that "the operators of the Magdalen Society initially attempted to describe the past of its clients in terms of the conventional seduction tale. The clash between the founders' preconceptions and the information presented to them by prostitutes" ultimately led to blaming women (and their class) for their "vicious" behavior (203).

14. See D'Emilio and Freedman, particularly pp. 171–221.

15. Stein began work on *The Making of Americans* in 1902. The project continued to expand as her conceptions of narrative and American character shifted over the next quarter of a century.

16. The narrator describes the same process when "one little boy does some-

thing to another little boy who does not like it, he shows no sign of reacting to it the little boy who does not like it" (378). The narrative thus generalizes this phenomenon of a delayed response to past events in "little ones" (379).

Chapter 2

1. The conclusions of the Moynihan report are based on the assumption that "the family is the basic social unit of American life; it is the basic socializing unit" (*Negro Family,* 5). It adds that "a fundamental insight of psychoanalytic theory . . . is that the child learns a way of looking at life in his early years through which all later experience is viewed" (5). According to the report, the "great discontinuity" in American family structure is "that between the white world in general and that of the Negro American." This difference is that white family structure is "stable," and "the family structure of lower class Negroes is unstable" (5).

2. Maxine Baca Zinn's excellent essay "Family, Race, and Poverty in the Eighties" describes and discusses both the cultural and the structural models for understanding the causes of the underclass. She shows how much these analyses depend upon a belief that only two-parent families can be economically successful, despite the decline of this family type in white as well as black communities and despite the existence of alternatives. Further, she shows that phrases like "the feminization of poverty" obscure what is happening to black men—economic disenfranchisement—and simultaneously reinforces "the public patriarchy that controls Black women" (87).

3. Historians have debated whether or not the paternalism of plantation owners should be understood as benign, though the arguments of Fogel and Engerman about the comforts provided by slave masters have now been discredited. Fogel and Engerman also denied that slaves were brutally exploited sexually.

4. "Ellison's law" is drawn from one of Ellison's pieces in the *New York Times,* "On Being the Target of Discrimination," April 16, 1989: 6–9.

5. In a chapter of *The Politics of Survivorship,* in which she discusses *Thereafter Johnnie* by Carolivia Herron (1991), Rosaria Champagne attempts to explain why father-daughter incest can be an effective trope for the institutionalization of slavery: "When violence becomes naturalized—that is, understood as common, ordinary, or even necessary to group cohesion and identity— . . . it conditions social patterns of oppression, which constitute all subjects who make up that culture. Since rape under slavery was called 'capitalism' and therefore, ostensibly, was not marked as abuse, rape for the society born of slavery—that is to say, our own— is an overdetermined symbol of citizenship and subjection" (165).

6. Special thanks to Thorell Tsomondo for discussing with me both Ellison's work and the problem of incest.—DH.

7. Sundquist's commentary is part of an introduction to a selection from Gunnar Myrdal's study of racism, *An American Dilemma,* See *Cultural Contexts for Ralph Ellison's Invisible Man: A Bedford Documentary Companion.*

8. Peter L. Hays notes that "Norton's investment is more than personal financial gain—it's a form of propitiation, a method of assuaging the guilt he feels

because of desiring his own daughter. His pathological interest in Trueblood reflects this. . . . So does his insistence on his daughter's purity; he describes her so five times in three paragraphs" (336).

9. Houston Baker writes: "From Freud's point of view, Trueblood's dream and subsequent incest seem to represent a historical regression. . . . And having run backward in time through the grandfather clock, Trueblood becomes the primal father, assuming all sexual prerogatives unto himself. . . . Insofar as Freud's notions of totemism represent a myth of progressive social evolution, the farmer's story acts as a counter myth of inversive social dissolution" (179–80).

10. Michael Awkward writes that "Baker's essay mirrors the strategies by which Trueblood (and Trueblood's creator) validates male perceptions of incest while, at the same time, silencing the female voice or relegating it to the evaluative periphery" (197).

11. Obviously, the incestuous making of generations can be gendered in other ways. In her novel *Corregidora,* for example, Gayle Jones depicts "making genera-tions" as a way for *women* to memorialize the crimes of a white Brazilian slave master who has raped one generation of women and incestuously assaulted the next. These women are not making monsters, they are revealing a monstrous maker. Knowing that officials may burn and distort documents, women must become vessels of a history of incest that might otherwise be erased and forgotten by reproducing daughters who will tell. The injunction of the Corregidora moth-ers to their daughters, "make generations," is a command to reproduce witnesses to the crimes of the past. Yet this process of racialized and gendered memory, Jones suggests, may dangerously contain and rebuke black women's individual capacity for pleasure in the name of a painful reproductive imperative. Certainly Trueblood's story about "making generations" has little to do with women's desires and pleasures.

12. In her novel *The Women of Brewster Place,* Gloria Naylor specifically reminds her readers of a black sharecropper's vulnerability and inability to protect his daughter from a white man's predation (in Ben's story). When he tells his story, Ben is a janitor who pathetically awaits a letter from the daughter he failed to pro-tect, unsuccessfully attempting to comfort himself by drinking. He and Lorráine bond because of their suffering, further emphasizing the black father's feminization and vulnerability. Clearly helpless in the face of larger socioeconomic forces, Ben cannot even protect his surrogate daughter from her devastating rape by the young black toughs of the neighborhood who feel insecure about their own masculinity in a society where white men's authority is still predominant.

13. See also David Lionel Smith's discussion of *The Bluest Eye* and Vanessa D. Dickerson's "The Naked Father in Toni Morrison's *The Bluest Eye.*" The novel does not make it easy to imagine positive alternatives to patriarchal norms. Even Mr. McTeer is described as remote and cold, though these qualities are explained as produced by his constant battle to provide his family with food and shelter.

14. Michael Awkward argues that Morrison "writes her way into the canon" by directly "taking Ellison to task for the phallocentric nature of his representation of incest which marginalizes and renders as irrelevant the consequences of the act for the female victim" (201).

Chapter 3

1. Because the stories Armstrong collected were about "true" experiences and informed by a political critique, Armstrong does not think that they can be classified with first-person testimonies that proliferated in the 1980s, which are no more than "stories." "All that began to get through were stories: battered women's *stories*, rape victims' *stories*, incest victims' *stories*" (*Kiss Daddy Goodnight*, 76). Presumably, the feminist incest story is the only one to offer a real critique of power and violence; other stories are mere rhetoric. However, as we will show, it is too simple to declare the feminist story the truth and other stories mere fabrications.

2. Armstrong begins one chapter of *Rocking the Cradle* by describing a young woman's furious response to a panel on incest: "You keep saying men! . . . You are wrong! Everything you are saying is wrong. I was sexually abused by my mother!" (59). Armstrong goes on to say that this was just one of a number of attacks that left her feeling perplexed. She does not deny that mothers can be perpetrators but argues that these are relatively rare experiences that do not make her gender-based analysis incorrect.

3. Tavris, in *The Mismeasure of Women*, approvingly cites Armstrong's *Kiss Daddy Goodnight: Ten Years Later* for its outrage about mother-blaming in the public and professional literature on incest (314–15). However, Janice Haaken makes a good point about the way incest narratives try to make women's relationships seem unproblematically sisterly and supportive.

4. This is the same Raymond Solokov who, in his review of *The Bluest Eye*, praised Toni Morrison for writing "a novel instead of a harangue" (95).

5. Armstrong briefly discusses this review in *Rocking the Cradle* but does not mention the problems associated with the book's cover.

6. Armstrong includes a chapter about a "swinging" father-daughter couple. The daughter extols her "closeness" to her father as she recounts a story of her subjection to his needs. Armstrong offers this story as proof that the daughter's desire for her father is really a sign of his power over her. Florence Rush confirms this view: "The call for sexual freedom in children . . . is transparently focused upon adult gratification" (*Kiss Daddy Goodnight*, 187). Not only does the power differential between adults and children compromise children's sexual "choices" but, as we have already seen, in earlier psychological literature, the child's "desire" is constructed so as to blame the "seductive" child as instigator of the father's assaults.

Sandra Butler's *Conspiracy of Silence* includes an interview that suggests the complicated ways in which this feeling of being vulnerable and seductive can be internalized: "My father reinforced my feelings as a child that I had no power to stave off his assault. But he also reinforced the notion that I had a lot of power, because if I hadn't had a lot of power, I wouldn't have seduced this grown man into sexually acting out. . . . But when I try as an adult woman to let some of that power, vitality, strength out, it gets misinterpreted in the world—the world of men. . . . I see this as being related to issue of sexism, of my being a woman and my options for expressing my power being culturally limited" (59). In these remarks, incest is said to elicit an eroticized power that is misinterpreted "in the world of men," but seemingly also "in the world of women," where incest is often equated only with powerlessness.

Diana Russell's chapter entitled "Can Incest Be Nonabusive?" asserts that some cases of incest between siblings or cousins may be positive, though she argues that a person's own feelings of being traumatized should not be used as the "sole defining criterion for sexual abuse" (42). She believes that abuse occurs, even if a person does not feel victimized, if there is an age or "power disparity" when sexual contact—or attempted sexual contact—occurred between relatives.

7. See "Three Men and Baby M" in *Feminism without Women.* Her analysis refers to such films as *Three Men and a Baby* and *Three Men and a Cradle* as well as to television programs like *My Two Dads* and *Full House.*

8. Herman entitles a chapter of *Father-Daughter Incest* "The Daughter's Inheritance." In *A Thousand Acres,* Jane Smiley expands upon the idea of incest as a paternal legacy.

9. Herman points out that this is also the therapeutic agenda of Henry Giaratto. However, in his *Integrated Treatment of Child Sexual Abuse: A Treatment and Training Manual,* this reinstalling of the bond could be understood as a disciplinary process that involves asking women to assume all primary parenting responsibilities. Herman both adopts this view and shapes it by imagining the utopian possibilities associated with the mother-daughter bond.

10. In the 1960s, clinical accounts of incest explain how maternal failures lead fathers to molest their daughters. See Lucy M. Candib's "Incest and Other Harms to Daughters across Cultures," which discusses this discursive tradition and addresses contexts of male dominance that lead to maternal practices that harm daughters.

11. Giaratto explains that the "context" in which incest takes place is "faulty marriage" (57), a familiar but much narrower parameter of understanding than is offered by Herman. One traditional defense of the father's incestuous assault of his daughter is that his wife does not meet his sexual needs.

12. In discussing the "social location" of concerns about threats to children, Joel Best challenges the "folk myth" that upper-middle-class parents are particularly susceptible to anxieties about threats to children. Studying the results of a *Los Angeles Times* survey, he finds that "the people who worried most about threats to children were people who must have seen themselves as especially vulnerable in uncertain times." Concern was "higher among categories of people who would seem more likely to feel socially vulnerable: women rather than men; blacks and Hispanics rather than whites; older—and to a lesser degree—younger people, rather than the middle-aged; the less-educated; and those with lower incomes" (173). Fear of threats to children is not simply a matter of white middle-class ideology.

13. The Child Abuse Prevention and Treatment Act became law in 1974, authorizing $86 million over three and a half years and establishing the National Center for Child Abuse and Neglect. (The states had earlier passed reporting laws in response to growing concerns about battered children.) Barbara J. Nelson has argued that issues like rape and incest became a part of the governmental agenda because they are represented as "deviance" and thus cannot claim to be protected by privacy of the family. The "deviance" model, she argues, turns policy "away from considering the social-structural and social-psychological underpinnings of abuse and neglect" (3), though she elsewhere acknowledges that domestic violence

legislation does highlight power in the family and power in society. Her view is complex: she sees that raising the issue of child abuse is often good for children and for enhancing the authority of professionals working on their behalf. However, in the 1980s, the problem of structural causes and long-established power relations faded from view for a number of reasons: Reagan's cuts to the budgets for research on abuse and neglect; media coverage shifting to the failure of state programs and the problems of reporting; a new focus on psychopathology (as in the Giaratto model).

14. Armstrong embraces Andrea Dworkin's theory of eroticized domination, which is based on an analysis of pornography as the key to understanding the condition of women. Armstrong does not examine the way that feminist criticisms of pornography converged with right-wing denunciations of sin in the early 1980s. Feminist morality can lose sight of its institutional and social effects.

15. Elayne Rapping discusses the influence that feminism has had on the recovery movement by encouraging women to seek "fairer, more rewarding" lives (164). She also acknowledges that the recovery movement has shaped feminist discourses about the politics of the self, about personal change and self-esteem. (For example, see Gloria Steinem's *The Revolution from Within*). Rapping writes: "The recovery movement, in adopting so many feminist ideas, only to twist them into the service of so many deeply reactionary ends, is a fascinating and compelling sign of the times" (9). These reactionary ends, she argues, are possible when women embrace an overly simple narrative to explain their unhappiness.

Chapter 4

1. In 1987, Bessel A. van der Kolk edited a group of essays called *Psychological Trauma,* based on the work of the Harvard Trauma Study Group, that included an essay by Judith Herman and van der Kolk, "Traumatic Antecedents of Borderline Personality Disorder." Van der Kolk, like Herman later, sees the contemporary interest in trauma as deriving from two important sources, (1) the women's movement and its concerns about consequences of rape and child abuse, (2) grassroot concerns of veterans about the psychological symptoms exhibited by returning Vietnam veterans. In *Trauma and Recovery,* Herman elaborates on this account, tracing interest in trauma back to the work of Janet that informed the study of shell shock in World War I. A rival genealogy, whose limits we discuss in chapter 1, has been created by Ian Hacking, who locates the origin of ideas about psychological trauma in the study of neuroses following railway accidents.

Both Herman and Hacking share a faith that their histories will recover the truth of the past. Such faith is hard to shake—and that is why both Herman, a recovered-memory advocate, and Hacking, a skeptic, share this belief. The discovery of historical patterns is a way of establishing what seems to be a solid relationship between the past and the present. The extent to which the origin of the chain linking past and present is not the past but shifting present concerns is frequently unacknowledged. The attraction of the canonical text, for example, is the belief that it both embodies the past and is a key to explaining the present, hence its seeming universality.

Our goal is not to decide on a true history but to show how Herman's text foregrounds ideas about trauma that shape and have been shaped by feminist ideas about narrative forms as both dangerous and empowering to subjugated women. In the 1980s, the literary canon becomes a crucial site for exploring this issue.

2. Feminist efforts to open up the canon have been criticized by John Guillory for their narrow understanding of representation: the assumption that authors and characters can stand for entire social groups and their key experiences and values; the way that opening up the canon becomes *the* definition of a progressive institutional practice to the point that diversity in the canon is assumed to be the same thing as actual social diversity. We appreciate Guillory's critique of the theoretical and political limitations of the practice of canon revision, but a sympathetic understanding of feminist criticism of the canon in the 1980s is nonetheless crucial to understanding the writing practices that we are discussing in this chapter.

3. In addition to the work of Baym, Froula, and McKay mentioned in this chapter, many other examples of feminist work written in the 1980s challenge the traditional literary canon, such as Joanna Russ's *How to Suppress Women's Writing*, Lillian Robinson's "Treason Our Text: Feminist Challenges to the Literary Canon," and Paul Lauter's "Caste, Class, and Canon" (1981), which was revised in 1987.

4. We explore this shift in feminist thinking and its grounding in the psychoanalytic theories of Melanie Klein and D. W. Winnicott in *From Klein to Kristeva* (Doane and Hodges).

5. Because the "witch hunt" metaphor pervades false-memory literature, it is not surprising that Miller's play has become a touchstone. While feminist critic Elaine Showalter deplores the credulity of readers who accept the truth of recovered memories, she repeatedly cites *The Crucible* as if it were a key to understanding both the past and the present, describing it as "prophetic" and calling her own last chapter "The Crucible."

What is surprising about her faith in the play's truth is that as a literary critic she might be expected to see it as something other than a simple mirror of reality, especially given its configurations of gender. *The Crucible* powerfully reinforces contemporary challenges to the evidentiary status of recovered memories while at the same time naturalizing a familiar logic of male innocence and female corruption. Miller rewrote the story of Salem making one of its male victims—John Proctor—into a younger, attractive, and virile man, and one of the accusers—the eleven-year-old Abigail Williams—older so that she could be a "harlot." This revision might well be explored not just as a vehicle for analyzing the McCarthy hearings, as is so often done, but as a characteristically 1950s version of the melodrama of beset manhood.

6. Pendergrast and Showalter make a similar argument about what the novel is saying, narrowly defining the work as a recovered-memory polemic.

Chapter 5

1. The foundation was started by Pamela Freyd after her husband was accused by their daughter, Jennifer, of sexual abuse. Its newsletter features parents and experts, but the organization has resisted scrutiny, so claims about its mem-

bership are open to question. Mike Staunton's "U-Turn on Memory Lane" explores how the FMSF has managed to strongly influence public opinion while itself trying to block articles critical of its own operation.

2. This book is widely cited in texts devoted to the memory wars. In addition to Ofshe and Watters, see, for example, Schacter; Loftus, *Myth of Repressed Memory;* and Lindsay and Read.

3. Erdelyi, by calling Crews's discussion of repression a "vast red herring," points to the way in which Crews is controlling his reader's understanding of recovered memory by making Freud and repression the objects of attack. Crews's rhetorical strategy of attacking Freud and repression makes therapy seem outmoded by obscuring ongoing developments in the psychological study of memory and trauma.

4. Sexual abuse survivor stories by adult males, long concealed by homophobia (responses to women's accounts often turn the victim into the "seductive" daughter; men fear being turned by the same logic into "seductive" boys) and the conflation of sexual abuse and incest (with predominantly female victims), are just now being widely explored.

5. In *Return of the Furies,* Hollida Wakefield and Ralph Underwager write: "Radical feminism, emphasizing the unique relational and contextual experience of women and claiming special knowledge of truth for women, abhors distinctions, principles, universals, or consistency" (39). This statement, is, in their view, a useful gloss on this one expressed by an editor of a textbook on feminist jurisprudence and cited in their book: "the feminist intellectual movement, like many postmodern movements, regards the truth of all propositions relating to society and certainly to law as depending on context, perspective, and situation" (39). The anxieties created by an increasing awareness of the problems of judging what constitutes a veridical memory are displaced onto feminism; antifeminism thus is associated with reason and an undistorted access to the past. Because Wakefield and Underwager offer a particularly wacky historical account of claims by adult children of repressed memories as social phenomena antithetical to the foundational (for them, Greek) ideas of civilization, they very much need to scapegoat feminism as the embodiment of unreason. Few of these commentators are able to recognize the complex debates between and within radical feminism, cultural feminism, ludic feminism, and so on.

6. Adrienne Harris has written about this passage: "Loftus's memory of an experience of sexual abuse in her childhood, which pops up *in toto* in her account, remains privileged and uncontested in a book in which personal conviction is regularly dismantled and disputed. At the same time, the language in which she describes her experience is achingly familiar to anyone working with abuse" (162).

7. In her novel *Push,* Sapphire depicts this kind of group as making possible new cross-race and cross-class alliances between women.

8. Donald Spence in "Narrative Truth and Putative Child Abuse" draws on this exchange to make his case that respondents to Tavris, like many others, were not willing to consider memories of early child abuse as "narrative truths," as "metaphors for a wide range of boundary violations which belong to both past and present" (289). Indeed in his view, a "tight narrative structure and an almost total absence of doubt or irrelevant detail is almost certainly false" (289) and thus prob-

ably honed to make a "legal or clinical argument" (299). On the other hand, "The most truthful account of an early childhood experience is probably one told haltingly in a rather disconnected manner with many internal contradictions, false starts, blind alleys, and all the other earmarks of a confused memory that refers to an event that took place many years ago at a time when details were vague, only partly known, and the world was just beginning to come into focus" (298). These assumptions about the marks of a true narrative demonstrate the growing power of the "fragment" as marker of the truth. While in our next chapter we will discuss the possible meanings of the fragment in incest tellings, we do not recognize only fragmented narratives as true.

    9. I would like to thank my students, Lara Henry and Monica McTyre, for directing my attention to this web site <http://www.a-team.org/nation3 .htm>. D.H.

Chapter 6

    1. Most of these memoirs were published by small presses and have not been reviewed, which has limited their accessibility. These memoirs include *A Miracle From the Streets* by Cherie Ann Peters (Nampa, Idaho: Pacific Press Publishing Association, 1997); *Annie's Attic: Surviving Sexual Abuse* by Sarah Anne Stevens (Scottsdale, Ariz.: Hubbard Publishing, 1995); *Because I Remember Terror, Father, I Remember You* by Sue William Silverman (Athens, Ga.: University of Georgia Press, 1996); *Cry the Darkness* by Donna L. Friess (San Juan Capistrano, Calif.: Hurt into Happiness Publishing, 1993); *Forgotten Memories* by Barbara Schave (Westport, Conn.: Greenwood Publishing Group, 1993); *In Search of My Heart* by Rebekah Huetter (Albuquerque, N. Mex.: Words of Hope, 1998); *The Little Girl Within* by Pamela Capone (San Jose, Calif.: R&E Publishers, 1991); *My Jewels Are Broken Glass* by Ella M. Heady (Baden, Pa.: Rainbow's End Company, 1997); *Living On Empty* by Mary Jane Hamilton (Colorado Springs, Colo.: Cook Communications Ministries, 1994); *Paperdolls* by April Daniels and Carol Scott (Curtis, Wash.: RPI Publications, 1993); *Prisoner of Another War* by Marilyn Murray (Berkeley, Calif.: PageMill Press, 1991); *No Place to Cry* by Doris Van Stone (Chicago, Ill.: Moody Press, 1990); *The Obsidian Mirror* by Louise M. Wisechild (Seattle, Wash.: Seal Press, 1988); *There Were Times I Thought I Was Crazy* by Vanessa Alleyne (Toronto, Ontario: Sister Vision, 1997). Kathryn Harrison's *The Kiss: a memoir* (New York, N.Y.: Morrow/Avon Books, 1997), while it recounts remembered incest, is an effort to depict and recall how the mind and body suffer unspeakable experiences.

    2. These memoirs are to be distinguished, then, from narratives produced as legal testimony. In *Troubling Confessions* Peter Brooks discusses narratives of recovered memory that were used in legal cases.

    3. In her essay "Not in This House," Elizabeth Wilson draws upon the work of Diana Russell, *The Secret Trauma* (1986), whose research suggests that "high-income background" is a risk factor in incest. Finkelhor and Araji in their *Sourcebook*, also published in 1986, do not make precisely this case, though they do claim that income and prevalence are not correlated, thus undercutting views that the

problem occurs only among the poor. However, *The Third National Incidence Study of Child Abuse and Neglect* (1996), written by Andrea Sedlack and Diana Broadhurst, provides statistics showing that children of families making less than fifteen thousand dollars a year may be at significantly greater risk (more than twenty-five times greater) than children from families in the highest income classification (making more than thirty thousand dollars per year). This study also argues that this risk cannot be simply explained as a result of the greater surveillance of the poor. As a result, the *Incidence Study* explicitly makes a plea for a stronger commitment to working with and increasing the incomes of those in poverty. Acocella's interpretation of such recent demographic statistics about sexually abused children tends to "forget" that these statistics hardly deny the existence of abuse in middle-class and high-income families, although the fact that the highest income classification is $30,000 per year suggests that the incident study has avoided scrutiny of the wealthy. However, the *Third National Incidence Study* finds that there is one case of sexual abuse in every two thousand families with incomes over thirty thousand dollars per year. Of course, how the data are collected and what they prove remain a matter of debate.

4. See, for example, van der Kolk and Van der Hart; Zola; and Brewin and Andrews. These writers are interested in exploring the contributions of neurobiology and cognitive science to our understanding of how memory works because they wish to replace repression and dissociation as explanations of forgetting.

5. For accounts skeptical about trauma theory, see especially Elizabeth Loftus's *The Myth of Repressed Memory.* Janice Haaken offers a nuanced and cautious critique of trauma theory in her *Pillar of Salt,* especially pp. 60–83.

6. In "We Shared Something Special," Jane F. Gilgun reports on her interviews with eleven incest perpetrators. She found that perpetrators understood incest as a form of "caring" behavior. Further, they saw children as "gatekeepers" for sexual relationships. Gilgun remarks, "The perpetrators, as adults and parents and parent figures, clearly had authority in these relationships, and to delegate their authority in circumstances where children had virtually no freedom of choice had to be highly confusing to children, as well as unfair and harmful" (276).

7. See Jennifer Freyd's extensive exploration of a child's adaptive need not to remember experience of childhood abuse. On the basis of growing evidence, Freyd argues that the most devastating and long-lasting effects of child abuse occur when a victim is abused by a trusted person in the child's life. The abused child will process this betrayal by blocking information about it, not to reduce suffering but to maintain an attachment with a figure vital to the child's survival, development, and thriving.

8. Writers about the experience of trauma emphasize, far more than do those who emphasize recovery, the limits of language. Betsy Warland eloquently speaks to this issue: "Memory is most true when not translated into words. A smell or taste, long forgotten then remembered—a sensation so vivid, stories so intact, they shock us. / With words we begin our forgetting. Tongue forgets taste, forgets touch, as it quickens to its work of words. / Words that force forgetting: memories then held in our senses, speaking through symptoms, nervous physical habits, inexplicable intuitions, redundant emotional culs-de-sac. . . . Memory saved in senses

translated into language: re / storying, remembering, re-storying. / Words to remember what we had no words for" (*Bat*, 14).

For academic explorations of the challenge trauma theory poses to the conceptual framework and to concepts of referentiality in many different disciplines, see Caruth, *Trauma* and *Unclaimed Experience;* and Caruth and Esch, *Critical Encounters.* For trauma theory's impact on pedagogy, see Felman and Laub. Suzette A. Henke in *Shattered Subjects* demonstrates the usefulness of trauma theory to an understanding of women's life writing. While not neglecting recovery and healing, all of these writers focus upon traumatized individuals' powerful feeling that their experience lies just beyond the capacities of representation, and that attempts at representation of these experiences thus demand new modes of response and listening on the part of their audience.

Chapter 7

1. The works of Sapphire and Allison make claims for realism as a resource for presenting fundamental truths of history and challenging oppressive forms of capitalism, claims Georg Lukács also made for realist modes of writing. However, Lukács could not have anticipated the alliance of realism and therapeutic discourses that has resituated the place of the individual in realist writing.

2. Allison's efforts to "refuse the language and categories that would reduce me to less than my whole complicated experience" are part of a project to "remake the world" (*Skin*, 213).

3. In some sense, Bone's problem is that she dreads reinforcing the cultural expectation, informed by the conventions of the southern gothic, that the lower-class southern family is predictably inbred (sexually abusive) and violent. Allison's novel replicates this model of the Faulknerian family yet also significantly revises it by making the female child's point of view visible and her abuse hard to explain as either inevitable or merely a metaphor for larger cultural conflicts.

4. In her collection of short stories, *Trash*, Allison includes an account of her "real" Aunt Raylene, who is married to a man who beats her. In *Bastard out of Carolina*, Raylene's situation is narrated as expansive with possibilities.

5. Rosaria Champagne relates incest and queer subjectivity in a different way: "The project of politicizing incest shares its closest kinship to that of queer liberation because of the social stigma patriarchy has attached to those outside its law (of 'normality') and also because both queer culture and survivor culture have strategically and historically constituted themselves in the closet and signified themselves through codes (nondiscursive symbols of inclusion or exclusion). In both constituencies, the closet has functioned historically as a site of subjectivity, and coming out of the closet has served as political performance" (6). While there are problems with this linkage (complex contexts for closeting and for coding identity are seen as the same for incest survivors and queer subjects), the performance of coming out—or trying to—does inform both kinds of narrative.

Works Cited

Acocella, Joan. "The Politics of Hysteria." *New Yorker,* April 6, 1998: 64–79.

Adams, P. L. Review of *Father-Daughter Incest. Atlantic,* October 1981: 108.

Alcoff, Linda M., and Laura A. Gray. "Survivor Discourse: Transgression or Recuperation?" *Signs* 18, no. 2 (1993): 260–90.

Alleyne, Vanessa. *There Were Times I thought I Was Crazy.* Toronto: Ontario: Sister Vision, 1997.

Allison, Dorothy. *Bastard out of Carolina.* New York: Penguin, 1992.

———. "Bone." In *The Women Who Hate Me.* Brooklyn: Long Haul Press, 1983.

———. *Skin: Talking about Sex, Class, and Literature.* Ithaca, N.Y.: Firebrand Books, 1994.

———. *Trash.* Ithaca, N.Y.: Firebrand Books, 1988.

———. *Two or Three Things I Know for Sure.* New York: Penguin, 1995.

Anderson, Jon. "Author Finds Ample Fodder in Rural Mid-West." *Chicago Tribune,* November 24, 1991: 1, 3.

Angelou, Maya. *I Know Why the Caged Bird Sings.* New York: Random House, 1970, c1969.

Antze, Paul, with Michael Lambek, eds. *Tense Past: Cultural Essays in Trauma and Memory.* New York: Routledge, 1996.

Armstrong, Louise. *Kiss Daddy Goodnight: A Speak-Out on Incest.* New York: Hawthorne Books, 1978.

———. *Kiss Daddy Goodnight: Ten Years Later.* New York: Pocket Books, 1987.

———. *Rocking the Cradle of Sexual Politics: What Happened When Women Said Incest.* Reading, Mass.: Addison-Wesley, 1994.

Awkward, Michael. "'The Evil of Fulfillment': Scapegoating and Narrative in *The Bluest Eye.*" In *Toni Morrison: Critical Perspectives Past and Present,* ed. Henry Louis Gates Jr. and K. A. Appiah, 175–209. New York: Amistad, 1993.

Baker, Houston, Jr. *Blues, Ideology, and Afro-American Literature: A Vernacular Theory.* Chicago: University of Chicago Press, 1984.

Barnett, Louise. *Ungentlemanly Acts: The Army's Notorious Incest Trial.* New York: Hill and Wang, 2000.

Bass, Ellen, and Laura Davis. *The Courage to Heal: A Guide for Women Survivors of Child Sexual Abuse.* 1988; New York: HarperPerennial, 1994.

Bass, Ellen, and Louise Thornton, eds. *I Never Told Anyone: Writing by Women Survivors of Child Abuse.* New York: Harper and Row, 1983.

Baym, Nina. "Melodramas of Beset Manhood: How Theories of American Fiction Exclude Women Authors." In *Feminist Criticism: Essays on Women, Literature, and Theory,* ed. Elaine Showalter, 63–80. New York: Pantheon Books, 1985.

Bell, Vicky. *Interrogating Incest: Feminism, Foucault, and the Law.* New York: Routledge, 1993.

Belsey, Catherine. *Critical Practice.* New York: Methuen, 1980.

Berlant, Lauren. "Race, Gender, and Nation in *The Color Purple.*" *Critical Inquiry* 14 (summer 1988): 831–59.

Best, Joel. *Threatened Children: Rhetoric and Concern about Child-Victims.* Chicago: University of Chicago Press, 1990.

Bobo, Jacqueline. "*The Color Purple:* Black Women as Cultural Readers." In *Feminism and Cultural Studies,* ed. Morag Shiach, 275–96. Oxford and New York: Oxford University Press, 1999.

Bonner, Helen. *The Laid Daughter: A True Story.* Austin, Tex.: Kairos Center Press, 1995.

Brewin, Chris R., and Bernice Andrews. "Recovered Memories of Trauma: Phenomenology and Cognitive Mechanisms." *Clinical Psychology Review* 18, no. 8 (1998): 949–70.

Brooks, Peter. *Troubling Confessions: Speaking Guilt in Law and Literature.* Chicago and London: The University of Chicago Press, 2000.

Brown, Laura. "Not Outside the Range: One Feminist Perspective on Psychic Trauma." In *Trauma: Explorations in Memory,* ed. Cathy Caruth, 100–112. Baltimore: Johns Hopkins University Press, 1995.

Butler, Sandra. *Conspiracy of Silence: The Trauma of Incest.* San Francisco: New Glide Publications, 1978.

Cain, Maureen. "Foucault, Feminism and Feeling: What Foucault Can and Cannot Contribute to Feminist Epistemology." In *Up against Foucault: Explorations of Some Tensions between Foucault and Feminism,* ed. Caroline Ramazanoglu, 73–96. New York: Routledge, 1993.

Candib, Lucy M. "Incest and Other Harms to Daughters across Cultures: Maternal Complicity and Patriarchal Power." *Women's Studies International Forum* 22, no. 2 (1999): 185–201.

Capone, Pamela. *The Little Girl Within.* San Jose, Calif.: R&E Publishers, 1991.

Carney, Vaughn. "Publishing's Ugly Obsession." *Wall Street Journal,* June 17, 1996: A14.

Caruth, Cathy. *Unclaimed Experience: Trauma, Narrative, and History.* Baltimore: Johns Hopkins University Press, 1996.

———, ed. *Trauma: Explorations in Memory.* Baltimore: Johns Hopkins University Press, 1995.

Caruth, Cathy, with Deborah Esch, eds. *Critical Encounters: Reference and Responsibility in Deconstructive Writing.* New Brunswick, N.J.: Rutgers University Press, 1995.

Champagne, Rosaria. *The Politics of Survivorship: Incest, Women's Literature, and Feminist Theory.* New York: New York University Press, 1996.

Chodorow, Nancy. *The Reproduction of Mothering: Psychoanalysis and the Sociology of Gender.* Berkeley and Los Angeles: University of California Press, 1978.

Christian, Barbara. "'Somebody Forgot to Tell Somebody Something': African-

American Women's Historical Novels." In *Wild Women in the Whirlwind*, ed. Joanne M. Braxton and Andree Nicola McLaughlin, 326–41. New Brunswick, N.J.: Rutgers University Press, 1990.

Crews, Frederick. "The Revenge of the Repressed." *The New York Review of Books*, November 17, 1994: 54–60.

———. *The Memory Wars: Freud's Legacy in Dispute*. New York: New York Review of Books, 1995.

Cutting, Linda Katherine. *Memory Slips*. New York: HarperCollins, 1997.

Cvetkovich, Ann. "Sexual Trauma/Queer Memory: Incest, Lesbianism, and Therapeutic Culture." *GLQ* 2, no. 4 (1995): 351–77.

Danica, Elly. Afterword to *Don't: A Woman's Word*. Toronto: McClelland and Stewart, 1990.

———. *Beyond Don't: Dreaming Past the Dark*. Charlottetown, Canada: Gynergy Books, 1996.

———. *Don't: A Woman's Word*. San Francisco: Cleis Press, 1988.

Daniels, April, and Carol Scott. *Paperdolls*. Curtis, Wash.: RPI Publications, 1993.

D'Emilio, John, and Estelle Freedman. *Intimate Matters: A History of Sexuality in America*. New York: Harper and Rowe, 1988.

Dickerson, Vanessa. "The Naked Father in Toni Morrison's *The Bluest Eye*." In *Refiguring the Father: New Feminist Readings of Patriarchy*, ed. by Patricia Yaeger and Beth Kowaleski-Wallace, 108–27. Carbondale: Southern Illinois University Press, 1989.

Doane, Janice, and Devon Hodges. *From Klein to Kristeva: Psychoanalytic Feminism and the Search for the "Good Enough" Mother*. Ann Arbor: University of Michigan Press, 1992.

duCille, Anne. *Skin Trade*. Cambridge: Harvard University Press, 1996.

Dworkin, Andrea. *Pornography: Men Possessing Women*. New York: E. P. Dutton, 1987.

Ebert, Teresa L. *Ludic Feminism and After: Postmodernism, Desire, and Labor in Late Capitalism*. Ann Arbor: University of Michigan Press, 1996.

Ehrenreich, Barbara. *Fear of Falling: The Inner Life of the Middle Class*. New York: Pantheon Books, 1989.

Ellison, Ralph. *Invisible Man*. New York: New American Library, 1952.

Erdelyi, Michael. "Letter to the Editor." *New York Times* (March 23, 1995). Reprinted in Frederick Crews, *The Memory Wars*: 266–70.

Evans, Wendy, and David Maines. "Narrative Structures and the Analysis of Incest." *Symbolic Interaction* 18, no. 3 (1995): 303–22.

Fabre, Genevieve, and Robert O'Meally, eds. *History and Memory in African-American Culture*. Oxford: Oxford University Press, 1994.

Felman, Shoshana, and Dori Laub. *Testimony: Crises of Witnessing in Literature, Psychoanalysis, and History*. New York: Routledge, 1992.

Fink, Deborah. *Open Country Iowa: Rural Farm Women, Tradition, and Change*. New York: State University of New York Press, 1986.

Finkelhor, David, and Sharon Araji. *Sourcebook*. Beverly Hills: Sage Publications, 1986.

Finkelhor, David, and Angela Browne. "The Traumatic Impact of Child Sexual

Abuse: A Conceptualization." *American Journal of Orthopsychiatry* 55 (October 1985): 530–41.

Fogel, Robert William, and Stanley Engerman. *Time on the Cross.* Boston: Little, Brown, 1974.

Foucault, Michel. Afterword to *Michel Foucault: Beyond Structuralism and Hermeneutics,* by Herbert L. Dreyfus and Paul Rabinow. 2d ed. Chicago: University of Chicago Press, 1983.

Foucault, Michel. *The Archeology of Knowledge* and *The Discourse on Language.* Trans. A. M. Sheridan Smith. New York: Pantheon, 1982.

Foucault, Michel. *The History of Sexuality. Vol. I: An Introduction.* Trans. Robert Hurley. New York: Vintage Books, 1980.

———. *Power/Knowledge: Selected Interviews and Other Writings.* Ed. and trans. by Colin Gordon. New York: Pantheon Books, 1980.

Frankel, Haskel. Review of *The Bluest Eye. New York Times Book Review,* November 1, 1970: 46–47.

Fraser, Sylvia. *My Father's House: A Memoir of Incest and of Healing.* New York: Harper and Row, 1987.

Freyd, Jennifer J. *Betrayal Trauma: The Logic of Forgetting Childhood Abuse.* Cambridge: Harvard University Press, 1996.

Friedan, Betty. *The Feminine Mystique.* New York: Dell, 1983.

Friess, Donna L. *Cry the Darkness.* San Juan Capistrano, Calif.: Hurt into Happiness Publishing, 1993.

Froula, Christine. "The Daughter's Seduction: Sexual Violence and Literary History." *Signs* 11, no. 4 (1986): 621–44.

Gallwey, P. L. G. Review of *Father-Daughter Incest. British Journal of Psychiatry* 142 (1983): 318.

Gardner, Richard A. *True and False Accusations of Child Sex Abuse.* Cresskill, N.J.: Creative Therapeutics, 1992.

Garrett, George. "No Wonder People Got Crazy as They Grew up." *New York Times Book Review,* July 5, 1992: 3.

Gartner, Richard B. *Memories of Sexual Betrayal: Truth, Fantasy, Repression, and Dissociation.* Northvale, N.J.: Jason Aronson, 1997.

Giaratto, Henry. *Integrated Treatment of Child Sexual Abuse: A Treatment and Training Manual.* Palo Alto, Calif.: Science and Behavior Books, 1982.

Gilbert, Olive. *Narrative of Sojourner Truth.* Chicago: Johnson Publishing, 1970.

Gilgun, Jane F. "We Shared Something Special: The Moral Discourse of Incest Perpetrators." *Journal of Marriage and the Family* 57 (May 1995): 265–81.

Gordon, Linda. *Heroes of Their Own Lives.* New York: Viking, 1988.

———. "Incest and Resistance: Patterns of Father-Daughter Incest, 1880–1930." *Social Problems* 33, no. 4 (1986): 253–67.

Guillory, John. *Cultural Capital: The Problem of Literary Canon Formation.* Chicago: University of Chicago Press, 1993.

Gzowski, Peter. Foreword to *Don't: A Woman's Word.* Toronto: McClelland and Stewart, 1990.

Haag, Pamela. "'Putting your body on the line': The question of violence, victims, and the legacies of second-wave feminism." *Differences: A Journal of Feminist Cultural Studies* 8, no.2 (summer 1996): 23–67.

Haaken, Janice. *Pillar of Salt: Gender, Memory, and the Perils of Looking Back.* New Brunswick, N.J.: Rutgers University Press, 1998.

———. "Sexual Abuse, Recovered Memory, and Therapeutic Practice: A Feminist-Psychoanalytic Perspective." *Social Text* 40 (fall 1994): 115–45.

Hacking, Ian. "The Making and Molding of Child Abuse." *Critical Inquiry* 17 (1991): 253–88.

———. *Rewriting the Soul: Multiple Personality and the Science of Memory.* Princeton, N.J.: Princeton University Press, 1995.

———. *The Social Construction of What?* Cambridge: Harvard University Press, 1999.

Hamilton, Janet. "Repressing Abuse: The Crime against Sylvia." *Quill and Quine* 53 (August 1987): 33.

Hamilton, Mary Jane. *Living on Empty.* Colorado Springs, Colo.: Cook Communications Ministries, 1994.

Harris, Adrienne. "False Memory? False Memory Syndrome? The So-Called False Memory Syndrome?" *Psychoanalytic Dialogues* 6, no. 2 (1996): 155–87.

Harrison, Kathryn. *The Kiss: a memoir.* New York: Morrow/Avon Books, 1997.

Hays, Peter L. "The Incest Theme in *Invisible Man.*" *Western Humanities Review* 23 (1969): 335–39.

Heady, Ella M. *My Jewels Are Broken Glass.* Baden, Pa. Rainbow's End Company, 1997.

Henke, Suzette A. *Shattered Subjects: Trauma and Testimony in Women's Life-Writing.* New York: St. Martin's Press, 1998.

Herman, Judith Lewis. *Trauma and Recovery.* New York: Basic Books, 1992.

Herman, Judith Lewis, with Lisa Hirschman. *Father-Daughter Incest.* Cambridge: Harvard University Press, 1981.

Hessinger, Rodney. "Victim of Seduction or Vicious Woman? Conceptions of the Prostitute at the Philadelphia Magdalen Society." *Pennsylvania History* 66, supplement (1999): 201–22.

Huetter, Rebekah. *In Search of My Heart.* Albuquerque, N. Mex.: Words of Hope, 1998.

Iannone, Carol. "A Turning of the Critical Tide." *Commentary,* November 1989, 57–58.

Ivy, Marilyn. "Have You Seen Me? Recovering the Inner Child in Late Twentieth Century America." *Social Text* 37 (winter 1993): 227–52.

Jetter, Alexis. "The Roseanne of Literature." *New York Times Magazine,* December 17, 1995: 54–57.

Jones, Gayle. *Corregidora.* New York: Random House, 1975.

Kaminer, Wendy. *I'm Dysfunctional, You're Dysfunctional: The Recovery Movement and Other Self-Help Fashions.* New York: Vintage Books, 1992.

Kaplan, Carla. "Reading Feminist Readings: Recuperative Reading and the Silent Heroine of Feminist Criticism." In *Listening to Silences: New Essays in Feminist Criticism,* ed. Elaine Hedges and Shelley Fisher Fishkin, 168–94. Oxford: Oxford University Press, 1994.

Kincaid, James. *Child Loving: The Erotic Child and Victorian Culture.* New York: Routledge, 1992.

Kitzinger, Jenny. "Who Are You Kidding? Children, Power, and the Struggle against Sexual Abuse." In *Constructing and Reconstructing Childhood: Contemporary Issues in the Sociological Study of Childhood,* ed. Allison James and Alan Prout, 157–83. London: Falmer Press, 1990.

Lambek, Michael, and Paul Antze, eds. *Tense Past: Cultural Essays in Trauma and Memory.* New York: Routledge, 1996.

Langs, R. *The Techniques of Psychoanalytic Psychotherapy.* New York: Jason Aronson, 1973.

Lauter, Paul. "Caste, Class, and Canon." In *Feminisms: An Anthology of Theory and Criticism,* ed. Robyn Warhol and Diane Price Herndl, 247–48. New Brunswick, N.J.: Rutgers University Press, 1991.

Leonard, John. Review of *The Bluest Eye. New York Times,* November 12, 1970: 35.

Lessard, Suzannah. *The Architect of Desire: Beauty and Danger in the Stanford White Family.* New York: Dell, 1996.

Lindsay, D. S., and J. Read. "Psychotherapy and Memories of Childhood Sexual Abuse: A Cognitive Perspective." *Applied Cognitive Psychology* 8 (1994): 281–338.

Lipstadt, Deborah. *Denying the Holocaust.* New York: Plume, 1993.

Loftus, Elizabeth, and Katherine Ketcham. *The Myth of Repressed Memory: False Memories and Allegations of Sexual Abuse.* New York: St. Martin's Press, 1994.

———. *Witness for the Defense: The Accused, the Eyewitness, and the Expert Who Puts Memory on Trial.* New York: St. Martin's Press, 1991.

Lundgren, Jodi. "Writing in Sparkler Script": Incest and the Construction of Subjectivity in Contemporary Canadian Women's Autobiographical Texts." *Essays on Canadian Writing* 65 (fall 1998): 233–47.

MacCannell, Dean, and Juliet Flower MacCannell. "Violence, Power, and Pleasure: A Revisionist Reading of Foucault from the Victim Perspective." In *Up against Foucault: Explorations of Some Tensions between Foucault and Feminism,* ed. Caroline Ramazanoglu, 203–38. New York: Routledge, 1993.

MacCowan, Lyndall. "Organizing in the Massage Parlor: An Interview with Denise Turner." In *Whores and Other Feminists,* ed. Jill Nagel, 232–41. New York: Routledge, 1997.

Males, Mike. "False Media Syndrome: "'Recovered Memory,' Child Abuse and Media Escapism." *Extra!* September–October 1994: 10–11.

Marvin, Patricia H. Review of *The Bluest Eye. Library Journal,* November 1, 1970: 3806.

Massé, Michelle A. *In the Name of Love: Women, Masochism, and the Gothic.* Ithaca, N.Y.: Cornell University Press, 1992.

McDowell, Deborah. "Reading Family Matters." In *Changing Our Own Words: Essays on Criticism, Theory, and Writing by Black Women,* ed. Cheryl A. Wall, 75–97. New Brunswick, N.J.: Rutgers University Press, 1991.

McKay, Nellie. "Reflections on Black Women Writers: Revising the Literary Canon." In *Feminisms: An Anthology of Literary Theory and Criticism,* ed. Robyn Warhol and Diane Price Herndl, 249–61. New Brunswick, N.J.: Rutgers University Press, 1991.

McNarrow, Toni, and Yarrow Morgan, eds. *Voice in the Night: Women Speaking about Incest.* Minneapolis: Cleris Press, 1982.

Miller, Arthur. *The Crucible.* New York: Penguin Books, 1976.

Milloy, Courtland. "A 'Purple' Rage over a Rip-Off." *Washington Post,* December 24, 1985: B3.

Modleski, Tania. *Feminism without Women: Culture and Criticism in a "Postfeminist" Age.* New York: Routledge, 1991.

———. *Old Wives' Tales and Other Women's Stories.* New York: New York University Press, 1998.

Morrison, Toni. *The Bluest Eye.* New York: Plume Books, 1994.

Murray, Marilyn. *Prisoner of Another War.* Berkeley, Calif.: Page Mill Press, 1991.

Nathan, Debbie, and Michael Snedeker. *Satan's Silence: Ritual Abuse and the Making of a Modern American Witch Hunt.* New York: Basic Books, 1995.

Naylor, Gloria. *The Women of Brewster Place.* New York: Penguin, 1982.

The Negro Family: The Case for National Action. Office of Policy Planning and Research: United States Department of Labor, March 1965.

Nelson, Barbara J. *Making an Issue of Child Abuse: Political Agenda Setting for Social Problems.* Chicago: University of Chicago Press, 1984.

Norton, Anne. *Republic of Signs: Liberal Theory and American Popular Culture.* Chicago: University of Chicago Press, 1993.

Ofshe, Richard, and Ethan Watters. *Making Monsters: False Memories, Psychotherapy, and Sexual Hysteria.* New York: Charles Scribner's Sons, 1995.

Okin, Susan Moller. *Justice, Gender, and the Family.* New York: Basic Books, 1989.

Olsen, Tillie. *Silences.* New York: Dell, 1983.

Painter, Nell. *Sojourner Truth: A Life, a Symbol.* New York: W. W. Norton, 1996.

Pangborn, Kenneth R. "A Nation without Fathers." <http://www.a-team.org/nation3/htm>. January 24, 2001.

Pendergrast, Mark. *Victims of Memory: Sex Abuse Accusations and Shattered Lives.* Hinesberg, Vt.: Upper Access, 1996.

Peters, Cherie Ann. *A Miracle From the Streets.* Nampa, Idaho: Pacific Press Publishing Association, 1997.

Petersen, Betsy. *Dancing with Daddy: A Childhood Lost and a Life Regained.* New York: Bantam Books, 1992.

Plummer, Ken. *Telling Sexual Stories.* New York: Routledge, 1995.

Powers, William. "Sapphire's Raw Gem." *Washington Post,* August 6, 1996: B1–B2.

Prescott, Peter. "A Long Road to Liberation." *Newsweek,* June 21, 1982: 67.

Prozan, Charlotte Krause. *Feminist Psychoanalytic Therapy.* Northvale, N.J.: Jason Aronson, 1992.

Rapping, Elayne. *The Culture of Recovery: Making Sense of the Self-Help Movement in Women's Lives.* Boston: Beacon Press, 1996.

"Real Incest and Real Survivors: Readers Respond." *New York Times Book Review,* February 14, 1993: 3, 27.

Ritchie, Leslie. "'Words Are for Forgetting': Incest and Language in Betsy Warland's *The Bat Had Blue Eyes.*" *Essays in Canadian Writing* 65 (fall 1988): 205–26.

Robinson, Lillian S. "Treason Our Text: Feminist Challenges to the Literary Canon." In *Feminisms: An Anthology of Literary Theory and Criticism,* ed. Robyn R. Warhol and Diane Price Herndl, 212–26. New Brunswick, N.J.: Rutgers University Press, 1991.

Rogers, David Laurence. "The Irony of Idealism: William Faulkner and the South's

Construction of the Mulatto." In *The Discourse of Slavery: Aphra Behn to Toni Morrison,* ed. Carl Plasa and Betty J. Ring, 166–90. New York: Routledge, 1994.

Roiphe, Katie. "Making the Incest Scene." *Harper's,* November 1995: 65–69.

Rose, Alison. "Polished Sapphire." *New Yorker* 71 (December 25, 1995): 48.

Rosen, Ruth. "Introduction." In *The Maimie Papers,* ed. Ruth Rosen and Sue Davidson. Old Westbury, N.Y.: Feminist Press, 1977, xiii–xliv.

Rosen, Ruth, and Sue Davidson, eds. *The Maimie Papers.* Old Westbury, N.Y.: Feminist Press, 1977.

Rush, Florence. *The Best Kept Secret: Sexual Abuse in Children.* Engelwood Cliffs, N.J.: Prentice Hall, 1980.

Russ, Joanna. *How to Suppress Women's Writing.* Austin: University of Texas Press, 1983.

Russell, Diana E. *The Secret Trauma: Incest in the Lives of Girls and Women.* New York: Basic Books, 1986.

Sanday, Peggy. *A Woman Scorned: Acquaintance Rape on Trial.* New York: Doubleday, 1994.

Sapphire. *American Dreams.* New York: High Risk Books, 1994.

———. *Push.* New York: Alfred A. Knopf, 1996.

Schacter, Daniel L. "Memory Distortion: History and Current Status." In *Memory Distortion: How Minds, Brains, and Societies Reconstruct the Past,* ed. Daniel L. Schacter, 1–44. Cambridge: Harvard University Press, 1996.

Schave, Barbara. *Forgotten Memories.* Westport, Conn.: Greenwood Publishing Group, 1993.

Scheper-Hughes, Nancy, and Howard F. Stein. "Child Abuse and the Unconscious in American Popular Culture." In *Child Survival: Anthropological Perspectives on the Treatment and Maltreatment of Children,* ed. Nancy Scheper-Hughes, 339–58. Dordrecht: D. Reide, 1987.

Sedlack, Andrea J., and Diane D. Broadhurst. *Third National Incidence Study of Child Abuse and Neglect* (NIS-3). U.S. Department of Health and Human Services, September 1996.

Shakespeare, William. *King Lear.* Ed. R. A. Foakes. The Arden Shakespeare, third series. Surrey: Thomas Nelson and Sons, 1997.

Shengold, Leonard. *Soul Murder: The Effects of Childhood Abuse and Deprivation.* New Haven: Yale University Press, 1989.

Showalter, Elaine. *Hystories: Hysterical Epidemics and Modern Media.* New York: Columbia University Press, 1997.

Silverman, Sue William. *Because I Remember Terror, Father, I Remember You.* Athens, Ga.: University of Georgia Press, 1996.

Simon, John. "Black and White in Purple." *National Review,* February 14, 1986: 56.

Smiley, Jane. *A Thousand Acres.* New York: Fawcett Columbine, 1991.

Smith, David Lionel. "What Is Black Culture?" In *The House That Race Built,* ed. Wahneema Lubiano, 178–94. New York: Pantheon Books, 1996.

Solokov, Raymond. Review of *The Bluest Eye. Newsweek,* November 30, 1970, 95.

———. Review of *Kiss Daddy Goodnight. New York Times Book Review,* August 6, 1978: 16, 20.

Spence, Donald P. *Narrative Truth and Historical Truth: Meaning and Interpretation in Psychoanalysis.* New York: W. W. Norton, 1984.

————. "Narrative Truth and Putative Child Abuse." *International Journal of Clinical and Experimental Hypnosis* 13, no. 4 (1994): 289–303.

Spillars, Hortense. "Mama's Baby, Papa's Maybe: An American Gramma Book." *Diacritics*, summer 1987: 65–81.

Sprengnether, Madelon. "Undoing Incest: A Meditation on Fathers and Daughters." *Modern Philology* 1996: 519–36.

Staunton, Mike. "U-Turn on Memory Lane." *Columbia Journalism Review,* July–August 1997: 44–49.

Stein, Gertrude. *The Making of Americans.* Normal, Ill.: Dalkey Archive Press, 1995.

Steinem, Gloria. *The Revolution From Within: a book of self-esteem.* Boston: Little, Brown, 1993.

Stevens, Sarah Anne. *Annie's Attic: Surviving Sexual Abuse.* Scottsdale, Ariz.: Hubbard Publishing, 1995.

Strong, Marilyn. "Talking Trash with Dorothy Allison." *San Francisco Focus,* June 1994: 61–98.

Sundquist, Eric J. *Cultural Contexts for Ralph Eliison's Invisible Man:* A Bedford Documentary Companion. Boston: Bedford Books of St. Martin's Press, 1995.

Sweetland, J. H. Review of *Kiss Daddy Goodnight: A Speak-Out on Incest. Library Journal,* June 15, 1978: 70.

Tal, Kali. *Worlds of Hurt: Reading the Literature of Trauma.* Cambridge: Cambridge University Press, 1996.

Tavris, Carol. "Beware the Incest-Survivor Machine." *New York Times Book Review,* January 3, 1993, 1: 16–17.

————. *The Mismeasure of Woman.* New York: Simon and Schuster, 1992.

Terr, Lenore. *Unchained Memories: True Stories of Traumatic Memories, Lost and Found.* New York: Basic Books, 1990.

Twitchell, James. *Forbidden Partners: The Incest Taboo in Modern Culture.* New York: Columbia University Press, 1987.

van der Kolk, Bessel A. *Psychological Trauma.* Washington, D.C.: American Psychiatric Press, 1987.

van der Kolk, Bessel A., and Onno Van der Hart. "The Intrusive Past: The Flexibility of Memory and the Engraving of Trauma." In *Trauma: Explorations in Memory,* ed. Cathy Caruth, 158–82. Baltimore: Johns Hopkins University Press, 1995.

Van Stone, Doris. *No Place to Cry.* Chicago: Moody Press, 1990.

Vogeler, Ingolf. *The Myth of the Family Farm: Agribusiness Dominance in U.S. Agriculture.* Boulder, Colo.: Westview Press, 1981.

Wagner-Martin, Linda. *Favored Strangers: Gertrude Stein and Her Family.* New Brunswick, N.J.: Rutgers University Press, 1995.

Waites, Elizabeth A. *Trauma and Survival: Post-traumatic and Dissociative Disorders in Women.* New York: W. W. Norton, 1993.

Wakefield, Hollida, and Ralph Underwager. *Return of the Furies: An Investigation into Recovered Memory Therapy.* Chicago: Open Court, 1994.

Walker, Alice. *The Color Purple.* New York: Pocket Books, 1982.

Warland, Betsy. *The Bat Had Blue Eyes.* Toronto: Women's Press, 1993.

————. *Proper Deafinitions: Collected Theorograms.* Vancouver: Press Gang Publishers, 1990.

Washington, Mary Helen. "'The Darkened Eye Restored': Notes toward a Literary History of Black Women." In *Reading Black, Reading Feminist: A Critical Anthology,* ed. Henry Louis Gates Jr., 30–43. New York: Meridian, 1990.

Whitman, Walt. *Song of Myself.* In *Leaves of Grass: The First (1855) Edition.* Ed. Malcolm Cowley, 25–86. 1961; New York: Viking, 1975.

Williams, Linda, and Victoria Banyrad, eds. *Trauma and Memory.* Thousand Oaks, Calif.: Sage, 1999.

Williamson, Janice, ed. *Sounding Differences: Conversations with Seventeen Canadian Women Writers.* Toronto: University of Toronto Press, 1993.

Willis, Susan. "Memory and Mass Culture." In *History and Memory in African-American Culture,* ed. Genevieve Fabre and Robert O'Meally, 178–87. Oxford: Oxford University Press, 1994.

Wilson, Elizabeth. "Not in This House: Incest, Denial, and Doubt in the White Middle Class Family." *Yale Journal of Criticism* 8 (1995): 35–58.

———. "Tell It Like It Is: Women and Confessional Writing." In *Sweet Dreams: Sexuality, Gender, and Popular Fiction,* ed. Susannah Radstone, 21–45. London: Lawrence and Wishart, 1988.

Wilson, Melba. *Crossing the Boundary: Black Women Survive Incest.* Seattle: Seal Press, 1994.

Winter, Angela Roorda. "'Faith in the Process': Reading Elly Danica's *Don't: A Woman's Word.*" *Essays in Canadian Writing* 60 (winter 1996): 187–98.

Wisechild, Louise M. *The Obsidian Mirror.* Seattle, Wash.: Seal Press, 1988.

Young, Allan. *The Harmony of Illusions: Inventing Post-traumatic Stress Disorder.* Princeton, N.J.: Princeton University Press, 1995.

Zinn, Maxine Baca. "Family, Race, and Poverty in the Eighties." In *Rethinking the Family: Some Feminist Questions,* ed. Barrie Thorne with Marilyn Yallow, 71–90. Rev. ed. Boston: Northeastern University Press, 1992.

Zola, Stuart M. "Memory, Amnesia, and the Issue of Recovered Memory: Neurobiological Aspects." *Clinical Psychology Review* 18, no. 8 (1998): 915–32.

Index